KEN MITCHELL COUNTRY

Edited by
Robert Currie

Coteau Books

Most of the selections in this anthology, or earlier versions of them, first appeared in *Prism International, Dandelion, Smoke Signals, Wascana Review, Canadian Forum, Saturday Night, Writing Magazine, The Fiddlehead, Canadian Fiction Magazine,* Pile of Bones Broadsheets, *Everybody Gets Something Here* (Macmillan), *Saskatchewan Gold* (Coteau Books), *Sundogs* (Coteau Books), *The Con Man* (Talonbooks), *Wandering Rafferty* (Macmillan), *This Train* (Playwrights Co-op), *The Hounds of Notre Dame* (Fraser Film Associates Ltd.), *The Meadowlark Connection* (Pile of Bones Publishing) and on CBC Radio. Others are published here for the first time.

Inside drawings by Denis Nokony.
Cover photography by Richard Gustin Photography Inc.
Cover design by Bob Barkman.
Produced by First Impressions Ltd.
Printed by Hignell Printing Ltd.

We gratefully acknowledge the assistance of the Saskatchewan Arts Board, the City of Regina and the Canada Council in the publication of this book.

Saskatchewan
Arts Board

Canadian Cataloguing in Publication Data

Mitchell, Ken, 1940—
    Ken Mitchell country

ISBN 0-919926-34-7

I. Title.
PS8576.I83A6 1984   C818'.5409   C84-091338-9
PR9199.3.M583A6 1984

coteau books

Thunder Creek Publishing Co-operative
Box 239, Sub #1
Moose Jaw, Saskatchewan
S6H 5V0

For Jeanne

Contents

KEN MITCHELL COUNTRY:
AN INTRODUCTION

by Robert Currie

Writing in the Toronto *Globe and Mail*, William French once noted that "there's nobody better than Ken Mitchell at portraying the godforsaken little towns of the prairies, especially in the winter—the muzzy jollity of the beer parlour, the passion for curling, the bleak physical and intellectual landscape, the forced heartiness of the inhabitants as they idly fill in time till spring...." Certainly, most people associate Ken Mitchell with the West. "If Canada is a country of extremes," Mitchell himself has noted, "the West is a region of violent extremes — a massive contradiction of fire and ice, jagged mountains and endless plains. This landscape has tempered a strange breed of Canadian, a kind of Super Canuck who strides from tooth-rattling February blizzards into the solar blast of a 100-degree July."

For Mitchell the tempering process began when he was born in Moose Jaw, an ideal spot for a writer to have his beginnings. "Born in Moose Jaw," says Mitchell, "gives a special claim to extraordinary status, like being born within the sound of

Bow Bells or on the banks of the river Ganges." He adds, "I went to school on South Hill, where to survive you either had to be the biggest, meanest kid around — or else the most dazzling liar (i.e., story-teller) in the school. I was small for my age and learned early how to develop verbal skills."

Those verbal skills have been his ticket to see a lot of country beyond the prairies and the University of Regina, where he now teaches. He's been a Visiting Professor at the University of Victoria and at the University of Nanking in China. He's lived in and written of both England and Greece. He's also spent a year in Scotland, as Scottish-Canadian Exchange Fellow, at the University of Edinburgh, as well as Writer-in-Residence at the University of Stirling. *Ken Mitchell Country*, one begins to suspect, is really the world.

Ken Mitchell is a writer whose employment record is admirably suited for the hands of those people who write blurbs for book jackets; he's been a pig farmer, journalist, ice cream porter, house painter, bartender, press operator, sign painter and professor. His writing skills are every bit as varied. In fact, he's been described as a one-man literary explosion because of his tremendous output of poems, plays, stories and novels — not to mention his criticism and scripts for radio, television and film. Critics have praised him for his "knockout theatre," his "humour, compassion and fine sense of dramatic climax." *Ken Mitchell Country* demonstrates the depth and power of Mitchell's achievement in fiction, drama and poetry by bringing together a selection of his best work, including *The Meadowlark Connection* in its entirety. Poking fun at everything from the CBC to the R.C.M.P., it is a Saskatchewan satire which, as Jim Christy pointed out in *Books in Canada*, is "a riot... that all-too-rare book that has you laughing out loud while reading, a thoroughly enjoyable bit of slapstick humour."

Mitchell is, perhaps, best known as a playwright. His first play, *Heroes*, was the Best One-Act Play in the Ottawa Little Theatre Nation: Competition in 1971 and has since been performed in over 40 different productions in Canada, the U.S.A., England and Scotland. *Cruel Tears* has been produced in England and the United States, had a very successful tour of Canada, and was one of the featured cultural events at the 1976 Olympics. *The Hounds of Notre Dame*, his feature film on Father Athol Murray, won praise at the Chicago International Film Festival for its "unusually sensitive script" and earned him a "Genie" nomination for best original screenplay in 1981. More recently, *Gone the Burning Sun*, his one-man play about Norman Bethune, was the feature presentation at the Guelph Spring Festival in May of this year where it was praised for its insight and power. Mitchell's success as a playwright may be due, at least in part, to his own experience as an actor, for CBC radio, and on stage in amateur and professional productions. He has the actor's feel for what will work on stage and the writer's skill at getting it into the script. And he never forgets that a writer has a responsibility to entertain.

Which may also be one reason why Ken Mitchell is such an effective story teller.

He believes strongly in the oral tradition of literature. In fact, he once read an entire novel *(The Meadowlark Connection)* to an audience who flocked once a week to Regina's Museum of Natural History to hear him perform. And "perform" is the right word, for a Ken Mitchell reading is a performance, approached with the same concentration about getting into character that one would expect from an actor.

What was, perhaps, Ken Mitchell's most difficult performance came one July evening in 1974 at Fort San, home of the Saskatchewan Summer School of the Arts, where — incidentally — Ken Mitchell served as Director of Creative Writing for five years and developed a major writing program. On this particular occasion, the students of the school — most of them music students and quite young at that — had assembled in the top-floor auditorium of James Hall for a poetry reading. What brought the majority of them out, I suppose, was the prospect of cokes and cookies by candlelight (a sort of wine and cheese party for the under-aged). It had been a scorching day, and possibly none of them realized that, even with the sun hidden behind the fabled hills of Qu'Appelle, the temperature in James Hall would still be somewhere over the ninety degree mark (this was, of course, in the good old days of Fahrenheit). If memory serves me right, the cookies were dry, the cokes were warm, and the poetry — provided by members of Anne Szumigalski's class — was good. Which is to say somewhat over the heads of so young an audience. By the time the poetry reading was finished, the auditorium was aswarm with writhing, sweating fidgeters, the inside temperature had risen several degrees, and it was Ken Mitchell's turn to read.

I remember thinking that if it were up to me I'd

simply say, "Listen, gang; it's too hot for this. Why don't we save it for another night?" Ken, however, saw in that contorted mass of music students a challenge.

He looked them over for a moment, long enough for the sounds of fidgeting to subside, though only slightly; then he began to read, using a microphone which sputtered and crackled so furiously that his voice was hardly more intelligible than that of a hoarse grackle. Finally, he shook his head and stepped away from the mike, moving closer to his restless and unwilling audience. It was when we noticed that his eyes were on his audience more than his book that his strategy became clear. He would concentrate on the kids at one table, staring at them until they had ceased whispering and squirming long enough to get hooked by the story; then he would turn his attention to the next table with similar results. Meanwhile, his voice brought to life a flamboyant old codger who got through the doldrums of the depression by listening to a radio run on stolen electricity, which he swore "by the Holy toe-nails of Moses" nobody had the right to cut off. It was his Canadian classic, "The Great Electrical Revolution," that he read, and long before Grandpa had his hilarious tug-of-war on the electric lead-in wire with the man from the National Light & Power, the hall was filled with laughter — the kind of laughter that is the most proper punctuation for a funny story. If there was another sound in all of James Hall, it could only have been made by sweat dripping from the bodies of those who were so completely held by the power of a story that they had forgotten how hot and miserable they had been only moments before.

No mean achievement.

But one that readers of this book will come to understand.

THE GREAT ELECTRICAL REVOLUTION

I was only a little guy in 1937, but I can remember Grandad being out of work. Nobody had any money to pay him, and as he said, there wasn't much future in brick-laying as a charity. So mostly he just sat around in his suite above the hardware store, listening to his radio. We *all* listened to it when there was nothing else to do, which was most of the time, unless you happened to be going to school like me. Grandad stuck right there through it all—soap operas, weather reports, and quiz shows —unless he got a bit of cash from somewhere. Then he and Uncle Fred would go downtown to the beer parlour at the King William Hotel.

Grandad and Grandma came from the old country long before I was born. When they arrived in Moose Jaw, all they had was three children— Uncle Fred, Aunt Thecla, and my Dad; a trunk full of working clothes; and a twenty-six-pound post maul for putting up fences to keep "rogues" off Grandad's land. Rogues meant Orangemen, cattle rustlers, capitalists, and Indians. All the way on the train from Montreal, he glared out the Pullman window at the endless flat, saying to his family:

"I came here for land, b'Christ, and none of 'em's goin' to sly it on me."

He had sworn to carve a mighty estate from the raw Saskatchewan prairie, although he had never so much as picked up a garden hoe in his life before leaving Dublin.

When he stepped off the train at the C.P.R. station in Moose Jaw, it looked like he was thinking of tearing it down and seeding the site to oats. It was two o'clock in the morning but he kept striding up and down the lobby of the station, dressed in his good wool suit with the vest, puffing his chest like a bantam rooster in a chicken run. My dad and Uncle Fred and Aunt Thecla sat on the trunk, while Grandma pleaded with him to go and find them a place to stay. (It was only later they realized he was afraid to step outside the station.) He finally quit strutting long enough to get a porter to carry their trunk to a hotel across the street.

The next morning they went to the government land office to secure their homestead. Then Grandad rented a democrat and took my Dad and Uncle Fred out to inspect the land they had come halfway around the world to find. Grandma and Aunt Thecla were told to stay in the hotel room and thank the Blessed Virgin for deliverance. They were still offering their prayers three hours later, when Grandad burst back into the room, his eyes wild and his face pale and quivering.

"Sweet Jesus Christ!" he shouted at them. "There's too much of it! There's just too damn much of it out there." He ran around the room several times, knocking against the walls and moaning, "Miles and miles of nothing but miles and miles!'' He collapsed onto one of the beds, and lay staring at the ceiling.

"It 'ud drive us witless in a week!''

The two boys came in and told the story of the expedition. Grandad had started out fine, perhaps just a bit nervous. But the further they went from the town, the more agitated and wild-eyed he became. Soon he stopped urging the horse along and asked it to stop. They were barely five miles from town when they turned around and came back, with Uncle Fred driving. Grandad could only crouch on the floor of the democrat, trying to hide from the enormous sky, and whispering at Fred to go faster. He'd come four thousand miles to the wide open spaces—only to discover he suffered from agoraphobia.

That was his last excursion onto the open prairie. (He did make one special trip to Bulkhead in 1928 to fix Aunt Thecla's chimney, but that was a family favour. Even then Uncle Fred had to drive him there in an enclosed Ford sedan in the middle of the night, with newspapers taped to the windows so he couldn't see out.) He abandoned the dream of a country manor. There was nothing he could do but take up brick-laying again in Moose Jaw, where there were trees and tall buildings to protect him from the vastness. Maybe it was a fortunate turn of fate; certainly he prospered from then until the Depression hit, about the time I was born.

Yet—Grandad always felt guilty about not settling on the land. It was his conscience that prompted him to send my Dad to work at a cattle ranch in the hills, the day after he turned sixteen. He married Aunt Thecla off to a Lutheran farmer at Bulkhead who threshed about five hundred acres of wheat every fall. Uncle Fred was the eldest and an apprentice brick-layer, so he stayed in town and lived with Grandad and Grandma in the suite above the hardware store.

I don't remember much about the cattle ranch my father eventually took over, except whirls of dust and skinny animals dragging themselves from one side of the range to the other. Finally there were no more cattle, and no money to buy more, and nothing to feed them if we *did* buy them, except wild fox-tail and Russian thistle. So we moved into Moose Jaw with Grandad and Grandma, and went on relief. It was better than the ranch, where there was nothing to do but watch tumbleweeds roll through the yard. We would have had to travel into town to collect our salted fish and government pork anyway. Grandad was happy to have us, because when my Dad went down to the railway yard to get our ration, he collected Grandad's too. My Dad never complained about waiting in line for a hand-out, but Grandad would have starved to death first. "Damned government drives us all to the edge," he'd say. "Then they want us to queue up for the God-damned swill they're poisoning us with."

That was when we spent so much time listening to Grandad's radio, a great slab of black walnut cabinet he had swindled, so he thought, from a second-hand dealer on River Street. An incandescent green bulb glowed in the centre of it when the tubes were warming up. There was a row of knobs with elaborate-looking initials and a dial with the names of cities like Tokyo, Madrid, and Chicago. Try as we might on long winter evenings to tune the needle in and hear a play in Japanese or Russian, all we ever got was CHMJ Moose Jaw, The Buckle of the Wheat Belt. Even so, I spent hours lying on the floor, tracing the floral patterns on the front of the speaker while I listened to another world of mystery and fascination.

When the time came that Grandad could find no more work, he set a kitchen chair in front of the radio and stayed there, not moving except to go to the King William with Uncle Fred. My Dad managed to get a job with the city, gravelling streets for forty cents a day. But things grew worse. The Moose Jaw Light and Power Company came around one day in the fall of 1937 and cut off our electricity for non-payment. It was hard on Grandad not to have his radio. Not only did he have nothing to do, but he had to spend all his time thinking about it. So he stared out the parlour window, which looked over the alley behind the hardware store. There was a view of the rear of the Rainbow Laundry, probably the dreariest vista in town.

That was what he was doing the day of his discovery, just before Christmas. Uncle Fred and my Dad were arguing about who had caused the Depression—R.B. Bennett or the C.P.R. Suddenly Grandad turned from the window. There was a new and strange look on his face. "Where does that wire go?" he said.

"Wire?" said Uncle Fred, looking absent-mindedly around the room. He patted his pockets looking for a wire.

"What wire?" my Dad said.

Grandad nodded toward the window. "This wire running right past the window." He pointed to a double strand of power line that ran from a pole in the back alley to the side of our building. It was a lead-in for the hardware store below.

"Holy Moses Cousin Harry. Isn't that a sight now!" Grandad said, grinning crazily.

"You're nuts!" Uncle Fred told him. "You'll never get a tap off that line there. They'd find you out in nothing flat."

Grandma, who always heard everything that was said, called from the kitchen: "Father, don't you go and do some foolishness will have us all electrinated."

"By Jayzuz," he muttered. He never paid attention to anything she said. "Cut off *my* power, will they?"

That night, after I went to bed, I listened to him and Uncle Fred banging and scraping as they bored a hole through the parlour wall. My Dad wouldn't have anything to do with it and took my mother to the free movie at the co-op. He said Grandad was descending to the level of the Moose Jaw Light and Power Company.

As it happened, Grandad was an experienced electrician. He had known for a long time how to jump a wire from one side of the meter to the other, to cheat the power company. I had often watched him under the meter, stretched out on tip-toe at the top of a broken stepladder, yelling at Grandma to lift the God-damned Holy Candle *higher* so he could see what the Christ he was doing.

The next day, Grandad and Uncle Fred were acting like a couple of kids, snorting and giggling and jabbing each other in the ribs. They were eager for the King William beer parlour to open so they could go and tell their friends about Grandad's revenge on the power company. There they spent the day like heroes, telling over and over how Grandad had spied the lead-in, and how they had bored the hole through the wall, and how justice had finally descended on the capitalist leeches. They came home for supper, but as soon as they ate they headed back to the King William. Everybody was buying them free beer.

Grandma didn't think much of their efforts, though she claimed to enjoy the benefits of electrical power. The line came through the hole in the wall, across the parlour floor to the kitchen and the hall. Other cords were attached which led to the two bedrooms. Grandma muttered in irritation when she had to sweep around the black tangle of wires and sockets. She had that quaint old-country belief that electricity leaked from every connection and with six of us living in the tiny suite, somebody was forever tripping on one of the cords and knocking things over.

But we lived with all that because Grandad was happy again. We might *all* have lived happily if Grandad and Uncle Fred could have kept silent about their revenge on the power company.

One night about a week later we were in the parlour listening to Fibber McGee and Molly when somebody knocked at the door. It was Mrs. Pizak, who lived next door in a tiny room.

"Goot evening," she said, looking all around. "I see your power has turnt beck on."

"Ha," Grandad said. "We turned it on *for* 'em. Damned rogues."

"Come in and listen to the show with us," Grandma said. Mrs. Pizak kept looking at the black wires running back and forth across the parlour, and at Grandad's radio. You could tell she wasn't listening to the show.

"Dey shut off my power, too," she said. "I alvays like listen de Shut-In program. Now my radio isn't vork."

"Hmmm," Grandad said, trying to hear Fibber and the Old-Timer. Grandma and my Dad watched him, not listening to the radio any more either. Finally he couldn't stand it.

"All right, Fred," he said. "Go and get the brace and bit."

They bored a hole through one of the bedroom walls into Mrs. Pizak's cubicle, and she was on Grandad's power grid, too. It didn't take long for everybody else in the block to find out about the free power. They all wanted to hook up. There were two floors of apartments above the hardware store, and soon the walls and ceiling of Grandad's suite were as full of holes as a colander, with wires running in all directions. For the price of a bottle of whiskey, people could run their lights twenty-four hours a day if they wanted. By Christmas Day, even those neighbours who *paid* their bills had given notice to the power company. It was a tolerable Christmas in a bad year—and Grandad and Uncle Fred liked to take credit for it. Which everyone gave them. There was a lot of celebration up and down the halls, where they always showed up as guests of honour. A funny feeling ran through the block, like being in a state of siege, or a revolution, with Grandad and Uncle Fred leading it.

One late afternoon just before New Year's, I was lying on the parlour floor, reading a second-hand Book of Knowledge I had gotten for Christmas. Grandma and my mother were knitting socks, and all three of us were half-listening to Major Bowes' amateur show. From the corner of my eye, I thought I saw Grandad's radio move. I blinked and stared at it, but the big console just sat there quoting the Major's tactful enthusiasm. I turned a page. Again, it seemed to move in a jerk.

"Grandma," I said. "The radio—"

She looked up from her knitting, already not believing a word I might have to say. I gave up and glared at the offending machine. While I watched, it slid at least six inches across the parlour floor.

"Grandma!" I screamed. "The radio's moving! All by itself!"

She looked calmly at the radio, then the tangle of wires spread across the floor, and then out the parlour window.

"Larry-boy, you'd best run and fetch your grandfather. He's over at McBrides'."

McBrides' suite was along the gloomy hall a few doors. I sprinted the whole distance and pounded frantically at the door. Someone opened it the width of a crack. "Is my Grandad in there?" I squeaked.

Grandad stepped out into the hall with a glass in his hand, closing the door behind him. "What is it, Larry?"

"Grandma says for you to come quick. There's something wrong with the radio!"

"My radio!" Like most small men, he had the energy of a race-horse. He started walking back up the hall, broke into a trot, then a steady gallop, holding his glass of whiskey out in front at arms length so it wouldn't spill. He burst through the door and skidded to a stop in front of the radio, which sat there, perfectly normal except that it stood maybe a foot to the left of his chair.

"By the Holy Toenails of Moses—what is it?"

Grandma looked up and jerked her chin ominously toward the window. Her quiet firmness usually managed to calm him, but now, in two fantastic bounds, Grandad stood glaring out the window.

"Larry," he said, turning to me with a pale face, "fetch your Uncle Fred." I tore off down the hall again to number eight and fetched Uncle Fred. When we entered the suite, the two women were still knitting. Grandma was doing her stitches calmly enough, but my mother's needles clattered like telegraph keys, and she was throwing terrified glances around the room.

Grandad had not moved. "Have a gawk at *this*, will you, Fred."

Uncle Fred and I crowded around him to see out. There, on a pole only twenty feet from our parlour window, practically facing us eye-to-eye, was a lineman from the power company. He was replacing broken glass insulators; God knows why he was doing it in the dead of winter. He could not have noticed our home-made lead-in, or he would have been knocking at the door. We could only pray he wouldn't look at the wire too closely. Once, he lifted his eyes toward the lighted window where we stood gaping out at him in the growing darkness. He grinned at us, and raised his hand in a salute. He must have thought we were admiring his work.

"Wave back!" Grandad ordered. The three of us waved frantically at the lineman, to make him think we appreciated his efforts, although Grandad was muttering some very ugly things about the man's ancestry.

Finally, to our relief, the lineman finished his work and got ready to come down the pole. He reached out his hand for support—and my heart stopped beating as his weight hung on the contraband wire. Behind me, I could hear the radio slide another foot across the parlour floor. The lineman stared at the wire he held. He tugged experimentally, his eyes following it up to the hole through our wall. He looked at Grandad and Uncle Fred and me standing there in the lit-up window, with our crazy horror-struck grins and our arms frozen above our heads in grotesque waves. Understanding spread slowly across his face.

He scrambled around to the opposite side of the pole and braced himself to give a mighty pull on our line. Simultaneously, Grandad leaped into action, grabbing the wire on our side of the wall. He wrapped it around his hands, and braced his feet against the baseboard. The lineman gave his first vicious yank, and it almost jerked Grandad smack against the wall. I remember thinking what a powerful man the lineman must be to do that to my Grandad.

"Fred, you feather-brained idiot!" he shouted. "Get over here and *haul* before the black-hearted son of a bitch pulls me through the wall."

Uncle Fred ran to the wire just in time, as the man on the pole gave another, mightier heave. From the window, I could see him stiffen with rage and determination. The slender wire sawed back and forth through the hole in the wall for at least ten minutes, first one side, then the other, getting advantage. The curses on our side got very loud and bitter. I couldn't hear the lineman, but I could see him—with his mouth twisted in an awful snarl, throwing absolutely terrible looks at me in the window, and heaving on the line. He was not praying to St. Jude.

Grandad's cursing would subside periodically when Grandma warned: "Now, now, father, not in front of the boy." Then she would go back to her knitting and pretend the whole affair wasn't happening, and Grandad's blasphemies would soar to monumental heights.

That lineman must have been in extra-good condition, because our side quickly began to play out. Grandad yelled at Grandma and my mother, even at me, to throw ourselves on the line and help. But the women refused to leave their knitting, and they would not allow me to be corrupted. I didn't want to leave my viewpoint at the window, anyway.

Grandad and Uncle Fred kept losing footage until the huge radio had scraped all the way across the floor and stood at their backs, hampering their efforts.

"Larry!" Grandad shouted. "Is he weakenin' any?"

He wanted desperately for me to say yes, but it was useless. "It doesn't look like it," I said. Grandad burst out in a froth of curses I'd never heard before. A fresh attack on the line pulled his knuckles to the wall and barked them badly. He looked tired and beaten. All the slack in the line was taken up. He was against the wall, his head twisted, looking at me. A light flared in his eyes.

"All right, Fred," he said. "If he wants the God-damned thing so bad—let him have it!" They both jumped back—and nothing happened.

I could see the lineman, completely unaware of his impending disaster, literally winding himself up for an all-out assault on our wire. I wanted, out of human kindness, to shout a warning at him. But it was too late. With an incredible backward lunge, he disappeared from sight behind the power pole.

A shattering explosion of wild noises blasted

around us, like a bomb had fallen in Grandad's suite. Every electric appliance and light that Grandma owned flew into the parlour, bounding off the walls and smashing against each other. A table lamp from the bedroom caromed off Uncle Fred's knee. The radio collided against the wall and was ripped off its wire. Sparking and flashing like lightning, all of Grandma's things hurled themselves against the parlour walls, popping like a string of firecrackers as the cords went zipping through the hole. A silence fell—like a breath of air to a drowning man. The late afternoon darkness settled through the room.

"Sweet Jesus Christ!" Grandad said. Then there came a second uproar: a blood-curdling series of roars and shouting, as all our neighbours recovered from seeing their lamps, radios, irons, and toasters leap from their tables and collect in ruined piles of junk around the "free power" holes in their walls. Uncle Fred turned white as a sheet.

I looked out the window. The lineman sat at the foot of his pole, dazed. He looked up at me with one more hate-filled glare, then deliberately snipped our wire with a pair of cutters, taped the end and marched away into the night.

Grandad stood in the midst of the total darkness and the ruins of his home, trying to examine his beloved radio for damage. Grandma sat in her rocking chair, knitting socks and refusing to acknowledge the adventure.

It was Grandad who finally broke the silence. "Well! They're lucky," he said. "It's just damned lucky for them they didn't scratch my radio!"

WILLIAM

June is the nicest time of the year in Sand Valley, but it nearly killed me this year. The weather, I mean. It was just too perfect, and it brought me to the depths of despair. It might sound weird to blame it on the weather, but after the rottenest winter in ten years and then a long slow grinding spring—it snowed on May 15—then June really got to me. I suppose it's only natural that when summer really hits, a guy can get pushed into doing things he never would have considered otherwise.

By then, the sun has been climbinb since about five o'clock in the morning, and around ten the river flats start cooking like a pancake on a griddle. You can actually see the vapour rising into the blue sky—as if all the lilacs and elm trees are breathing out at once. And on that kind of day, people start getting ready to deal with *hot*—hot pavement, hot car seats on the skin, hot passions.

I knew as soon as I locked my bike outside the school that I'd never last the day inside and if I'd been a bit smarter, I'd have just cut and run right then. But I went inside and sat in class for two hours, with all that bright yellow sunshine pouring in the windows behind my back. Finally, I couldn't stand it any longer and, clutching my head, I staggered down the hallway to the principal's office. I convinced the principal's secretary I was near death due to a sinus-splitting headache and was given a sick slip to go home.

The relief when I hit the sunshine outside was incredible. I could hardly keep from screaming "Freedom!" at the top of my lungs and racing in circles around the school on my ten-speed. Nearly a whole day lay ahead—without algebra. Without French!

I stopped at Sand Valley Pool Hall to check out the action there, but it was still empty at that time of the day, so I left after a couple of runs at Donkey Kong and a hot dog. I drifted past the Avalon Theatre, and discovered that Wally was running a couple of movies at a one o'clock matinee. One was an old Clint Eastwood western and the other was a weird effort called *Teen-Agers From Outer Space*. I'll watch any Clint Eastwood movie, especially a Western, so I bought a ticket and went in to the empty theatre. Naturally the other show was playing first, so I had to sit through a couple of hours of watching these aliens take over the earth, all of them dressed like fifties greasers. Really I don't know where Wally finds these epics, because they sure don't pull in the crowds at Sand Valley. I was the only person in the theatre, and I decided I'd stay only as long as Wally's girl friend Marge didn't come in from her popcorn machine and make me douse my cigarette.

Then as I was sitting with my feet propped up on the seat in front of me, I noticed a girl come in.

She sort of fumbled her way through the empty theatre in the darkness, bumping into the seats along the aisle. She couldn't see me, and she sat a couple of rows ahead of me, across the aisle. It was pretty strange, seeing her there. Girls never go to the show by themselves, but then I suppose she was a bit older than most, maybe 21 or even older. Not exactly a knockout, but not plain either. Her hair curled in waves down her shoulders, gleaming a bit in the darkness as she stared up at the screen, trying to make sense out of the weird teen-agers. I couldn't quit looking at her, at the hair caressing her shoulders, and forgot all about the movie as I wondered just what the hell she was doing there. Sand Valley isn't that big a town, and I thought I knew everybody around.

When the movie ended, a preview came on the screen and I had worked up enough courage to go and sit beside her. First I went to the lobby to buy a box of popcorn. Marge looked at me suspiciously. "Why aren't you in school today?" she said. "Does your mother know you're here?"

I hunched back into the theatre just as the East-wood was getting started. This time it was me that was blinded by the darkness and I had to stumble around to find her, spilling my popcorn in all directions. I sat down beside her finally, faking intense interest in the movie credits. I had to jam my feet under the seat in front to keep my knees from trembling. I shifted the box of popcorn toward her. "Popcorn?"

My voice squeaked. Popcorn rattled out of the box and bounced into her lap.

"No thank you," she said, not even looking at me.

My arm was shaking like a poplar leaf. I drew it back and it collapsed onto the arm of the seat. I was ruined. I was paralyzed. I was trapped. Clint galloped off across a thousand miles of desert, not even caring about me. I was left behind, choking in the dust.

But suddenly, through my haze of misery, I saw her hand lift from her lap and dip into the box of popcorn. She lifted a kernel toward her mouth and as I stared in amazement, began crunching it between her teeth. The mass of wavy hair rose and fell with the chewing movement of her delicate jaw. I fell in love with her. For some reason, a teardrop glittered on her lower eyelash, flickering in time to the images on the dusty screen.

We remained that way for some time. She watched the movie and demolished my box of popcorn. I watched tear after tear tremble and slide from the eyelash down her cheek. The box emptied. Her hand went back to her lap.

"More popcorn?" I ventured.

She shook her head, but I was already rushing toward the aisle, banging into chairs. Marge glared in outrage as I bought a package of red licorice. I ran back to my seat and ripped the end of the package. She never took her eyes from the gun duel raging onscreen as she accepted one of the long red strips. In a few minutes, the entre package was gone.

This time as I ran from the theatre, I stumbled over a strange pair of legs in the darkness and I realized the place was slowly filling with people. I already had a bag of jujubes in my hand, facing Marge, when I realized I was out of money.

"I'll be right back! I'm going back in!" I

waved my ticket stub at her and ran outside for my bike. This time I was totally blinded by sunshine, and could barely see through my watering eyes as I pedalled madly toward the pool hall. By that time, school was out. The place was packed with high school students. I found my buddy Moon at a snooker table.

"Quick, Moon—gimme a buck!"

"You nuts? What for?"

"Bag a jujubes."

Everybody laughed. "Look, his eyes are all red. Bag a jujubes!"

Moon said, "How come you skipped school, Bunion? The principal was looking all over for you."

My stomach went cold, but I took the dollar and dashed back to the theatre. Again I couldn't find her, and frightened quite a few movie-watchers as I peered into their faces along the rows. I finally found her again and waved the bag of candy. "Hi. Jujubes."

She selected a yellow one and leaned toward me, opening her mouth to speak. I couldn't breathe.

"You missed the love scene," she said in an accusing whisper.

I was immediately on fire with self-hatred. I wanted to tear out my hair, kick myself in the shins, bite my nose. There'd been a love scene, and I had abandoned her, without so much as a shoulder to sigh on. I was a disgrace to Clint Eastwood, a failure in my first love affair.

She finished the jujubes as the movie gunfights raged to a conclusion. I was only aware of the time speeding by, Old Scratch the principal, outside somewhere searching for me in the streets. My spending money for the week was gone. *Teen-Agers from Outer Space"* was coming back onto the screen.

"This is where I came in," I whispered, a touch of panic already gnawing through my innards.

She studied my face for a minute. Whoever she was, she was gorgeous. Large brown eyes, a full mouth. She adjusted her shoulder-bag and stood up, moving toward the aisle. I followed behind.

We stood for a minute on the sidewalk, dazzled by the sun glaring off Main Street. My bicycle was there, chained to the fence beside the theatre, but I was now in a world beyond such a childish toy. But could I even talk adult talk? Would I be able to stall long enough to get a driver's licence and a car?

My dream woman began to walk down the street, not even allowing a good-bye. I ran to catch up.

"If it's okay with you, I can walk you home."

She looked at me, dubious.

"Or anywhere, for that matter. I'm pretty free."

Her eyes seemed to go up and down, taking in the Diefenbaker High School Dragons team jacket, the pimples I had been fighting on my forehead, my big nose. Teen-ager from outer space. People going by in the street stared at us.

"You're not trying to pick me up, are you?"

"No, no!" I assured her. "It's just—I saw you crying! I thought maybe I could make you—feel better—"

A hard look crossed her face. "How?"

"Oh, I could be a—friend. If you're all alone."

"What would you know about it?" she sneered. "You're just a kid!"

"Oh well—I'm pretty mature for my age."

"So—keep maturing."

There was nothing else to be said, but I followed her anyway as she walked away, shrugging one sun-tanned shoulder. I couldn't keep my eyes off the long dark hair swinging back and forth across the back of her neck. She wandered down Manitoba Street and toward the river road. It was the opposite direction to my way home, but still I followed.

We walked by the playground in the Kinsmen Park, where a few kids were scrambling on the swings and monkeybars. She stopped to watch them play and, without any warning, suddenly began to cry again. Once more she began to walk in this aimless fashion toward the edge of town, until we stood at the edge of the river valley. After a moment she sat down, gazing into the Sand River as she had gazed at the Avalon movie screen. The late afternoon sun was turning it all golden.

"It's nice in the summer," I said.

"What is?"

"The valley. Just being here can be nice. It's the only good time of the year. I'll probably have a car next year. We could go driving. I'll be finished high school—could get a job. I could just give you a call—"

She smiled, still staring at the river. "What's your name?"

"William."

"It's been a real nice afternoon, William."

"It's okay. Any time."

"My name's Florence."

"Hi."

The moment had come to make my move. I reached out to touch her hair.

"Don't do that."

"Why not?"

Tears began springing from her eyes again. She shook her head.

"What's wrong, Florence?"

"Nothing! Oh, I don't know! I'm all confused —"

"You're going out with somebody already—is that it?"

She suddenly fell toward me, her head on my chest, crying. "I'm married! I mean—I *was* married—! Oh, I don't know what to do. Ron's gone away somewhere. He hasn't been home for three days. I just left my baby at the neighbour's—!"

"Baby?"

A lump of ice dropped into my belly, despite the hot day. I had been offered a sudden, fractured insight into adult life and couldn't quite handle it. I heard a distant voice call, "Williammmm!" It was my mother.

I looked up and saw a car stopped on the gravel road, only a few yards away. It was my father's Chev sedan. He was inside it, looking grim. She was standing anxiously beside the open door of the car. I leaped up in a panic, reaching for my bicycle. I needed a fast getaway from this nightmare. Too late, I remembered it was chained beside the theatre.

"What the blazes is going on here?" mother said, moving toward me like a storm cloud.

"Nothing."

"They said at school you left there at 11 this morning, saying you were sick. We've been looking all over town! At the movie theatre, they told us you were headed out this way. William—what—is—go-ing—on?"

"I have to go," Florence said. "It's getting late."

"Who is this person, William?"

"Hey, don't worry about it! Just somebody I met."

"We'll discuss this later."

"All that happened was I forgot to phone and tell you where I was going. My headache cleared up and I went to the Avalon. In fact, my bike's still there. I can show you, if you don't believe me!"

Mother's face turned bright red, then livid again. "You get over there and climb into the car right now!"

I walked before her, turning once to look for Florence, but she had disappeared. The valley seemed to be dust-laden once again, empty of life as the sun faded beyond the hills. The ash trees were already changing from green clouds into dark silhouettes.

THE CATHOLIC WARS

Catlick, catlick, sittin on the fence
tryna make a dollar outta fifteen cents!

This was the war with the Catholics.
It began the autumn we had to walk,
the year the school bus quit running.
Our gang took the long route home
walking the ruts of Willowbunch Trail
across the virgin prairie, rolling
through the cactus down Buzzy's Hill
two miles of valley past the dam.

The scholars from St. Joe's met us
at the top of Buzzy's on the third day.
We jeered for hours through the grass
before arranging a mutual retreat.
On the seventh day of the war
we elected Vern Poole our champion.
We never heard the name of theirs
but he looked as big and stupid.

In each engagement of the war
the gladiators were circled
within our ring of lunch-pails
on the grass. A fury of punches
would connect like bags of blood
as they rolled in the sage
noses exploding in bright bouquets
tatters of skin everywhere.

The silent watchers on the fence,
Catholics and whatever we were —
Protestants if you will —
stood jostling in the circle
breath halting and panting
eyes staring, panting hard
as our heroes fought and bled.

> *If they can't make a dollar,*
> *fifty cents will do.*
> *If they can't make fifty cents,*
> *they take it out on you.*

THE WITCH

The witch traversed our neighbourhood
at least three times a week
uttering crazy curses at our upright lives.
She tramped her warlock hordes
in strict formation
through the pansy beds in Gerlachs' yard
to the back alley, across several rows
of Mr. Birley's Sweet Bantam corn,
past Kingsway Clover Farm store
to the soccer field at St. Joe's School.

There she called her legions to a halt,
her long white hair whipping in the wind
while we snickered in the weedy ditches.
She'd raise her sunbright sword
(strip of chrome
from a forty-eight ford
hammered to a cross)
and harangue her invisible minions
in a wild jabbering whinny
that turned our brains to slush
jabbing her bright blade at the ranks
of green-trimmed houses in our street.

And one time at us five
crouched giggling in the pigweed.
Corbett Elstrom, our hero and bully,
leaped up and pitched a stone
while we flattened the weeds laughing
at her furious yammering retreat.
But within a month Corbett
met a train on the high-level
CNR trestle and though
we followed his slow spinning
flight to the river
with great attention —
we never found him
for the funeral.

COMING OF AGE

The moon hung on a silver thread
the first night I drank
Bohemian beer, bobbled
among the baby shoes dancing
under Duncan's rear-view mirror
nearly hidden by the yellow fog
of smashed grasshopper
sweeping over Duncan's windshield.

Jolly Gerry Erwin drove,
his head stuck out the side window
like a CPR engineer,
ducktail haircut blowing wild
as we cannonballed through
the dusty ruts in a farmer's oats.

My friend Keenan yelled "The cops!
The cops!" at every pair of headlights
topping a rise on this empty plain.
Then bottles of Bohemian
flew like foaming depth charges
into that clover-smelling sea.

We bayed Old Black Joe
at that silver moon
we could barely see
(through the baby shoes
and hopper guts)
and went home bombed,
reeling.
Like men.

LUCK

It was almost midnight when I went over to Phil's Lunch and Eats, to wait for Robby to get off work. Phil was there alone, except for a bunch of his buddies from the States sitting at one of the tables down at the back of the café. Mrs. Phil and all the other kids had already gone home.

"Tony," Phil said. "How'n hell are ya?" Phil always said that.

"Where's Robby?" I asked.

"He took off early," Phil said. "Gone up to the lake with a couple of his friends. Some dance or something."

Robby's kind of a friend of mine. What I mean by kind of is he's a couple of years ahead of me in school, but sometimes he takes me along to dances and stuff. He doesn't get much time off from his dad's lunch counter, but once in a while he leaves early if they're not too busy. Sometimes we play pool. Robby's one of the best shots in town, but he doesn't like to play much with other guys.

"I guess I'll have a Coke, Phil," I said.

"We're closing up," he said.

I looked around at Phil's buddies from the States sitting in the booth. They were smoking cigars and drinking out of paper cups which they kept covered with their hands. Phil's buddies came up here every summer from the States. They sat around at Phil's Lunch and Eats all day, and played poker in the kitchen at night when the restaurant closed. They were very cagey about it, but it wasn't much of a secret. They always got tanked up around four in the morning and started hollering at each other. Or else they would turn the radio up loud and wake the whole neighbourhood. Mrs. Phil hated having them around, but she never said anything to Phil. Actually, she took it out on Robby. She wouldn't let him even match pennies. For instance, if she found out he was down in the pool hall, she would come shooting downtown and haul him out, in front of all his friends.

"We got enough gamblers in this family," she would say. You could hear her right to the back of the pool hall. "If you want something to do, go and do your schoolwork."

Even if Phil gambled a lot, though, nearly everybody in town liked him. Phil was sort of an easygoing guy, fat as a hog. He was the fattest guy in town. A few years ago, he brought his family up from the States for a holiday and never went back. I guess they must have been at loose ends, because Phil up and bought Irwin's old grocery store. He turned it into a lunch counter and had a sign-painter come out from Moose Jaw and paint PHIL'S LUNCH AND EATS right across the front of it. We get a few American tourists up here for the summer, camping at Sand Valley Park, and Phil figured he could make money. But why he'd want to move from Omaha to a little Canadian whistle-stop like Meadowlark, I don't know.

The whole family worked in the café, from Phil on down. They had a whole gang of kids, and *all* of them worked in the restaurant if they weren't in school. Robby worked there every night, and all summer when school was out. Phil never hired any help. He figured the whole family got the benefits so they should all help out, washing the dishes and waiting on tables. Mrs. Phil cooked in the back and Phil stayed out front. He liked keeping the customers happy. It was all very good, until Phil's buddies from the States started coming up every summer. Mrs. Phil always got upset and banged her pans when they came in and sat at the table down at the back. Phil would give them free hamburgers and stuff.

"Wait a minute," Phil said to me. "Maybe I can give ya a Coke after all." He reached down behind the counter and pulled out an empty whiskey bottle.

"It's about the booze," he said. "See?"

I nodded.

"I'll give y'a Coke if ya run over to Dave's and get me another bottle just like this one," he said.

Dave keeps bottles of whiskey over the weekend for people that run out on Sunday afternoons. Dave isn't a real bootlegger; he does it as a community service. Probably he only makes a dollar a bottle.

"Awright?" Phil said.

"What the hell. Give him a buck, Phil," one of the buddies said.

"Okay, give ya a buck. Awright?"

"Okay," I said. I took the money and went over to Dave's and knocked on his door.

"What do *you* want?"

"Phil sent me over for a bottle of rye," I said. I gave the money to Dave.

"Tell Phil I can't sell liquor to minors," Dave said. He handed the money back.

"It's illegal for you to sell liquor to anybody." I handed the money back again and Dave looked at me. "Besides, he's paying me a dollar for getting it."

Dave gave me a bottle of rye and I took it back to the café. Phil and four of his buddies were sitting around a table in the little kitchen, playing cards.

"Took ya long enough," one said.

"Tony," Phil said. "Tony, why don't ya stick around for a while? We might need ya to run some more errands. Ya can earn some money. Keep ya in jawbreakers."

"Sure, Phil," I said.

I sat at the counter in the front of the restaurant, playing solitaire. There was just enough light coming through the serving window so I could see my cards. Phil's gang was quiet for an hour or two, just swearing a bit if they lost a pot, and telling jokes between hands. Then Phil hollered at me to bring in a fresh deck of cards. He said somebody kept slipping kings into the deck, but he was only joking. Then I heard him holler the ace of hearts had already gone by.

"I seen it go by!" he yelled. His buddies quieted him down, but he kept mumbling about it. Pretty soon, he was hollering again. "Tony! Tony, go over to Dave's and get another bottle of whiskey."

I stuck my head through the door and told him I didn't have any money.

"One a you guys give him five bucks," Phil said. "The least you can do is buy the booze." His eyes were all bloodshot, and he was sitting at the table with the front of his shirt wide open. His big belly was hanging out, and sweat was dripping on it from his face. The place was solid with cigar smoke. One of the guys gave me a five.

"What about the dollar?" I said.

Another guy picked a one out of his wallet and tossed it at me. There weren't any ones on the table. It was covered with twenties and fifties.

When I got back with the bottle of rye, Phil was bent over the sink in the corner, running cold water on his head. All his buddies were sitting around the table, joking through the cigar smoke and looking at Phil once in a while. He dried his head off with a dish towel and sat down at the table. He took the cap off the whiskey bottle and banged the bottle down in the middle of the table.

"Awright," he said. "We gonna play poker or we gonna play poker?" He glared around the table. All his buddies looked at one another and then looked at him.

"Maybe we better knock off for one night, Phil," one of them said.

"Knock off, hell. We gonna play *poker*. Awright?" He looked over at where I was standing in the door, and his eyes took a minute to focus. "Get that kid the hell outta here," he said.

It was getting pretty late anyway, so I decided to go home to bed. I thought about going over to Mrs. Phil and telling her about the poker game, but then I thought I better keep my nose out of it. For one thing, it was past midnight and it's not good to upset people in the middle of the night.

The next day, I went to the pool hall to ask Robby or one of the other guys about the dance. Robby wasn't there, but there was some kind of uproar going on. Nobody was playing pool except a couple of old geezers at the back. Everybody was standing around in bunches, arguing and waving their hands.

"What is it?" I said. "What's happening?"

"Phil," somebody said. "Phil went and shot hisself."

"Phil?" I said. "Phil's Lunch and Eats?"

"Yeah, Phil. He up and shot hisself. Lost the café in a poker game. One a his buddies from the States."

"Phil's Lunch and Eats?" I said. He'd been losing money in the game, but he always lost money. Who ever thought he would bet his lunch counter? Phil always figured it would turn into a real moneymaker, if he ever got a reputation. Phil's Lunch and Eats.

"That's crazy," I said. "What would those guys want with a café? They don't know nothing about cafés."

Stan Crewe came up, jerking his arms and cracking his knuckles, like he always does.

"They all blew town this morning," he said. "They got Faversham at the real-estate office looking after the café. Bill a sale and all. They're trying to sell it for fifteen thou. Prob'ly worth at least twenty. The just wanta dump it."

"Phil's Lunch and Eats?" I said.

"Yeah, whatsa matter? You stupid or somethin'?"

"Where's Robby? Does he know?"

"He's at home with Mrs. Phil and the kids. They closed the café up for the day."

"Didn't have much choice, did they?" somebody else said.

"I guess the shotgun woke the whole family up," Stan said. "The poker game musta wound up around six this mornin'. Old Phil, I guess he went straight home and got the shotgun outta the basement. Blew the back a his head off. Right in the middle a the front hall. Blood and brains all over the place."

"That's the fourth time you told us," somebody said.

"Robby, he wasn't home then. Off horsin' around at some dance up to the lake. He just got back to town in time to open up the café. It musta bin him found the note."

"Note?" I said.

"Yeah, note. On the cash register. Said he was sorry about leaving the family in a tough spot and all. Just said he lost the café and didn't think he could live and face it. Said he wished them luck," Stan said. He cracked his knuckles. "Howzat fer a laugh? Luck!"

Nobody saw Robby all weekend. He stayed in his house and never went out. Just him and his mother and the kids in the house. Some people went over to try to talk to them. Mrs. Phil would answer the door and stand there, not saying anything. She wouldn't let people in the house, so they'd mumble a few words and then go away. The funeral was on Monday, and Mrs. Phil and all the kids went. They didn't say anything to anybody. The whole town was at the funeral, except Robby. Somebody said he had got a job out at the pellet plant, and was out there working.

Robby couldn't stand to talk to anybody. He

even worked a double shift out at the plar... Out
there sixteen hours a day, not talking to anybody. I
guess the only person he talked to was Bill Faver-
sham, the real-estate agent. Bill was trying to sell the
café for Phil's buddies down in the States. He put
an ad in the paper, advertising the place for sale.
"Excellent business opportunity in progressive com-
munity," it said. I don't know why he had to do
that—everybody knew it was up for sale. Nobody in
town wanted to buy it, either.

Faversham was telling about it one day in Roy's
barbershop when I went in to get a haircut. It
sounded like he'd been telling it all day.

"Right in the middle of the night," he said.
"Young Robby. Phil's boy. I answered the phone
after it had rung about ten times. Maybe more, I
dunno—I was asleep. The old lady got me outta
bed.

"This Bill Faversham?" he says. I say yeah,
who the hell is this, phonin' me up in the middle of
the night?

" 'Robby,' he says. 'You got that ad in the
paper,' he says.

" 'Ad? What ad?' I say.

" 'The café,' he says.

" 'Oh,' I say.

" 'Git it out,' he says. 'Git it out or I'll shove it
up your nose!' Then he hung up. Just like that.
Scared the pants off me." Faversham sat back in his
chair, shaking his head.

"What did you do?" Roy said.

"I got it out," Faversham said.

The next Saturday, I was down at the pool hall.
It was payday at the plant, which usually results in a
lot of action. When I walked in, there was a gang

standing around the big table at the front.

"What's going on?" I said. "What's up?"

"Ssshh, Ssshhh," everybody said.

I squeezed through the crowd, and there was Robby, walking around the table with a pool cue in his hand. He was playing poker-pool with three other guys from the plant. He still had his work-clothes on. He must have collected his pay and come right off the night shift into the pool hall.

"Hey Robby," I said. "You winning?"

"Hi Tony," he said.

Then I saw the bills on the side of the table. They were playing twenty bucks a hand. One of the guys sank the five ball and Robby said to him, "You out?"

"No," he said and Robby said, "Good," and picked up his cue and rammed the nine ball home off a double bank. He threw his cards down.

"My game. You guys going for another?"

"I'm in," one said. He put a fifty-dollar bill down on the table. The other two dropped out, but Jay Shaw stepped forward and picked up a cue. He had been standing there watching.

"Now you're getting into my league," Jay said. He's the best shot in town. Sometimes he goes into the city to play for money. He threw a fifty in and looked at Robby. Robby put down his fifty and picked up a clean deck of cards.

"Low card breaks?" he said.

"Jesus, he's playing way over his head," Stan Crewe said. "That Shaw is a shark."

"Shut up, Stan," somebody said.

I got Robby a soft drink from the cooler. His face was white as the cue ball. The guy from the plant broke and got the ace, but he missed his next shot. Jay took his cue and lined up on the eleven ball.

"Watch him clean up now," Stan said.

Jay sank the jack and then he put away the three and the four balls. He tried to bank the six, but he missed. He swore and banged his cue on the floor. Then Robby put his cards face up on the edge of the table. He had an ace and a four, five, six, seven straight. That meant he still had to sink the last three, but it was crazy to show his cards like that when he still had three balls left to sink.

"Christ," Stan said. "He's throwing the game away."

"Why don't you keep your stupid mouth shut?" somebody said.

Robby banked the five in and came up on the seven. Perfect shape. He drove it in, but got left behind another ball. He couldn't see the six at all. He walked around the table for a minute. You could hear everybody breathing.

"End bank to the corner," he said. He hardly even lined it up, just powdered it down the long end, and in went the six.

"You're lucky," Jay said. "I had a pair of sixes left."

"Uh-huh," Robby said. He picked up the money. "You guys sticking?"

Robby kept playing like that all day, away over his head, against all the best players in town. He didn't even act nervous. He just kept walking around the table playing his shots and picking up the money. Maybe he lost three or four games.

I had to go home for supper and when I got back he was still playing. Just about everybody in town was down in the pool hall. I brought him back a couple of sandwiches from my Mom, but he didn't stop playing. He just set them down on the edge of the table and walked around, taking a bite once in a while between shots.

About eleven o'clock, there was a bigger mob than ever. You couldn't get anywhere near the table, and they had to keep pushing guys back so Robby and Jay and the two other guys could shoot. Finally, Robby missed a dead-on shot to the corner, an easy shot, and Jay finished off the game.

"Tony," Robby said. He took some handfuls of bills out of his shirt pockets and pants. "Count this for me, will ya?" he said.

I took the money and counted it out in piles, straightening out the bills. It was all tens and twenties and even a couple of fifties. Everybody was crowding around me, keeping count while I laid it out. There was $2,723. I handed it back to Robby.

"I'm beat," he said. "I gotta quit."

Somebody in the crowd started to clap their hands, but another guy said, "Shut up, willya?"

"Is Faversham here?" Robby said.

"Yeah," said a voice at the back.

"I've got twenty-seven hundred here. Will you take that as a deposit on the café?"

"That suits me," Faversham said.

"Okay, send a receipt to my mother."

Everybody did start clapping then. They hollered and whistled and cheered and carried Robby around the pool hall and then out to the street and down toward his house. They even carried Jay Shaw. Maybe they figured he deserved some of the credit. Cars were honking their horns and people were coming out their doors hollering, "What is it? What is it?", and somebody would yell back:

"It's Phil's son. He got the café back. He won it playing pool." Then the people in the house would cheer and wave their arms. It looked like it might go on all night, but when we got to Robby's house, Mrs. Phil came out and walked up to the guys carrying Robby.

"Put him down," she said.

They put him down and he stood there, so tired he was almost falling over. Mrs. Phil waved her finger in his face and said, "If you ever go near that pool hall again I'll skin you alive." She grabbed him by the arm. "Now all you people get home and leave him alone. You ought to be ashamed of yourselves."

Then she took Robby into the house, and we could see all the kids peeking out their bedroom windows at the mob standing around in front.

"He was crazy," Stan Crewe said. "He was playing way over his head. Nobody has that kinda luck."

EVERYBODY GETS SOMETHING HERE

It was at this Portage place—Portage la some-thing—where Milt and me ran into this Koffman guy. We pull into the town just beat. It's later than hell, and it's been raining on and off all day. The Chev is giving us problems again, and we're low on cash. So we decide to take a break. We go to one of the local juice-joints to see if there's any action around town. The waiter tells us there's some kind of local fair in town, and something should be hap-pening over there. Well, we didn't even get a chance to investigate, because this jerk comes in while we're sitting there cooling out, and if I ever figgered there was a carny type, this guy was it. The waiter sends him over to our table.

"You boys local?" he says.

"No, we're not," says Milt, and I give him a boot in the shins. He never learns to let me do the talking.

"We move here and there," I says.

This joker is looking for guys to work a wheel game. He says he knows a guy who'll pay twenty bucks a day each for a couple of smart boys. Forty bills sounds pretty sweet to us, what with the Chev giving us such a bad time, so we say okay. The fair is starting up the next day, so we crash in the car, and in the morning we find out the grounds are on a big island in the middle of some river that runs through the town. So we walk across this bridge, from the town to the carny, sort of like crossing the border at Blaine, Washington, from one country to another.

Nothing is started up yet. It's all quiet. When the rides aren't full of people all laughing and hollering, they're just dirty, greasy machines and the place looks like a crummy one-street town with no people around. After a while, though, the midway guys start opening up their fraud shops just like main-street storekeepers getting ready for the day's business.

Milt and me find the wheel game we're going to work, and I ask for the boss. Koffman comes out, and he's nearly enough to send us back to the Chev, missing cylinder and all. He's a real beaut—greasy and fat and sweaty, with a big Jew nose, and a black jaw that looks like it's bashed out of a rock.

It turns out we are getting hired on as shills, to help three others who seem to be there permanent. One of them is the guy that picked us up in the boozer. The deal is this: we pretend we're playing the wheel until a mark comes in, and then we all sort of crowd around him and make bets and talk it up about how this mark is winning all the money, and all the time Koffman is hollering about how the guy has to double his bet or he won't get any money, until before the guy knows it he's out fifty or a hundred bucks, and gets out of the game. Our job is to make it hard for him to get out, by pressing around and getting him to bet and saying how lucky he is.

Koffman is one of the best operators I ever seen. He can spot a mark clear across the midway and bring him into the game. And goofballs! This guy snaps off goofballs, holding them in his hand and flicking them into his mouth like he was eating peanuts. Just like an old steam locomotive he is, starting out of the station first thing in the morning. Chuff, and then in a little while another chuff, until he gets up a little more goofball steam, chuff, chuff, so by the middle of the afternoon he is cannon-balling down the track at seventy per, and nothing can stop him, chewing on those goofballs and baiting the marks, sweat pouring off his nose like engine grease.

Jesus, he knows how to handle people. He cons them when they want to get out of the game, and he insults them when they want in. All the time he's hollering, "Everybody gets something here!" then spinning the big wheel and chuckling to himself. "*Everybody* gets something here."

Except pretty soon Milt, he can't take it. After we get a couple of good marks in and take them each for seventy-five or so, Milt sours and says if I want to stay, I can meet him later in the bar. That's like Milt; no jam. I mean, I don't like the job either, but if the citizens of Portage are going to throw their money away, we might as well get it as Koffman and his clowns. And we need it if we're going to make it to Toronto. So I'm determined to stick it out.

The only thing that made it really tough was the people that bitched, like the girl, and later on, the Chinaman. You had to hand it to the girl, who was with some young farmer we got in before Milt faded. This mark never knew what hit him until his loot was all gone, and he *still* wasn't too sure then. But she knew. She must have stood out in front of the wheel for an hour, yelling, "You sons-a-bitchin' cheats! Goddam goons!" till even Koffman looks a little bothered by her.

After Milt leaves I get pretty tired, standing all the time, leaning on the counter and trying to stay interested in the game. When things are slow, I watch the teenies bopping past in their stretchy pants, but after a while I don't even get a charge out of them. They're all so high and excited with this two-bit carny, they don't see that even the rides and candy-floss stands are part of this whole con game. It's hotter than hell, sort of muggy, and I'm sweating so bad I scare myself. Koffman goes on and on, never letting up, and we're taking in all this loot. I think maybe I'm going to heave my cookies at one point, but we need the twenty bucks, so I stay.

That's when this Chinaman and his wife come along, and Koffman brings him in by throwing a handful of money into the crowd and hollering: "Free try. Free game once a day." The Chinaman is a little wee guy with a nice grey suit, probably the local café-owner or something.

Anyway, he starts laying on the money, and he's got a lot of it to lay on. His wife is beside him looking lost; she keeps grabbing him by the sleeves, trying to haul him the hell away from there. He's playing the game real serious, and keeps watching the wheel go round, working out the odds. I figure him for a local two-bit gambler, who probably thinks he knows what he's doing. But nobody, not even Jack the Hack in Vancouver, could win on this game.

After a while the Chinaman starts to see he isn't getting any money back. "Wait," he says. "You explain rules again, please." He doesn't talk English too good, and is pretty hard to understand.

"Whaddaya mean, explain the rules!" yells Koffman. "I explained 'em to ya three times awready. Ya in the game, or ya out?"

"No, I want you explain rules. When do I get money?"

"I tole ya before. Ya got sixty bucks winnin's. One a the big winnuhs today. All ya have to do is put up another sixty bucks ta back it and ya win ninety. Come on, come on. Ya in or out?"

"I want sixty dollar *now*."

"Ya can't do that. You DPs never listen to the *rules*. Ya wanta take your money out, ya gotta hit a *red* peg on the *doubles*. Ya gambler or what? Let's go. Everybody gets somethin' here!"

"Okay, one more. Then I get money, okay?"

"Okay, we'll spin her again. Everybody wins! This is the big game where everybody wins! There she goes, there she *goes*, and where she stops, nobody knows. Aw, that's too *bad*, my friend. Can't win every time. Everybody's luck runs out once in a while."

The Chinaman flips. "You cheat!" he hollers. "You cheat me! You take my money." He is so mad he's shaking, and now his wife is pulling on his arm with her heels dug into the ground.

"Ya know what your problem is, my friend?" says Koffman. "You're a poor loser." He points to all us shills standing around and says, "Look at these gennelmen. They've been losin' all day. They ain't complainin'."

The Chinaman looks at us, one to another, all

the way around, and I can see his mind turning on. "House men," he says, quiet. "These all house men."

"Okay, move along, move along. Yer holdin' up the game."

"You don't do this. I professional gambler. I been at Los Vegas," says the Chinaman, and he pulls a little white card from his wallet and hands it to Koffman. Koffman looks at it, and stops his act for the first time all day. He starts to laugh. O Jesus, he laughs. He passes the card around to the shills, and starts to whoop and snort like the clown in the Crazy House. I see the card over one guy's shoulder. It says that the Chinaman is a "certified Las Vegas gambler," and is signed by "U.R. Aloozer."

The Chinaman grabs the card and takes off, hauling his wife along behind, while Koffman is hollering at him: "Cheapah rates for perfessionals! Come on back and try ya luck!"

This keeps him chortling and sweezing for a good fifteen minutes, till the Chinaman comes back with a cranky-looking Mountie.

"This man says he was cheated on your game. Let me see your licence, please."

Koffman takes a paper out from under the counter and the Mountie looks at it. "Okay, that's all right. Now sir," he says to the Chinaman, "you want to tell me what happened?"

The Chinaman starts squeaking about how he got taken, but he isn't making any sense, partly because most of it is in Chinese and partly because he doesn't really know what happened, anyway. The Mountie stands there, nodding his head and trying to make sense out of it. Finally the Chinaman gives up and sort of dancing and shuffling at the same time, keeps repeating, "Dam' cheat. Dam' cheat."

"What have you got to say?" the Mountie says to Koffman. By now there's a gawking, pushing crowd around the front of Koffman's wheel, but he isn't rattled a bit.

"Ya know how it is, officer. Everybody says they're cheated when they lose. But they keep comin' in and losin'. That's human nature. We run a clean game." Koffman looks innocent as hell, and leans across the counter to the Mountie. He says, loud enough so everybody in the crowd can hear:

"Besides, this Chinaman is a perfessional gambler. He's got a card in his wallet that says so."

The cop looks at the Chinaman, who has tears in his eyes by this time. You can see he can't believe what's happening to him. He takes the card out and gives it to the Mountie, ashamed of it.

"I *see*," the Mountie says, and shakes his head at the Chinaman, as if he should have known better. The Chinaman just stares at the ground, and then turns and wanders off, his wife trailing behind. After that the crowd drifts away, disappointed.

Then things start moving again and keep moving. Koffman and his boys are hauling the loot in by the handful. I'm getting spinny as hell with all the noise and the sweat, with nothing but hot dogs for scoff, but I got to hold on for that twenty bucks. I can't even remember it getting dark, but around eleven the crowd thins, and no more marks are coming in, just kids with dimes. Koffman tells me to go and get him a coffee.

When I come back, he's closed the game and is laying the money out on the counter. All the shills are standing around waiting. Koffman glances up at me. "We'll need ya tomorrow," he says. "I'm going to hold back half your pay just to make sure ya show."

I think, Christ, that's only ten bucks. But I got no plans for coming back tomorrow, so I keep my mouth shut. Koffman peels three ones off a great Jesus stack in his hand and lays them down one after the other. "There's your pay," he says.

And there's me. The last mark of the day. What I'd like to do is jump over his counter and paste him one in the mouth, but I remember how he *never* makes a mistake. I look around, and see his boys are all grinning, waiting for me to move. One guy hitches his pants up. I stuff the three bucks in my pocket and start to move out, but Koffman isn't going to let me get away that easy.

"See ya in the mornin'!" he hollers. I'm past his circle of boys and it's pretty hard to keep my mouth shut, but I keep walking.

"See if ya can talk ya buddy inta comin' back and workin' tomorra," he yells, and his shills laugh. I turn around once to say something, and they all quit laughing to listen, but I just look at them for a minute, then I keep on walking.

By the time I get back to the bar they've quit serving and I can't even get a beer. Milt is there, swacked out of his head. He's been drinking all afternoon, finishing whatever money we had. He doesn't look too enthusiastic when I sit down.

"So ya stuck around for the payoff," he says.

I tell him yeah, I got the money, but I blew it all riding on the merry-go-round.

He starts to say something clever, but I give him a look, and he shuts his mouth again.

"Oh," he says. "Like that."

"Yeah. Like that. I got three bucks for gas, so let's start trackin' for Winnipeg."

He's going to give me a lot of goofy back-talk, so I had to kick his ass out of there and get us back on the road. I swear I have to do all Milt's thinking for him. He'd be lost on his own.

LOFT

The old grey barn my father built
is burning down
under a column of oily smoke,
releasing all the delicious seizures
our hearts felt in the hay loft
when we plunged like stricken swans
to the prickly billows of sweet alfalfa.

The ruined bunkers of our mock wars
lie buried under this monument
of black smoke: the pyramid bales
the long labyrinth tunnels
of wheat straw bleached to silver
are crumbling into slag.

The rough cough of pine timbers
popping their knots in fiery rage
silences the eerie echoes of Tarzan yells
that swung in long looping yodels at the end
of my father's lariat tied to the beam
of the black-hipped roof, my brothers
and cousins flashing out and in
among the flares of dusty sunshine
sifting down from the cupolas.

As it burns we cry at the loss.
Not the barn — next month father
will cart a new one in on timbers
chained to a dozen wheels,
hauled by a Mack truck. No.

The loss of days we laid
on the tops of breathing stacks
of oat straw, hearing the pigs munch
orange rinds on the floor below,
gazing at the squared rafters
where bluebar pigeons muttered unaware
of the angry flames which threatened
their airy sanctuary.

POEM FOR A GRADUATION BANQUET

Here I stand before you now
embalmed in respectability —
an illustrious graduate — honoured guest —
bearing this solemn invocation to success.

You are waiting — dully glaring —
waiting to hear the saga of my fortune —
my long catalogue of triumphs
in the Great Tournament of Life.

Yes, I see the groans in your eyes already —
eyes glazed from creamed corn and boredom —
eyes bartering a shred of attention
for an early ending and the dance —
so I will be brief.

This I beg you —
don't betray these last few
seconds of your ignorance —
that sweet dumb innocence
radiating from your polkadot
bow ties and stuffed brassieres.

Tomorrow will seem like freedom
after the absurd apprenticeship
of galvonometers and Bliss Carman
you endured like stoics for twelve years
but listen to me.   Tomorrow

you'll all be fighting for an office
with orange shag rugs —
brass fittings in the bathroom —
registered retirement savings plans.

So go out tonight and boogie your brains out —
sample the sweet poison of lemon gin —
make fools of yourselves — play basketball
at midnight naked in the old school gym.

Because the world is not your golden plum
waiting to be plucked and nibbled.
No it isn't, I'm afraid.
It's not.   It   is   not.

THE DANGERFIELDS

I don't usually stop for hitch-hikers out on the highway, especially when I'm blacktop-barrelling homeward for the weekend, but this kid was standing there in the middle of winter beside the road, with his thumb hanging out like a frozen banana, feeling sorry for himself in the blowing snow. So pity got the drop on my good sense, and I geared the old GMC down to a walk and picked him up.

"Where ya headin', brighteyes?"

"Saskatoon," he says, just like Saskatoon was the only stop on this highway, even though it was still a hundred and fifty miles up the road. A city-kid, just like I figured.

"You're in luck, buddy. I'm goin' right through to Maidstone. Ever hear of it? I'll drop you right off at your house."

"I'm not going home. I'm just gonna hang out with some friends of mine. They got a big bash all lined up. It's pub-nite at the MUB."

"You go tuh university or something?"

"You bet your socks, Zeke. I'm an Engineer."

"Zatta fack? Lotsa money in that, I giss?"

"Well yeah—if you get a degree. Yuh gotta pass classes and stuff, and that can be a drag. I flunked both English and calculus at Christmas. But—gonna buckle down and tackle the old books one of these days."

"That's fer sure. Got 'em with ya?"

"Hey. This is a weekend off! What are you, some sort of workaholic?"

Well, I dropped *that* subject like a scoopful of pig-shit. I get dangerous when it comes to name-callin'. So we're rollin' along the highway, doin' a little foot-tappin' with Tammy and Waylon on the radio, when just about Aylesbury or thereabouts, he turns and says, "Hey, I know a guy from Maidstone."

"Yeah? Who's 'at?"

"Dangerfield. Lewis Dangerfield!"

I nearly fell out the door a my goddam truck. "You know Lewey?"

"Yeah, him and me were at Air Cadet camp together a couple a years ago. Fantastic guy."

"Well, I'll be goddamned to a week in a hoor-house! You know why I'm going home right now? And losing a whole goddam Saturday's overtime at the warehouse? 'Cuz we're throwin' a twenty-first birthday party for Lew tonight at our house. He's my cousin!"

"Go on! Your cousin?"

"No shit."

"Fantastic guy."

"Hell of a fantastic guy."

"Him and me used to sneak outta camp on Friday nights and go into Moose Jaw to that dance hall they had. Got torn down last year."

"Temple Gardens."

"Yeah, Temple Gardens. Fantastic place. One time, they tried to bounce Dangerfield out of there cause some a the townies were trying to get a fight together. They thought he was an airman, see? They really hate the pigeons there. Whew! Ever seen a bouncer get bounced before? They finally hadda call the cops."

"Yup, that's Lew Dangerfield awright. One time he came drunk to a curling bonspiel in Maidstone. Pissed right out of his head. They aren't gonna let him on the ice, and ya know what he done? Picked up one a them curling rocks and took a bite outuv it!"

"Tuh hell!"

"Hey, I was there. I seen it! Bit a chunk right out a the side of it."

That held him for a while, till we got about as far as Bladworth, and the kid says, "Yuh know, I haven't got a hell of a lot to do in Saskatoon, really. I'm not even sure I can find these guys. Whuddaya say we pick up a six-pack of Boh and I'll go along with you to Lewey's party? I could use a good celebration."

"Don't see why not. He'll probably get a big charge outta seein' you."

Anyway, we got to bull-shittin' and carryin' on all the way to Saskatoon, where we split the purchase of a dozen Boh and an extra bottle of rye just in case we ran out before the party started. Good thing we did, too, because we'd pretty well wasted the box of beer by the time we got to Maidstone, and it wouldn't have been too cool to show up for the party with nuthin' in our hands but the time of day.

We got to my folks' place in good time to clean

up a bit. While I was changing from my work clothes and takin' a shower, the kid was tellin' my old lady what a great life he was living at the Engineering College and all the stunts they were pulling, like hoisting an old car up on to the top floor of the Education Building, and beer-keg rolling contests and that sort of stuff, till my old man finally came into the bathroom.

"Jeeze, these city-boys are some bullshit-artists, eh?" he says. "Didjah hear that about carryin' the car up to the fourth floor of one a the university buildings?"

"Yeah."

"Spouts more b.s. than a bunged-up Black Angus bull. Wherejah find him?"

"Hitch-hikin' from Regina. He's an old friend of Lewey's."

"That figgers."

"Came fer the party."

"Hope yuh thought to invite the Mounties. Last time, they busted half the party between here and the access road. All that was givin' *them* the pip was they wasn't asked."

"Pa, it ain't that kind of party. It's a family celebration. His parents are comin' and all."

"That's what you said the last time. Where's this kid gonna sleep tonight?"

"Dunno. Giss he kin have my bed, and I'll crash in Grampa's bed."

"Just make sure ya clear Grampa this time, okay?"

"Just make sure he don't try and climb into Gramma's bed after he gets a skinful a whiskey, okay? Last time there was nearly a fatal gun accident. Mounties ain't gonna like that."

"Another thing. Yer old lady izzen too keen on a lot of hollerin' and carryin' on after the sun comes up."

"Yeah, yeah, we'll shut her down. Loan me yer razor a minnit, will ya? Hey Paul!" I hollered at the kid. "Ya wanta have a shower er anythin'?"

"Naw, I'm okay."

"Shave?"

"Naw, that's cool. I'm startin' a beard."

This broke Pa up some, so he hadda go and lay down on the front sofa and snicker for a while.

We thought it would be a hoot if we didn't tell Big Lew about his friend Paul, so's we could unload a big surprise at the party. And that's what we proceeded to do. This meant going down and killing some time at the Maidstone Hotel in town.

Actually, I only planned to take him down there and let him relax for a while till the party got rolling good, but the little guy turned out to be so entertaining, I got carried away and stayed down there with him. He was funnier than a randy one-legged rooster, with all his jokes and those crazy stories about the Engineers. He was such a big hit with the old boys, they were buying the beer for him like a visiting celebrity. But one thing proceeded to another, and it wasn't long before he had to demonstrate a triple-bank takeout on Jerry's old shuffleboard, and not only did he take out the rock, he took the end out of the shuffleboard itself, and sent the rock flying through the air right into the back of Elsie Grunwald's head, and that was it for the imported entertainment, even though some of the oldtimers said it was the best live act they had seen since George Wiens the Hutterite quit bitin' the heads offa chickens for a beer.

Anyway, we were pretty well hammered by the time we got back on the road out to the Dangerfield Homestead, which is about five miles out and one mean stretch of winter road, because of the drifting in the hollows. We had a fair suck on the Seagram's we discovered in the glove compartment along the way so the kid was totally blitzed by the time we rolled into the farmyard, dogs barking and yammering like coyotes, on account of the excitement. There was about thirty cars and trucks in the yard, even a couple of snowmobiles. I reckoned three quarters of them were Dangerfields.

We staggered up the front steps and while I was trying to kick the door in, the kid leaned over beside the front step and puked his toenails up in the lilac bushes. Just then Old Man Dangerfield, Lew's father, opened the door.

"Arnie!" he says. "Glad you could make it!"

"This here's Lewey's old buddy Paul, from Boy Scout camp. A twenty-first birthday surprise. All the way from Regina."

"Air cadess," Paul insisted, wiping drool off his chin.

"Well come on *in*, boys! *Lew!* An old friend of yours from the Boy Scouts. Come all the way from —where did you say you were from, son?"

"Regina."

"Wagner! Hey! Paul Wagner!"

Lew comes roaring up from the other end of the living room, a bottle of Blue in one hand and a hunk of birthday cake in the other, and leaps at the little bugger, nearly flattening him against the front door.

"Arnie, where the hellja find this guy?"

"Brung him up from Regina. He looked like he

could use a little wringin' out.''

"Hey folks! This here's my old pal Shorty Wagner, the hottest air cadet since Billy Bishop. Tell 'em about the time we flew the Link Trainer through the top floor of the Robin Hood Flour Mill, Shorty!''

To cut a long story short, it was a great bash, with the booze flowing non-stop. There must have been at least ten Texas mickeys and two fridges were crammed full of beer. All my sisters were there with their husbands and boy friends, and most of our cousins and uncles, so Shorty was having the time of his life, playing the city big-shot to all these folks, with Lew and me eggin' him on. My uncle Wayne got his electric guitar out, and they soon had an accordion and a busted-down violin just going at the Old-Time music like a dog full of splinters. The whole place was jumping up and down, better than twin waterbeds. It was only when the musicians wore out and the record player started up with some classical Rock'n'Roll that we noticed that the kid had dropped out of sight.

"Paul, you shrunken little chicken-turd! Where are ya?'' Lew was bellering at the top of his lungs, but that didn't uncover him. Him and me and a couple of others looked in all the rooms, even the clothes closets, but he'd just up and disappeared.

"The little bugger musta gone out to take a leak, and got lost in the storm!'' Lew yells. So we all had to get our parkas and snowmobile suits on, then run around outside, looking in all the cars, even checking the machine sheds, but he was nowhere in sight. We were all getting a little pissed-off at the stupid little son of a bitch, who couldn't do the simplest thing without causing a riot in the rhubarb-patch. After we all marched back inside, we sat around the kitchen having another beer and tryna decide whether to send out a search party. Just then the basement door opens and there he is, standing in the doorway with nothing but his jockey shorts and this stunned look in his eyes, like he'd just woke up, stretching and looking around.

"Where am I?"

Laugh? Paw bust his stitches—he said later he could actually hear them snap.

"You're standing in the middle of my kitchen, ya little creep. Where the hell ya bin? We bin out scouring the back forty, lookin' for you."

"Hmph. Well, I just woke up on some sofa downstairs, under a bunch of coats and stuff. Where's my clo'es?"

"You don't know where your clothes are?"

"Musta took 'em off to lie down."

"Well bugger me with a bent fork, if he isn't the saddest looking sight I've seen for a while. Arnie, you git down there and help him find his clo'es before he freezes somethin' vital and winds up in the Pope's choir!"

Well, I went down to the basement and looked around, but I couldn't find them anywhere, though I discovered he'd been flaked out for the last hour or two on our old sofa. There was a bunch of old coveralls and the like he'd burrowed under, so nobody'd see him. I took a set of these old coveralls back upstairs. Somebody'd put on the old Elvis and Buddy Holly records and there was a Fifties-style Jive Contest goin' on, with the kid just wailin' away in his orange jockey shorts, and Dangerfields standing five-deep hootin' him on.

We finally had to call a stop to it when he grabbed a hold of Gramma, and had *her* up jivin' away, tryna flip her over his back and throuᵍh the air. A regular ball of fire, he was, though Gramma was pretty cool to the operation, hollerin' at him to let her go. We finally had to stop the show for humanitarian reasons.

"Listen," I says to him. "Where's yer clo'es?"

"Dunno. Did I come with clothes on?"

"Yeah, you came with clo'es on. Whujuh do with 'em?"

"Dunno. What did they look like?"

"You had an Edmonton Oilers sweat-shirt and a pair of blue jeans."

"Wasn't me, officer!"

"All right, little soldier. We're gonna send you beddy-byes before you really embarass yourself. Come on."

"No. Wanna dance."

"Dancin's over. Time fer serious drinkin' now, and I reckon yer past that. Let's go."

I put him in my bed, though I had a few second thoughts about that, figuring he'd wake up and fling his cookies all over the bedroom, but I was gettin' past the point of no return myself.

In fact, I don't remember a lot more until about ten the next morning. I realized something was wrong when I woke up in my own bed, with a hell of a racket going on down the hall.

"Get out!" somebody was screaming. *You filthy pig! Get out!*

I was just in time to see Shorty Wagner somersault out of Gramma's bedroom, and her right behind him in her night-gown, whacking away on his bare back with her blackthorn cane. Before I could move, he'd gone skidding into the next door down the hallway. It was Mom and Pa's bedroom, and that stopped him pretty cold, too.

He turned around then, staring at me with this agonized look on his face. I could see he was in real difficulty. "Where's the can?" he whimpered.

"Can?"

"The john! Bathroom!"

"We don't have a bathroom, Paul. Just—you know—piss-pots, or the backhouse."

He looked at the back door with terror in his eyes. "I woke up on some wreck of a sofa in the basement. Without my clothes! And I remember dancing with some old lady. I hope I didn't—!"

"Naw, you were okay."

"Arnie, I have to take a crap—real bad!"

"Well, there's the toilet, outside."

He ran to the kitchen and peered out the back window. The shit house was sitting about forty yards from the back door, big drifts of snow piled up around it. Even the path was blown in.

"I can't go out there! Where's a piss-pot?"

"Well, okay—but it's in Gramma's room—"

"I gotta *go!*"

With that, he leaped to the back door, and grabbed one of the Old Lady's hooked rugs that was lying there for wiping boots on. It was purple and yellow, with a big bouquet of flowers in the centre. The kid yanked it up and threw it over his shoulders like a cape. Not even stopping to test the temperature, he flung open the door and jumped into a pair of the Old Man's heavy rubber boots standing there. Then he was gone, flying off the backstep and running like fury as soon as he hit the snow.

I jumped to the window to watch as he went leaping like a kangaroo through the drifts, ploughing a deep furrow all the way to the shitter. With the mat flying backwards in the breeze, he looked like some kind of runty Superman, trying to take off into the air like a wounded duck.

Then he hit the door. It was closed by a simple wooden latch which he just ripped off the nail as he charged through not even bothering to close it as he hucked himself onto the seat. The door slowly swung closed behind him.

By then Gramma and Grampa, even the Old Man, had run out to the kitchen to see what the commotion was all about. "Who the hell was that?" Grampa said.

"That was Lew's buddy from the city, Grampa. He was sleepin' in the basement. Seems he got caught short."

"Why didn't you give him the goddamn pot?"

"I was going to, but it was under Gramma's bed, and—well, he was in a big hurry."

"Poor little bugger. Look at him out there— freezin' his nuts off!"

Just then the door swung open again, and the kid stepped out into the snow, lookin' bluer than a pail of skim milk, you could see his boots were full of snow to the knees. He took one more step, and stopped, like he was all set to give up and die on the spot. Your heart had to go out to the little bugger.

Then he looked up and saw us in the window, staring at him with those dumb flowers wrapped around his shoulders. He straightened up and began marching back through the snowdrifts, for all the world like one of them Buckingham Palace guards.

"Now that's dignity," Pa said.

Even Grampa bust out in a cheer.

By the time he got to the back door, he was stiffer than a length of barnboard, but we had a couple of blankets ready to throw around him. Pa lifted him out of the rubber boots, and we carried him into the living room to lay him down on the sofa. Ma had found his clothes by then, stashed in the bottom of the broom closet, beside the basement door.

"Kid," the Old Man says. "You come back here and visit the Dangerfields any time you want. Even if y'are a city-boy. You're gonna be a legend in these parts."

Paul just smiled and closed his eyes, already drifting off to sleep, one relieved little engineer.

TRUCKIN'

I thought George was gonna swallow his Ole Port ceegar when he saw that orange Redi-Mix truck come barrelling up the drive toward the farmyard. We were sitting on the back step after dinner, while Adele was watching TV and doing the dishes.

"Look at that crazy bugger," George says. The truck was all shiny in the noon sun, just a-churning up George's driveway from the grid road, great Jesus clods of gumbo flying in all directions, and the ceement mixer on the back going full-tilt.

"It's gotta be a Yewkeranian!" George says. "*Lookit* that crazy bugger!"

All of a sudden the truck hits the soft grade, and she's swerving all over the road like a gopher with crushed nuts. Any second she's going to go shooting off into the summerfallow.

"I told 'em!" George says, "I told 'em to get it in here before ten o'clock!" It rained like hell the day before, and overnight there was a heavy October freeze. The road had stayed solid till around ten in the morning, but after eleven that driveway of old George's turned into the slickest grade this side of the Panama Canal.

"Better git down there," he says, "and stop that there Yewkeranian before he ends up in thuh summerfalluh."

I'm still standing beside the house with my mouth hanging open. "He might make it," I says, not wanting to get my cowboy boots all muddy. They're a real good pair with two-tone leather tooling. It was a Saturday and I was supposed to have the afternoon off to go into town and have a couple of games of pea pool.

"Get goin'," George says.

"Can I take the John Deere?"

"*No*, dammit! *Run!*"

I take off down the road, trying to stop him before he hits the dip near the dug-out. But what with stopping every ten yards to kick lumps of mud off my boots, I couldn't run worth a pinch of badger shit. It must've took me a good five minutes to go the quarter mile. All the time I'm hollering *stop*, *stop* and waving my arms like a Frog, but he didn't even slow down.

When he hits the dip, the ass end of the truck goes slewing off the side of the road like I expected, but the front end keeps on going, kind of sideways. It looked just like George's old red boar, the time he got the grain auger dropped on his back, and kept dragging himself around the farmyard with his front legs, going slower and slower till he finally groaned to a stop.

The driver jumps out and gallops around the truck, the wheels mired down in the gumbo. The mixer on the back was turning, making the truck slide further into the ditch. Right beside the ditch was George's dug-out, and it was full. Full of water twenty feet deep and full of trout George had planted in there last spring.

"Yuh *dope!*" I says, ploughing up to him. "Don't yuh know it *rained?* This ain't thuh Trans-Canada Highway, yuh know."

But he isn't even listening to me. He leaps back into the cab and grabs one of them two-way radio mikeraphones. "Six-five!" he yells. "This is one-three. Hello six-five! *Hello, six-five!*"

"Hey!" I says. "Don't yuh know it *rained . . .?*"

"Hold on a sec. *Hello*, six-five! This is one-three. *Come in*, six-five!"

Only a young guy he was, looked like one of them university students, tall and sort of skinny with a set of glasses—but he couldn't 've been, or he would've been at school. He looked like a Uke, too, with this bushy hair sticking straight out from his head.

"Nobody there," he finally says, throwing the mikeraphone down and scrambling around the truck again, kicking the wheels. He was in a fix okay. Every time the ceement mixer turned, the truck slid another inch toward the dug-out. Oh, a real fix.

"Listen," he says, "there's six yards of concrete in here for your granary floor. It's gonna *tip over!* Where's your tractor? Maybe we can pull it back on the road.

"Isn't my granary floor," I says. "It's George's granary floor."

He smacks himself in the forehead with his fist. *Whap*, just like that, and that's when I knew he was a Uke for sure.

"Why don't you shut the mixer off?" I says. "Won't slide then."

"You ever spent eight hours chipping concrete out of a mixer? Come on! Let's go and get that tractor!"

"Not my tractor, yuh don't," George says, slogging up in his old rubber boots. He's gasping and wheezing for breath, but still got the Ole Port stuck in his face.

"I never bin on the inside a one of them things," I says, climbing up on the back to see inside.

"Listen, do you guys want this concrete or not?"

"Never ordered it for no one o'clock in thuh afternoon," George says. "I told 'em to get it up before ten. Before thuh road turned soft."

The kid wallops himself in the head again. "All *I* know is I was supposed to deliver six yards for a granary. You got a granary, *right*? Now do you want this stuff or don't you?"

"Don't want her here," George says. "Want her up there." He points up behind the barn where him and me laid out all the plywood forms the day before.

Just then, the truck sort of shudders sideways another six inches, and the kid leaps at the side of it, heaving with all his might and trying to lift it back onto the grade.

"Give me a hand!" he yells at us from under one arm. "Or I'll have to dump it out here!"

George, he hawks a big gob, right beside the kid's feet where they're sliding into the ditch, making long gouges in the mud. "Don't hurt me none," he says. "Ceement ain't mine till she's slung into thuh granary."

The kid looks at George and at me and at his truck shivering slowly into the ditch. His face is so red, I'm afraid he's going to rupture himself, but finally he lets go and grabs the mikeraphone out of the cab again. "Mayday!" he hollers at the top of his lungs. "*Mayday!* In the ditch! Losing truck! Is anybody out there? MAAAAYDAAAAYYYYY!"

We all listen for an answer, but all there is is static. He shuts the mikeraphone off, and stares at it. "Guess they're all out for coffee."

"They Yewkeranians too?" George says.

"I'm not a Ukrainian!"

"Oh." George grins at me.

"Listen," the kid says. "Be reasonable. Why *can't* we pull it with your tractor?"

"Oney drag the tractor into the dug-out, too. Or get it bogged down in this here gumbo. Either way, it's too risky. Now if your truck was *empty*," he says, flicking his cigar ashes at it, "wouldn't be no problem."

"I can't just *dump* it. They'll dock it off my wages."

"It's a bugger awright," George says.

The kid thinks for a minute. "If I shut off the mixer maybe we could—*haul* the concrete to your granary. In barrels or something."

George gives me a funny kind of questioning look, which makes me nervous, 'cause I'm still planning to spend the afternoon playing pea pool at the Royal Billiards.

"Maybe the old stoneboat," I says. "If we can find some barls."

"Sure!" The kid looks brighter right away. "Sure, that'll work!"

"Okay," George says to me. "You take him and get the stoneboat and thuh John Deere, and we'll see what we kin do for this Yewkeranian."

"I got my good clo'es on, George. I was gonna go to town today. Siggie and Carl are meetin' me..."

"I'm not a Ukrainian," the kid says.

"Gotta get that grainry finished before freeze-up, Nick," says old George.

"This is my goddam day off," I says. "If you think I'm gonna get all dirty haulin' ceement—"

"Move!" he says.

The Uke shuts the mixer off, the truck stops sliding, and me and him hit off for the buildings. George, he stays behind to keep an eye on the truck. The kid keeps getting ahead, waving and yelling at me, but I keep plodding along to the yard, taking my time. By the time I get to the machine shed and start the John Deere, the kid has pulled the stoneboat across the yard by himself, which isn't a bad stunt. We sling it on behind the tractor with a chain and clevis.

I manage to find three gas barrels with the tops cut out. They weren't really enough, but there was no time to go around cutting any more, so the kid just throws them on the stoneboat and we chug straight out the yard and down the drive. He keeps hollering something, but I can't hear him over the engine and the racket of them barrels clanging against each other. I got the throttle opened to the hilt, and the tractor is showering the stoneboat with so much mud it looks like the kid's following the wrong end of a manure-spreader. But he just keeps waving *faster, faster*, so I'm pouring it to the old John Deere.

When we get back, George is leaning against the truck, useless as tits on a bull. The Uke is off the stoneboat in a flash, his legs a-going like pistons.

Right away, the mixer's rolling again, and by the time I get the tractor and stoneboat out in the field behind the truck, he's got the chute all set up. Not even stopping for breath, he zonks the ceement into them barrels and you could tell he was going to get every last yard of it hauled or bust a gut trying. He filled them to the top, but even so, they didn't hold half of it.

Next thing we know, he's jumped onto the seat of the John Deere, and it's all I can do to get myself on the stoneboat before he takes off. We go slithering around the field in circles a couple of times before he finally gets back on the driveway. I have to grab the barrels and hang on, or else get pitched off in the mud. There isn't much to choose between, though, what with George's summerfallow zipping by and the ceement flying out of them barrels in waves every time we hit a rut. It's sure making one hell of a mess out of my good black Western shirt with the mother-of-pearl buttons.

Just as we make it back onto the drive, I hear this funny screech—and there's old George churning along behind, like a Guinea hen in rubber boots, his arms stretched out trying to catch us. I lean way out and manage to grab one hand just before the kid hits the throttle, and we go most of the way to the yard like that, towing George through the muck by one arm like a busted-down water-skier. I finally manage to get him hauled onto the stoneboat just before we go sailing around the barn and pull up at the grainry.

The ceement forms are set in a square where George wants the floor, so the kid and me dump the barrels and fling them on the stoneboat to head back for another load. But old George is looking a little thoughtful. "Hold on," he says. "We gotta *level* this ceement before she sets."

The kid looks at George with a grin. "Ceement's yours when she's slung into the granary," he says, and leaps back onto the tractor. I grab George before he can think of an answer, and we pile onto the stoneboat as the kid roars off to pick up another load.

We're just swinging past the house when suddenly the kid jams on the brakes and everything goes off like an explosion, barrels flying in all directions, banging and gonging like church bells. I come plunging out of the sky, scrambling on my hands and knees through the cinders in the yard, and hear the John Deere go skidding into a pile of storm windows George had stacked up on the other side of the house, waiting for me to put on.

"*What the hell?*" George is roaring from the stoneboat. His chin is bleeding where he got uppercut with a barrel, but at least he didn't go overboard and scour the knees out of his only pair a brand new GWG's. "*What the hell?*"

Meanwhile, the kid is running up to the house. "Cream cans!" he yells, pointing at a couple of Adele's cream cans sitting on the back step waiting to be filled. "We gotta get it *all* this time."

Adele must have heard the cans banging, because she comes trotting out the door with a dish towel in her hand, just in time to see this Ukrainian taking off with her cream cans.

"Halt!" she screams. "Halt or I'll shoot!" Adele gets a lot of stuff from TV, but the kid doesn't know that. He freezes, standing there with the cans like a statue of Louis Pasteur or something, till George says, "For chrissakes Adele, it's *okay*!"

They're for the ceement!"

She looks kind of blank, staring at us standing there in the yard, plastered with mud and ceement from toenail to teakettle, blood dripping from George's face. Then she says all hands to the rescue or something, and goes running into the house and out again with her old straw hat down over her ears.

George, he spies a five-gallon grease pail over by the machine shed and goes after that, while the kid is shouting "Let's go! Let's go!" But Adele is already galloping back to the house, squeaking about the milk pails. Then I remember a rusty old separator bowl out in the weeds by the back-house, so I go threshing through the nettles looking for it and I'm just digging it out when here comes Adele running out with her arms full of milk pails.

"The butter churn!" George hollers at her when they meet in the yard. "*Where the Christ is the butter churn?*"

Meantime, the kid is going bats up there on the John Deere, roaring the engine and yelling at everybody to get on the stoneboat. George manages to fall aboard with the butter churn, and we're off zooming down the drive again with him clutching the churn against his overalls. I find myself holding on to Adele so she won't fly out on her head.

"What the dickens is going *on*, George?" she keeps saying, ducking and bobbing while the clods whistle past her ears. But he isn't paying any attention, just screaming at the kid to let her rip, all the way back to the truck.

I thought for sure we'd get it all this time, with all the extra pails and everything, but there was still a lot of it left. The kid isn't even fazed. He just takes one look around at George—and dumps the rest of it into the stoneboat. There wasn't much else he could do, because there was no time for another load. But George and Adele wouldn't get in the stoneboat, which was six inches deep in ceement, and they made me go in and hold the barrels.

All the way back to the grainry, I'm watching the ceement washing up against the sides of the stoneboat, rising up and down my good Western boots like a tide. George, you son of a bitch, I think, this is the last Saturday I'm going to be here to work for you, I don't care if you are my old man. You never treated me like a son, so there's no reason I should hang around being loyal.

It was like pulling guts through a barb-wire fence, trying to get all that ceement into the grainry. It must've took a good half-hour, 'cause by then it was drying out into big pasty chunks. All the time George is going at it with a plank and trowel, trying to get it levelled. There is a big pile of ceement in the corner where we shovelled it out of the stoneboat.

"Well," the kid says, scraping out the last barrel, "we did her."

"You fought the good fight," Adele says.

"Never mind that," I says. "Who's gonna look after getting my boots clean?"

"Your boots! What am I gonna do with *this*?" George points to the tower of ceement in the corner. It must've been a good four feet high. Adele is trying to pry some of it off into a milk pail, but getting nowhere.

The kid looks at the ceement pile for a minute. "You could put a brass plaque on it," he says. "Call it a Ukrainian Sculpture."

George, he gets this constipated look, but Adele just smiles and says, "I thought you done real *good* for a Yewkeranian."

The kid bashes his head again, and goes galloping off down the drive to his truck, jumping into it on the dead run. He guns her back and forth in the summerfallow till she comes roaring back onto the road in a burst of flying mud. He doesn't even stop, but with the truck already cannon-balling backwards down the drive, he opens the door and hangs out, one foot on the running board, to wave at the three of us standing there in the grainry.

"I told you he was a Yewkeranian," George says, watching him as he disappeared down the road with a big grin and the wheels throwing up big Jesus clods of mud all over the countryside.

LOOSE RUCK

Happy and me are playing Starship Destruction in the pool hall. After twenty games we are nearly tied for top score, a hundred and eighty thousand kills on the Electronic Laserbeams. Happy is just about to score big, when all hell breaks loose at the front of the pool hall. Brennan comes running in like Intergalactic war has just been declared. "*Happy*! Where's Happy Hunchuck?"

This blows Happy's cool. He misses a couple of Alien Starships, and one of their weapons blasts his fighter off the screen. He's blown his chance at the big one-eight-oh. "Ya fackin' dipstick!" he snarls at Brennan. "Look at that! The screen's gone dead! I was gonna beat the fackin' record!"

"Geeze, I'm sorry, Hap. But there's a game on in Regina this aft! In half an hour."

Brennan is the manager of Moose Jaw Gophers Rugby Club. He never has enough players, because he doesn't know how to get them organized. It's a big joke. In the winter, he manages the broomball team and they're even worse.

"A rugby game?" Happy says.

"Where's your cleats, man?" Brennan moans. "We gotta get movin! We're short at least three players."

"How come nobody told me about this game?" Happy forgets all about Starship Destruction. "You think I'm gettin' too slow or somethin'? Not good enough for you guys any more? Wut's goin' on?"

"No, Hap! No!" Brennan pulls off his POOL hat and starts twisting it with his hands. "If you'd only 'a come to practice on Thursday, you woulda known about it. What do you want me to do? You guys never want to come to practice all summer long. Everybody wants to play on Saturday, but nobody wants to practice on Thursdays. Everything gets left to me. You think I enjoy it or something?"

"Aaaa, shut up," Happy says. "Who we playing, the Condors?"

"Yeah, the Condors. And everybody's buggered off to the lake for the weekend. Same old story. Nobody's ever around in August."

"Yeah, maybe you're right. It's too hot to be running up and down a rugby field kicking the shit out of the Condors. How about a game of snooker, Brennan? I'll spot ya twenty points."

Brennan nearly swallows his POOL hat, he's squeezing his hands so hard on his head. "Hap— we're really stuck! Piston and Wombat both took off to the mountains for two weeks, and we got nobody to play in the second row! And if we don't have a second row, the Condors could *beat* us."

"Aaaa. That bunch of pansies? How about Alex?" Happy points to me with his thumb. "He kin play second row."

Brennan looks me up and down, looking kind of glum, just like he does whenever I go to Thursday practice. "Yeah—maybe."

"I got nuthin' else to do today anyways," I say. "And I think I remember the off-side rule now."

"It isn't just the off-side rule," Brennan says to Happy. "He's always tryna rip some guy's head off."

"I been practisin', Brennan! I know the rules. It's only that I get excited."

"Yeah. And we get the penalties. It was your dumb penalties in Edmonton that lost us the game against the Barbarians."

"If Alex doesn't play," Happy says, "I don't play."

Brennan doesn't like this one bit, but without big Hap in the scrums and the loose rucks, the Gophers aren't going to get any ball for their running backs, and he knows it. "Okay," he says, "let's go."

Outside on the street, it's like walking into a furnace. I mean it's about one o'clock and *nothing* is moving on the sidewalks of old Moose Jaw. Brennan's car, a bright yellow fifty-seven Caddy, is waiting at the curb, and we climb in. This is the first time I ever got a ride in it, a real dynamite machine he's been fixing for years.

"Man, this hot is *extreme*," Happy says. "Let's grab a box of beer and head out to the lake!"

"The Condors got some booze laid on after the game!"

"Yeah?" Happy says, looking interested again. "Maybe they're gonna act human."

"Well, actually, they're givin' us a barbecue. It's gonna be on Willow Island. Wives and girl-friends. And they're inviting a bunch a nurses."

"No shit!" Happy brightens right up. "Well,

let's go! Stop by the Cecil on the way to my place and we'll pull a case of beer.''

"Well—okay. After we get your equipment. And no drinking in the car, okay? The cops are always pulling me over for a check.''

"Aaaa—get rid of your pair a noya," Happy says. I look around inside the car for pair a these noyas, but all I see is some foam rubber dice hanging from the light. Maybe that's where Brennan keeps his dope stash or something. Inside of them.

Happy and me chip in and buy a two-four of Labatt's plus a couple of jumbo potato chips. Neither of us had any breakfast yet. It's only a half-an-hour till the game by the time we get out on the Trans-Canada Highway, and Brennan won't break the speed limit. He's scared of cops ever since he got pinched one time for riding his bike double across Fourth Avenue Bridge. It's nuts, really, because the highway is four lanes all the way to Regina, straight as a donkey's cock and barely a car on it.

"Brennan," Happy says, reaching one hand into the back seat so I can put a bottle of Labatt's in it. "What's the point of having a machine like this if you don't burn highway? Aren't we supposeta be late or something?"

"It isn't for racing. It's a show car!"

"Come *on*, man! You're lettin' all these Volkswagens and Datsuns *pass* us! And there izzen a cop in sight! When are you gonna give these goobers the benefit of all that double-carb and high suspension you put into this pig?"

"Hey, you guys! I said *no drinking* in the car!"

"Aaaa, don't be a pill, nobody asked you to drink it! If I don't get some liquid, I'll never last five minutes in this heat. You want us to win, doncha?"

All the time we are guzzling away on the La-
batt's, Brennan is checking in his mirrors and win-
dows for the sight of a cop car suddenly appearing
out of nowhere. With Happy egging him on, he fin-
ally starts passing the odd car. It isn't long before
some kid in a Duster pulls up alongside, moving
about seventy. He revs the engine a couple of times,
then Brennan takes off in a roar, leaving the kid
with his mouth hanging open in the fast lane. That
Caddy of Brennan's feels like a rocket taking off.
He could make a fortune if he wasn't so chicken-
shit of racing.

Anyways, we polish off about half the beer be-
fore pulling up at the Condors' field. The match is
already started. All the Gophers are running around
in their green-and-white uniforms and hollering for
us to get onto the field. They're getting beat twelve
to zip. Everybody is blaming Brennan for it like al-
ways. "Brennan, ya turkey!" they're yelling. "Did-
ja stop for a wank or what? Cummon ya dumb bas-
tard, get those guys out here! Didja bring that fack-
in' water jug?"

They're three players short, so they need me to
play second row with Happy. By the time we get our
cleats on and actually hit the field, the score is fif-
teen-nothing against, but the Condors are a bunch
of cream-pouffs anyway, nobody figures we'll have
any trouble straightening them out once we have a
full side. Happy always makes a difference.

At the first lineout, he stretches way up and
grabs the ball coming in, not even bothering to pull
it down for a loose scrum. He just takes off, his
bloodshot eyes glowing like bike reflectors, blasting
through the Condors' pack and heading for their
goal line. As soon as he busts through the for-

wards, he runs straight at their half-backs, levelling his head at them like a battering ram and picking up speed all the way, making his noise sort of like *hooooooom! hooooooom!* daring them to get in his way.

Naturally he scores a try right away, and our boys start breathing a little easier. With Happy and me in the second row, we can shove the scrum all over the field. The only problem I'm having is in the loose rucking, when the ball bounces all over the place and everybody's trying to pick it up and getting their fingers smashed. As soon as somebody touches it you drill him. The only way is just to get in there and hammer away with elbows or heads or boots or whatever. But there's offside rules too, which I can never get straight, so once in a while we get a penalty.

"Alex, you big dummy!" Brennan hollers from the wing. "Just the guys in *blue*! And only when they're carrying the *ball*!"

Sometimes I get carried away and try to break somebody's leg, so I got to try and remember what our team colour is. The whole game is slow going on account of the sun, but Happy and the backs manage to keep on scoring. We finally beat them about forty to thirty. Everybody is just shagged by the end of the game, soaked in sweat and ready to fall over at the side of the field. They shouldn't allow rugby in August. Really, it could kill somebody.

But both teams get buddy-buddy soon enough, singing songs in the showers and making dirty insults about each other, which Happy says is what rugby is all about. It's a neat game like that. There's one set of rules which makes everybody hate each other on the field, so they can be friends off it. A guy who kicks your teeth out will always buy you a beer fifteen minutes later.

The Condors' barbecue was a rip-off though. They brought about six boatloads of beer over to Willow Island, and no hamburgers. There was twenty cartons of buns and not a single chunk of meat to put inside them. Somebody said we should cut up Brennan and barbecue *him* because he's such a jerk, but he gets let off if he agrees to sing ten verses of "The Hairs on Her Dicky-Die Do."

It doesn't take long for the usual zoo to get going because there's three drunk rugby-players there for every woman; pretty soon people are chasing each other through the trees. Somebody from the Condors has brought good dope for once, and I manage to be standing in the right place at the edges of the crowd while a few joints of this Colombian is going around. Being stoned makes the entertainment seem funny which is how you have to see guys whipping their jeans down and flashing their asses at the crowd. After a couple of times this gets boring, unless you're one of them doing it.

Happy is making out pretty good with one of the nurses, but when she won't go with him for a stroll into the bushes, he grabs Brennan by the arm and says, "Fack it. Let's go and get us some Big Macs! I'm starved! Alex, you coming?"

I am still hanging out by the guys with the weed, and happy enough to stay there, but he pulls me back to the ferry boat, which carries us to Brennan's car. Considering there must be a hundred McDonald's Hamburger Drive-ins in Regina, they're not easy to find. The city is all one-way streets heading in the opposite direction. What with

Happy screaming directions from the back seat where the beer was, and Brennan pretty stunned at the best of times, we are lucky we don't run over some poor bugger on the street, because it's about five-thirty in the afternoon, rush hour is on and the downtown is crawling with pedestrians. Some of them would have got a Cadillac "V" stamped on their asses if they hadn't jumped right smart.

Brennan is wheeling down this street near Victoria Park when Happy suddenly yells, "Am I goin' blind, or is that a hot dog stand?" Down the next block is a shopper's mall, the kind of place where they put up barriers to keep cars out and fill the street with park benches and little barrels full of geraniums. Smack in the centre of this mall is an old streetcar which somebody fixed into a little snack stand. A sign on top of it says, "MARVIN'S DINER ON THE MALL."

"Haaaard *left*!" Happy yells. Brennan, like a dummy, does it. You can imagine the look on old Marvin's face when this yellow Caddy comes blazing down the street and screeches to a stop in front of the window where he hands out his Weenies-on-a-Stick. He stares at us, and back up the street where gangs of pedestrians are still scrambling for cover. Here and there a few tubs of pine trees are spilling their guts onto the pavement.

"Three weenies, pardner," Happy says to him. "And make it snappy, eh? We gotta be on our way in thirty seconds."

Brennan is revving the engine, feeling nervous about all the attention we are getting. There is a couple of sexy-looking bubblegummers giving us the eye from down the street and Happy brays at them in his best hog-calling style, "Heya sweet-thighs! Wutcha doin' tonight?''

All of a sudden these four cops just *appear*, running up behind us and wailing away on the roof of Brennan's Caddy with these huge wooden clubs. Well, I dunno man, this is no way to come down out of a cloud of Colombian dreams, not knowing whether to run, fight, or just shit bricks.

Brennan flips out completely of course, flooring the old gas-pedal. We roar off in a cloud of burning rubber and flying cops, through a big squealing U-ie back the way we came in. It is *weird*, this mall full of cops jumping out of doorways and pouring around every corner like a big riot was on. They must have put on extra patrols because of the rugby game.

It doesn't do much for Brennan's nerves to see this horde of fuzz coming at us like a horror scene in a drive-in movie. He whips through a few fancy power turns among the litter-bins and park benches, past all the cops and heading fulltilt for the entrance at the far end of the mall. We are just about to fly off the curb when this big cop steps up right in front of us. He has gold braid all over him, probably the chief, holding his arm up like some bigshot anyway, expecting us to stop. This is totally the wrong approach for Brennan. He goes spaz, tramping the gas through the floor and aiming straight at the cop along the hood like an Electronic Laserbeam.

Somehow the chief flings himself off to one side as we leap the curb and head down the street. We'd have made a clean getaway, no problem at all, except that Brennan starts to *think* about all this. At the next red light, he jams on the brakes and brings the Caddy screeching to a stop.

"*What* the *fack* are you *doin'*?" Happy screams, frantically stashing all the beer under the back seat. "*Lay rubber*, ya turkey!"

"Fack you too!" Brennan yells back. "You want me to lose my licence for running a lousy red light? Doncha think they got my licence number back there? I'm not stupid, ya know!"

The two of them start hollering at each other as the fuzz run up, about ten of their fastest sprinters I guess, and they don't make any mistakes this time. They haul us out of the car in about one second, throwing us face down on the hood and slamming our feet apart. They did a search that would have found the wrinkles on an elephant's ass, banging our heads on the hood a few times just for laughs.

"Okay," the chief says, hauling Happy to his feet, "what's your name, sunshine?"

"John Wayne!" Happy snarls back at him.

"Yeah? Smart guy, eh? Let's have a look at this I.D." He flips through the cards in Happy's wallet until he finds his driver's licence. "Says here your name is Harold Hunchuck. Is that your name or is this document stolen?"

"You figure it out, Kojak!"

The chief turns to Brennan, who pissed his pants all down the front. "What's your name?"

Brennan looks around for help, not knowing whether to make a break for it or beg for mercy. "John Diefenbaker," he says. Probably the first thing that came into his head.

"Okay, I'm through playing games. Take these jokers down to the shop, while I find out what's going on here."

Brennan falls onto his knees, blubbering, "I'm not with these guys, officer! I just gave them a lift in my car, see? I was on my way down here for this rugby game. I'm the manager of the Gophers, the Moose Jaw Gophers, and these guys all needed a ride—''

"Moose Jaw?" the chief says, going squinty-eyed. "Rugby game? Constable, check that car and see if there's any liquor in there."

One of the cops rips the back seat out and they find the remains of our two-four of beer. They start carrying it out with these thirsty looks on their faces. You couldn't blame them, either, in that heat.

"Any of you even 19 yet?"

The other guys look at me, so I say, "I guess I am."

"And who are you?"

"Alex Dinwoodie. My dad's a lawyer."

"Well, you'll need him. We're going to lay charges against you punks till you can't count them. Lock them up till they're ready to co-operate!"

Down at the cop shop they take away all our money and keys, then our T-shirts and shoelaces in case we want to hang ourselves. Brennan looks like he might too. We are in a row of cells where we can talk to each other, so we try to put together a story the cops will believe.

"I know!" Happy says. "We'll tell them we came down to enroll at university. Cops love university students. They get away with everything."

"Are you nuts? You gonna try and tell them Alex is a university student? He never got out of grade six!"

"I can say psychology," I remind Brennan.

"Okay, nice and simple," Happy says. "As soon as we got to Regina we went to Wascana Park for a job, and we're filling out the applications in the employment office when this dude in there, the head guy, asks us all down to the pub for a beer. *He* bought the beer, right?''

"That'll never work," says Brennan. "They don't buy guys like us beer."

"How be if we asked *him*?"

"Shut up, Alex. Let's concentrate. Okay, we meet this dude in the street, some friend of Alex's—"

"I don't know nobody in Regina. I've only been here once!"

"We're makin' it *up*, fer crissakes!"

Just then the cops figure we've sobered up enough to haul us down to the interrogation room. The chief is waiting there with a look on his face that would have cracked ice.

"Students, eh?" he says.

We all nod, not sure how far to take this lie. Brennan does evening classes at the Tech, and I'm still registered at the Adult Education Centre, but Happy's been out of school for a year.

"To hell, you're students!" he explodes. "You're all bums! Criminals! And I'll make sure you never hold a job in decent society again! We'll exterminate you!"

Brennan starts whimpering and crying. "Wha-wha-what're we charged with, your honour?"

"Shut up! I'm talking! We could charge you with a dozen things. Dangerous driving. Obstruction of police. Carrying open liquor in a car! Being a public nuisance! Buying liquor under age. And one that you don't even know about! The *worst* one!"

"What-what-what's that?"

"A week ago we heard that some gang of hoods was going to knock off the Woolworth Store at closing time today. We mounted a special surveillance operation. I had twenty men waiting for *four hours*. Then you idiots blundered along and scared them off!" He is getting redder by the minute, thinking about it.

"We're sorry, sir," I tell him. "We're very, very sorry."

He stares at me for a minute. "Get out!"

None of us can move, just stand there gaping at each other, hardly believing our own ears. He picks up a phone and yells, "Somebody come in and throw these punks out of here before I shoot them!"

Well these two enormous detectives come bashing in and chuck us straight into the street, throwing Brennan's car keys after. It is nearly sunset, the sun just going down, but you can still hardly breathe in the heat. That doesn't slow Happy down. He goes charging back to the door of the police station and gives it a huge kick that rattles the building.

"Hey, are you guys gonna give us back our beer?" he yells up at the window. "*How about our fackin' beer, huh?*"

Brennan and me grab him and hustle him down to the compound to get the Caddy, which is sitting there all dented where the cops did their number with the clubs. All the way out of the city, going the wrong way down these one-way streets again, Happy is badmouthing the cops. "Whaddaya expect from the pigs?" he says. "You could tell they had it in for the Moose Jaw Gophers! They hated us, man! Hey Brennan, we goin' down to Winnipeg to play at Labour Day?"

"I think I got the off-side rule figured out now," I tell him.

Brennan won't say nothing, just keeps doodling along at twenty miles an hour, muttering about his car getting worked over.

"Cummon Brennan," Happy says. "Don't be a pill. It's just a car, right? A pile of fackin' metal. It coulda bin worse—we mighta lost the *game*! And the game is life, right?"

"Right on!" I chime in, but it will take a lot to cheer Brennan up tonight. I gotta try to remember the off-sides next Thursday.

THE MEADOWLARK CONNECTION

1 THE RUSSIAN WOMAN

On the Canadian prairies, summer days are always long. In Saskatchewan in June, the sunshine seems to last forever.

RCMP Constable James Ashenden glanced at the Timex Marlin on his wrist. It was ten thirty p.m. He was bone-tired after sixteen hours on the job, barely able to keep his steely blue eyes focussed on the radar graph in front of him. It was nearly dark. Traffic on No. 15 Highway to Moose Jaw had ended for the day. And Ashenden still hadn't issued his quota of speeding tickets. He sighed.

Sub-division would be getting after him again. But at least today there had been that great tip from the mayor's wife about the drugs. Perhaps that would satisfy his superiors that he was good for something besides catching speeders. If only he could get permission for an investigation.

That morning he had set up his radar trap about a mile north-east of the town of Meadowlark, where a clump of aspens screened his cruiser from the already blazing summer sun. He had risen at six and enjoyed the usual breakfast at Ellie Sanders' boardinghouse: creamy-smooth oatmeal porridge, three crisply fried eggs, a stack of toast slathered with butter and crabapple jelly.

He knew, as he drove to the pre-selected spot, that it would be another scorcher of a day. The heat was bad for that time of year. The broad Saskatchewan plains are usually blessed with heavy rains in mid-June, the better to nourish the freshly seeded wheat crops which have made the area "Bread Basket of the World." But on June 15, 1973, there had already been a solid week of relentless sunshine and the farmers were restless. Ashenden was worried. 1973 was the year of the Centenary Anniversary of the Royal Canadian Mounted Police, and Ashenden didn't want a lot of truculent wheat farmers stirring up trouble and besmirching his public image. He had been warned by sub-division office in Moose Jaw to keep a low profile.

After two hours and not one speeder, Ashenden was ready to break for coffee, when he saw a tower of dust on the access road coming from town. A big car squealed onto the pavement of the highway, and accelerated hard toward him.

Ashenden stared at the radar graph, sweat trickling from his temples. The car zipped past his scanner. Seventy-six m.p.h.! Seeing the trap too late, the driver hit his brakes, then seemed to hesitate, as if considering a get-away. He skidded to a stop about fifty yards down the road.

As the cloud of dust settled, Ashenden observed a large black Buick with Saskatchewan licence plates. A sudden apprehension churned through his stomach. His first pinch of the day was Phil Boothroyd, the mayor of Meadowlark.

The car door swung open and Phil stepped out,

chewing on his morning cigar. He was a large man, and the straw cowboy hat perched on top of his skull made him seem even larger. Ashenden could make out the thin red veins lacing through the mayor's eyeballs. This might get nasty, he thought. A meadowlark trilled innocently from a nearby fencepost.

"Morning, Mayor," he ventured.

"What the hell's going on, Ashenden?"

Mayor Boothroyd's voice sounded as though he had swallowed half the gravel dust.

"Seventy-six miles per, Mayor," Ashenden observed, taking his book from his hip pocket.

"But I'm in a hurry—on town business."

"All the more reason to set a good example for the others, Mayor." Ashenden began printing out the ticket in neat block letters. "Maybe it would help if you repeated it to yourself as you drove along: sixty m.p.h. in the day, fifty m.p.h. at night, sixty m.p.h. in the—"

"What are you doing out here, anyway, Ashenden? Last week you were on the south side. Why can't you stay in one place?"

Ashenden chuckled modestly. "But that's the whole point, Mayor. Where would law and order be if my movements were known to every criminal in town?"

"Criminal!" The mayor spat his cigar onto the road. "While you're out here pestering the citizens of Meadowlark, vice and crime are running rampant through the district!"

Ashenden handed the mayor his speeding ticket and gazed at him with level eyes. "Is that so? Maybe you should tell me all about it, Mayor."

Boothroyd hesitated. "How come you're never

around when that Russian woman's barrelling along the roads at ninety miles an hour?''

Ashenden's ears quivered alertly. "Russian?''

"Well, Yewkerainian or whatever she is. That Madam Karmakov. She comes tearing over from Shakespear every day like a bat outuv hell! But you're never out there to catch *her*!'' Mayor Booth-royd climbed back into his car and slammed the door shut.

"One minute, if you don't mind, Mayor. Why does she come to Meadowlark every day?''

The mayor leaned out the window of his car. "Let's get this straight, Ashenden—I do not go around telling tales. But there's something going on between her and that Englishman!''

"Englishman? Jeremy Pules-Feltham? The janitor at the John G. Diefenbaker Composite School?''

The mayor nodded. "That's right. She comes tearing over from Shakespear every day and night —to visit him at the school. God knows *what* goes on when them foreigners get together.''

Ashenden had been keeping his eyes on Pules-Feltham for a long time—ever since he had gone into the office of the Meadowlark *World-Spectator and Times* and seen the Englishman in there with his Ascot tie and elegant manners. Pules-Feltham had been trying to persuade Mel Ringer, the editor, to publish some "poems,'' which he had insisted on reading in his fruity English accent. Mel had told him where to take his poems quick enough.

"He's a real dilly,'' Ashenden said.

"You know how he got that job, don't you?''

"No—how?''

"Over my dead body is how. Last year, before

you were posted here, old Froggy Fenchurch was the school janitor. Then he up and run off with that Collins girl—"

"The Grade Twelve cheerleader?" Ashenden had heard oblique references to the case.

"Yeah. They took off in the thirty-seater school bus and haven't been heard of since. Anyway, a lot of the local boys could have used that janitorin' job. But this greenhorn Englishman showed up and said he had some degree or other from Oxford or one of them places, and I'll be damned if those old turkeys on the school board didn't decide they wanted an 'educated' Englishman around the school."

"The fools!"

"Anyways, as chairman of the board, I told them it was a lot of bull-wash, and that his degree was a phoney, but they wouldn't listen to common sense. Well, now they're finding out. I don't know what's going on with that Madam Karmakov, but they aren't playing no cricket game."

Ashenden had always suspected Pules-Feltham of perversion. He lived in a small bungalow on the south side of town, right across the playground from the school. This made it convenient for him to lure naive young schoolgirls into his clutches. Or maybe even—boys.

Ashenden was printing furiously in his notebook. "What do they *do* when they get together, Mayor?"

Mayor Boothroyd revved the Buick's engine. "I don't have time to explain the facts of life to you, Ashenden. If you want to hear the gory details, why don't you go and listen to my wife for a few minutes?"

"Maybe on my lunch break. Sounds like a possible morals conviction. Sorry about the speeding ticket, Mayor. How are plans coming along for the Sports Day?

"That's why I'm rushing into Moose Jaw! Have to get a permit at least a week in advance. Today's the last day before the deadline."

"Well, don't speed now, Mayor. And remember, repeat to yourself, sixty m.p.h. in the day—"

The mayor tramped on the accelerator, and the Buick shot north towards the city. A coat of dust settled slowly onto Ashenden's fawn-coloured Stetson as he gazed thoughtfully off into the distance.

"Russian, eh?" he said to himself.

After Ellie Sanders' lunch of roast pork loin and gravy, Ashenden stopped by the Boothroyd home. It was a large square house with an elaborate porch, the kind of solid structure which suited a mayor of Meadowlark and the town's largest farm machinery dealer. He did not look forward to the interview with the mayor's wife. She was forever tickling him in his ribs to make him blush. Whenever she talked to him, she made his horse-shoe tie clip all damp.

He tapped on the screen door.

"Who is it?" Mrs. Boothroyd cooed from inside.

Ashenden removed his hat in the broiling sun, trying to peer through the screen door into the darkness of the front hall. "It's me—Constable Ashenden. Can I ask you some, uh, personal questions?"

She burst into a gush of giggling. "Ohohohoh-oh, you come on in and ask me anything you want to—Jimmy."

He pushed open the screen door and stepped in. He was alarmed to observe that she wore a gaudy house-dress half-unbuttoned down the front, where an assortment of bulges gleamed.

"Phil said, uh—" he began, staring at his hat in his hands.

"Oh don't you worry about Phil—he's gone to Moose Jaw!" She giggled again, quivering like a fat threshing machine. "Bet you're all worn out today, eh Jimmy? Chasing them waitresses around the bus depot lunch counter till all hours of the night!"

Her hand suddenly shot out to tickle his ribs; Ashenden had already moved nimbly aside.

"I'd like to ask you about two persons who may be engaged in illegal activities, Mrs. Boothroyd!"

She stopped in her pursuit. "Who?"

"Madam Karmakov and Jeremy Pules-Feltham!"

Mrs. Boothroyd erupted into another spasm of giggling. She was beginning to get on his nerves.

"Have you noticed anything suspicious about their activities? For example, why does she come here every day from Shakespear?"

Mrs. Boothroyd rolled her eyes and covered her mouth with her pudgy fingers. "*Well!* Far be it from me to go around spreading malicious gossip—but did you know she stays inside his house? All night, sometimes!"

Ashenden took out his notebook and recorded the information. "Anything funny going on at the school, that children might be—exposed to?"

"Well, there's no telling what happens in the janitor's room when those two get together."

Ashenden nodded. "She might be Russian. What makes you think she might not be?"

"I thought she was Yewkerainian. What's the difference?"

"What's the *difference*?" Ashenden was shocked. "Russia is the source of international revolution! Siberian slave camps! State control of hockey!"

"No! Really?"

"Ha! That's the first thing you learn in criminal matters, Mrs. Boothroyd. Never take *anything* for granted! Do you know what Sgt. Fred McLeod told me?"

"Who's he?"

"Security Services, Training Division. He said: 'Show me an innocent—and I'll show you a Sudo Communist.' Now answer this question carefully, Mrs. Boothroyd. What is going on inside that school?"

"Well, I guess they—fool around."

"Fooling around, you call it? With innocent children? Come now, Mrs. Boothroyd! And why is he working as a *janitor*, with all that Little Lord Fauntleroy get-up? Have you ever heard of an Englishman *working*, with his bare hands? Ever?"

"No," she admitted.

"Then what in heck are they *doing*?"

Mrs. Boothroyd shrugged. "Drug-peddlers?" she suggested.

Ashenden staggered as if he had been struck by a post-maul. Drugs? In *Meadowlark*? No! Still—he had received a directive just the week before from the sub-division Officer Commanding, Inspector Angleton J. Heavysides, warning all detachments in the Moose Jaw sub-division of a wave of drug-peddling ravaging the province.

Ashenden preserved a calm appearance. There

was no point in alarming Mrs. Boothroyd and getting the whole community in a panic until he had investigated this thoroughly.

"That is a remote possibility," he said. "Please keep this information confidential until I check it out."

"Jimmy?" she sighed. "Wouldn't you like a fresh piece of chocolate cake? Just baked it last night."

Ashenden jammed his hat onto his head and marched out the door, saying good-bye firmly. He had work to do. Madam Karmakov and Jeremy Pules-Feltham didn't know it yet but their nefarious activity, whatever it was, would soon come to an end.

2 THE BLUE STING RAY

For the rest of the day, Ashenden had sat under the thin shade of the aspens, baking inside his cruiser like one of Ellie Sanders' bran muffins. He had waited for Madam Karmakov to come speeding past, turning over in his mind the bizarre plot to ensnare the pupils of the John G. Diefenbaker Composite School.

It was a very long day, almost the longest day of the year, and the purple haze of dusk had gradually deepened into starry night by the time Ashenden packed up his radar equipment and started driving home. He took the long way around as he had one last look for the elusive Madam Karmakov—south to Shakespear, and then up the Sand Valley road to enter Meadowlark from the west.

As the cruiser approached the entrance to Sand Valley Regional Park on the outskirts of Meadowlark, swooping across the small iron bridge over the Sand Valley Creek, Ashenden suddenly felt a stirring of bristles on the back of his close-cropped neck, an intimation of danger.

On an impulse, he swerved the Pontiac into the park. It was empty these days, before the annual influx of summer tourists began on July 1. But it still attracted under-age beer-drinkers, and young couples who drove out in their parents' cars to spend the night cavorting.

He cruised slowly past the clumps of Manitoba maples and chokecherry, running his searchlight over the picnic tables and barbecue stands. Flashing his headlights onto high beam, he saw a sudden glint of light in a stand of willows beside the creek.

He switched off the lights and edged the cruiser closer. A Chevrolet Corvette Stingray. Dark blue Saskatchewan licence plates: 212-345. It was Madam Karmakov.

He threw the switch on his overhead red flasher and flicked on the siren. Skidding the car to a stop, barely missing a picnic table, he flung himself out the door and sprinted to the Stingray, hoping to reach it before she swallowed any evidence.

He pounded on the roof of the Stingray with his hand. "This is the RCMP!" he barked. "Open the door and climb out slowly. I've got you covered and surrounded."

Ashenden could see a dark shape thrashing wildly about inside the car. He stepped behind the protection of a small chokecherry bush and drew his .38 calibre Special Smith & Wesson Military and Police Model 10 from its leather holster on his belt. He cocked the revolver. The door on the driver's side opened and a figure stepped out into the glare of Ashenden's flashlight. Jeremy Pules-Feltham.

Ashenden barely resisted an urge to run forward and slam the car door shut on his arm. Instead he stepped from behind the bush, his revolver held in front of him. "Keep your hands out where I can see them," he snarled. "Step away from the car."

Pules-Feltham's pale face turned toward him, trying to peer in the darkness. "I say," he said. "What the devil is going on?"

Ashenden scrutinized him closely. Pules-Feltham was breathing hard. His beady little English eyes were red-rimmed and irritable. He had all the appearance of a perverted dope-fiend.

"I'll ask the questions, if you don't mind," he

said coldly. "Who have you got in that car?"

Pules-Feltham buttoned up his shirt, stalling for time. A typical Englishman, with his la-di-da accent and fancy poetry. Well, Ashenden was hard to impress.

"Quit stalling!" he barked. "Are you by yourself?"

"Would it not seem peculiar to you, Constable," Pules-Feltham said, fastening his cufflinks, "if you came across someone parked in the local lovers' lane by *himself?*"

"Never mind the smart-aleck questions. I'll do all the asking."

"You go right ahead."

This caught Ashenden off guard. He paused, thinking of a good question. "Is this your car?" he said casually.

"No, it isn't."

"So you admit it!" Ashenden reached for his notebook, momentarily forgetting the revolver in his hand. "And whose is it?"

"Is mine, polisman," a woman said inside the car, her voice vibrating sensuously in the night air. It was Madam Karmakov.

A tall woman with dark hair and deep brown eyes stepped into the light. Ashenden was stunned. He had expected a heavy-set older woman, wearing overalls and a polka-dot *babushka* like the Russian peasant women in his training films who slaved their lives away on Siberian forced-labour collective farms.

But this woman was—he tried to think of the word—*stacked*. The front of her blouse was slightly open, and her rich, deeply tanned flesh seemed to pout toward him. She smoothed her skirt, heightening the curves of her hips as she leaned forward toward the car. She rested her bosom on the roof of the Stingray and smiled at him.

Ashenden blushed. "You must be the Russian lady," he said.

"*Rossian*?" She turned her head and spat toward the creek. "Not Rossian, polisman! Born and raised in Kiev. The Ukraine I am from!"

"Can you prove that?"

"For you, polisman, I quote from Taras Shevchenko, national poet of Ukraine."

"Just a minute," Ashenden muttered, tearing his eyes from the top of the Stingray, "I'll write that down." He put his revolver on the ground to get the notebook and pencil from his tunic pocket.

"Here, let me help," the Englishman offered.

"Ha! No, you don't! Back up and keep your hands where I can see them!"

Taras Shevchenko. He committed the name to memory. He would have to be careful with Madam Karmakov. She was clearly a more dangerous enemy than the puny Englishman. And women were especially treacherous. At Depot Division, stories were told of what women were capable of in subverting law and order. He shuddered.

"I say," Pules-Feltham said. "Aren't you supposed to inform us what the purpose is in all this?"

"You'll find out. Just stand over there by the tree. I am going to search this car thoroughly. And if I find anything incriminating, you're going to wish you'd never left merry old England."

"Perhaps if you just told us what you're looking for, we would get it out for you."

Ashenden gave him a cold steely look and wrenched the car door open. He checked the ashtrays and waste-baskets. Any place that could hold a kilo of heroin. Nothing. He started under the floor mats, working meticulously from front to back. No luck. He went through the engine—air cleaner, starter, radiator, windshield washer tank— all the time enduring the snide insults of the scrawny little Englishman.

Finally, at 1:34 a.m. by his Timex, Ashenden struck pay dirt. Reaching under the rear seat of the car, his fingers found a metal container jammed between the springs. He held it in the beam of the flashlight. It was a brass tank-like container with knobs and a glass device on the top. It looked like a kerosene lamp, but Ashenden was willing to bet a dollar to a doughnut that inside that tank he would find a stash of white powder.

He went back to the two suspects who were whispering at a nearby picnic table. They leaped apart as the constable approached.

"Perfectly innocent, eh?" He flashed the container in front of Pules-Feltham's eyes. "How about *this*?"

There was a shocked silence for ten or fifteen seconds, and the Russian woman screamed sharply, startling Ashenden. "Oh polisman!" she cried. "You heff found it! Jheremy, zhe polisman has found it!"

"You're gol-darn right I found it. Now stand up slowly, the two of you—"

"Oh sank you, polisman, you heff found for me my antique coal-oil lamp! You remember, Jheremy —we bought at auction in Shakespear?"

"Coal-oil lamp?" Ashenden said, watching them carefully.

"Where you found it, polisman?"

"Under the back seat."

"Jheremy! Giff him a five-dollars reward for finding my antique lamp." She kept up a pretty good act, Ashenden had to admit.

"I hope," he said coldly, taking out his notebook and pencil again, "that you are not trying to offer me a bribe." They weren't playing around with some Mexican border cop. This was the RCMP they were dealing with.

The Englishman put the five-dollar bill back in his wallet.

"Oh Jheremy," Madam Karmakov sighed. "Zhees Mounties! Zhey are so disciplined!"

She'd see how disciplined he was when she was standing in the prisoner's box in the court room in Moose Jaw, spilling her story as she broke down under the crushing evidence he was even now assembling for the Crown attorney.

"I'm going to let you two go for the time being," he said. "But I don't want you to leave the district without letting me know. Failure to comply with this condition could result in your arrest."

"My dear fellow," Pules-Feltham sighed. "Where could one *possibly* ask to go?"

Ashenden was tempted to arrest him anyway, for indecent exposure. His turn would come. He patted the fake dope-filled lamp, and the outline of a confident smile crossed his clean-shaven face. Madam Karmakov would be his first big bust.

3 A MOUNTED POLICEMAN'S WEEKEND

A Morals conviction would be simple, he thought as he drove toward Meadowlark. But it was the Narcotics Act that Ashenden wanted to hit them with.

The memo from Inspector Heavysides, his O.C., had said that drugs appeared first in the schools, spreading their cancerous tentacles into the community. Last month's news bulletin, in fact, had told of a corporal in Saskatoon who had put on a wig and a weird set of clothes and started going to local high school classes. Within three months, he had nailed half the Grade Twelve class for trafficking in marijuana, and given the vice-principal a good scare with a warning for possession.

Now Ashenden had his chance. He hurried into his detachment office with the lamp, chuckling to himself. His satisfaction lasted until 4:30 a.m. when he finally bashed the seams of the lamp apart and discovered—coal oil. It was impossible to repair. He would have to take it over to Gordie Gompers' Garage. Gordie would re-assemble it so it could be returned to the foreigners and no questions asked. The twenty-dollar mechanic's fee Ashenden would have to pay from his own pocket.

But they had not stymied Constable Ashenden for a minute. Without even pausing for a nap, despite his fatigue, Ashenden ploughed on through the night. First he had to fill out a report for Inspector Heavysides, detailing his suspicions of the drug-peddlers and proposing an investigation. It was wise in such situations to keep oneself covered.

If the inspector approved, he might even send the divisional Narcotics Squad from Regina to assist Ashenden. If the case was successfully prosecuted, there could be a transfer in it for Ashenden. Perhaps a promotion. After he had sealed the envelope and dropped it into the mail slot at the Post Office, his day's work was done and the sun had already risen on a long June day.

The alarm clock blasted him out of bed at noon, precisely twenty minutes before the last call at Ellie Sanders' lunch-table. This meant leaping out of bed, dressing quickly, washing, shaving, brushing his teeth, making his bed so taut a quarter would bounce on it, polishing his boots, ironing a fresh shirt and tie, brushing his jacket, giving his single room a quick sweep, and sprinting down the street a full block to the boardinghouse.

"Jimmy!" Ellie smiled her motherly smile. "Darn near time, too. I was just going to ring the bell."

He smiled and tucked into one of Ellie's *great* lunches: rib-sticking bean-and-carrot soup; cold roast beef topped with rich brown gravy; rhubarb crumble with fresh cream. Then he sauntered outside to enjoy his Saturday off.

There was work to be cleaned up first, however. Because he had spent the whole night on the Karmakov case, it meant a lot of typing to catch up on. There was no point in complaining. In a one-man detachment you either got the typing done or drowned in paperwork. "Heavy Step" Heavysides was a stickler.

He picked up his mail at the Post Office on his way back to the detachment office. The office occupied one half of a small brick building on Antelope Avenue; the other half was his living quarters. The mail was rich for a Saturday. A letter from his mother in Niebelung, Manitoba; the June issue of *The Western Horseman*; a bill from Mintenko's Feeds; a large carton full of new memos and regulations from the sub-division HQ; and two "Wanted" posters from division HQ. The latter he pinned up on his bulletin board. For six minutes, he studied the faces, committing the scars and the shapes of their ears to memory. Then he turned to the typing.

There was his weekly report, several daily reports, and a mid-month report; reports in investigations, accidents, prosecutions, incidents, and discipline problems. Typing was by far the most practical skill Ashenden had learned during his six-month training, though he had been disgusted by it at the time. He had looked forward so long to the joys of karate and horsemanship.

It had turned out, to Ashenden's shocked disappointment, that horsemanship was no longer considered important to a modern technological police force, though it had once been the centre of a proud tradition. Gone were the days—fondly recalled by older hands—of a rookie being assigned his own horse. Gone were the long hours of stabling and grooming the horses. Gone was the hallowed tradition of scrubbing its genitals with a toothbrush, twice daily.

Ashenden finished the typing and went to supper with a light and carefree step. It was Saturday night but he was not attracted to television or the fleshpots of the Meadowlark Hotel. He was going to visit his horse, Trooper.

Before he could leave the boardinghouse, Ellie's

telephone rang. Pearl Dumba, the telephone operator, was on the line. She had "accidentally overheard" a conversation between Barclay Campbell's daughter Eleanor and young Charlie Sigurdson.

"I'm not one to go around poking my nose in, Jimmy," Pearl said. "But he told her he was going to take her to the dance in Sand Valley tonight. Well, I know from the police-court column in the *World-Spectator and Times* that you had him up last week for dangerous driving and his licence was suspended. Just thought you might like to know."

"Thanks, Pearl," Ashenden said. "I'll keep my eye on him." Darn it all, he thought. There went his Saturday night. If young Sigurdson got away with it, the whole Rural Municipality would descend into lawless chaos.

By midnight, after waiting by the Campbells' farm for three hours, he realized that Charlie Sigurdson had taken the back road out of the farm. Ashenden accepted his defeat wearily and headed home to bed.

The next morning, Ashenden allowed himself the luxury of sleeping in until 10 a.m. before driving to Healey's farm a mile south of town, to visit Trooper. A special bond had been steadily growing between the two of them since Ashenden had bought Trooper at the Moose Jaw Horse Sale six weeks before. It had been a case of love at first sight.

All afternoon, Ashenden washed and curried Trooper's sleek chestnut coat. He scrubbed the white star in the middle of Trooper's forehead, and the neat white stockings above the hooves. Lifting her tail, Ashenden applied his old toothbrush with a will to the folds and wrinkles. Trooper nickered with contentment.

Ashenden led Trooper around the farmyard on the halter. He hoped to find somebody in town who could give him riding lessons. It was embarrassing for a Mounted Policeman to ask for them. But it didn't matter, because together they were happy.

That night he felt fulfilled, ready for another week's work. Madam Karmakov and her puny sidekick were at a disadvantage in the looming battle of wills. How could he know of the new and darker excitement about to invade his simple life? Or that his relationship with Trooper would never be the same again?

4 THE GIRL IN THE YELLOW MG

Monday morning saw Constable Ashenden once again manning his radar unit, this time on the south-west side of Meadowlark, on the highway to Wheat City and Shakespear. His duties did not allow him to spend the day pursuing suspected drug traffickers. He was expected to fill his quota of speeding prosecutions, come heck or high water. With luck, he would have a bagful by noon and get on with his investigation.

By 10 a.m. the sun was high over the surrounding fields, now carpeted green with wheat reaching the shot-blade stage. He knew it would be another hot, baking day. Once again his legs would broil inside his knee-high leather boots and heavy serge breeches.

Yet Ashenden was a career man, committed to the proud traditions of his obsolete costume, and he could never question its practicality. The uniform had been one of two reasons Ashenden had joined the RCMP, the other being his desire to become a horseman. Unlike other members of the Force, Ashenden had welcomed the directive that "encouraged" him to wear his breeches and boots on duty. Nevertheless, it did not improve his outlook on the day to know that his toes would be pickling in the quarter-inch of sweaty brine which would collect inside the boots by twelve o'clock noon. Already the leather Sam Browne strap across his back felt like a branding iron.

Suddenly Ashenden heard the whine of a car approaching from the south. His mind snapped into place, alert for action. The whine grew into a roar, and he knew he had a customer for the radar trap.

Over the crest of a low hill on his left, a car shot into view in a blast of dust. Ashenden's hand moved to the siren switch, his eyes glued to the radar receiver. The car whistled past. Ninety-six miles per hour! He flicked the switch. The sharp scream of his Sterling Model 20 siren blasted through the dozing countryside. Gophers in the community pasture two miles away lifted their heads in smart attention.

The effect on the blur was uncanny, as it caught the full force of the siren's blare and seemed to leap sideways off the road, skidding toward the ditch with tires shrieking, swerving left, then right, as the driver fought to gain control—barely missing a "CAUTION" sign and spinning ninety degrees before roaring back across the road again and through the opposite ditch, crashing into the barbed-wire fence guarding Barclay Campbell's field of tender young flax. The three strands of tautly strung barbed-wire trampolined the car back across the ditch and onto the road, where it halted almost directly in front of Ashenden's cruiser, facing in the direction it had come.

As the dust settled, Ashenden realized to his surprise that it was not Madam Karmakov's Stingray, as he had hoped, but a mustard-yellow MG convertible with Ontario licence plates. Tourists. He sprinted toward the car. Luckily, the top was down. He could just reach in and—

Ashenden stopped in amazement. The driver was a girl! She was unconscious, collapsed onto the passenger's seat. Her deep-red hair, blown about by the wind, enclosed her face like a flaming halo. She was the most beautiful girl Ashenden had ever seen. He stopped, dumbfounded at the sight of her tanned bronze skin, which even in unconsciousness, gleamed through the stretched fibres of her white pant suit.

"Are you—are you okay?" he said hesitantly.

Her eyes snapped open. "Was that *your* siren? *Ass-hole*?"

Ashenden staggered back a pace and straightened his Stetson so she could see it better. She must be in a state of shock, he thought, doesn't know what she's saying.

"Um—you're all right, are you? No—broken bones?"

"Keep your hands *off* me—bully!"

"Eh?"

She sat up and fixed him with a glare. "All right. You wanted me to stop. What's on your mind?"

"On my—mind?"

"Look," she said, tossing her hair impatiently, "you did blow a siren, didn't you?"

"Oh. Oh yes. Well, you were speeding, you see—"

"Bull*shit*!"

"But I clocked you at ninety-six miles an hour!"

She looked at him with undisguised contempt. "You mean you run a *radar trap*?"

"Well—yes."

"Oh, all right, let's get it over with. Just hurry up."

"Driver's licence, please."

As she reached toward the glove compartment, her pants stretched with awesome tension. Ashenden caught a glimpse of black underwear and looked quickly toward Barclay Campbell's flax crop. Barclay had been spraying the crop, but was now standing on the seat of his tractor, watching the proceedings. He waved cheerily. Ashenden turned back.

The girl handed over her licence. He quickly took down the particulars. Name: Sharon Sharalike; Address: Apt. 1215-499 Whitman Street, Toronto, Ontario.

"Tourist?" he asked.

"No."

"Are you staying around here?"

"At the motel in Shakespear."

"Oh. Visiting friends?"

"No."

Ashenden resolved to be polite despite her coolness. After all, he had given her a bad scare. "Working in Shakespear, then?" he said, making out the speeding ticket.

"I'm doing a documentary, if you want to know."

"Documentary?"

"For CBC television."

"You don't say! What on?"

"Ethnic Minorities of Canada," she sighed, lighting a cigarette. "No. 123 in the series. I've tracked down the only Pitcairn Islander in the country. He lives in Shakespear."

"Old Max Christian, you mean? The tapman in the beer parlour?"

Sharon Sharalike's dark green eyes grew newly interested in Constable James Ashenden. She smiled warmly. "You know him?"

"Sure. I played Rummoli with him all last winter."

She laughed a golden laugh. "Say, are you taking a coffee break?"

"Coffee?"

"Well—whatever you break for. I'd like you to tell me about Mr. Christian."

"You want information on Max Christian? Sure thing. Tell you what— We'll get your car turned around, and then I'll treat you to breakfast at Ellie Sanders' boardinghouse." He grinned shyly. "That's where I eat."

Sharon Sharalike smiled an enticing smile. "Far-out," she said.

Ellie was pleased to have a guest for breakfast, especially such a pretty one, for Jimmy's sake. She bustled maternally about with her pancakes while Sharon questioned Ashenden on Max Christian's mores. What kind of books did he read? Nurse stories. What were his favourite television programs? "Lassie" and "The Three Stooges." How did he feel being the only Pitcairn Islander in Canada? Okay. She pumped him for half-an-hour.

As they finished their coffee, which Ellie had brewed to perfection, Ashenden turned the conversation.

"Do you like horses?" he asked suddenly.

She stared at him for a long moment, her delicate eyebrows arched politely. "I beg your pardon?"

"Horses!" Ashenden exclaimed. "That's why I joined the RCMP! I wanted to be a *Mounted* Policeman. But now they're phasing horses out, you see." He leaned over to whisper: "So I bought my own horse. I rent a stable at Healey's farm, just outside of town."

She lit a cigarette. "That's—nice," she said.

"Maybe if you're not in a big hurry—if you

have lots of time—you might like to—go out and visit—"

"I'm allergic to horses."

"Oh." A gloom settled over the table. "Like another coffee?"

"No thanks. I really have to split."

"Gee, I hope you're not mad about the scratches on your car—or my scaring you like that with the siren. That's my *second* big goof this week."

"No kidding," she said, standing up and tossing her hair. "What was the other one?"

Ashenden wondered if he could take Sharon Sharalike into his confidence. One glance at her deep, emerald green eyes reassured him. "I nearly made a false arrest for drug-peddling," he confessed. "Lucky for me I checked the suspected drug-shipment container first. It was empty."

"Oh, *really*?" She sat down again and smiled seductively.

"You see, the school janitor is—well let's say a *good friend*, if you know what I mean, of this Russian lady in Shakespear and—"

"*Russian* lady?"

"I *think* she's Russian. You see, they're setting up a drug-ring in the school."

Sharon Sharalike gazed at him for a long moment. "Listen," she said. "Where did you say your horse is tied? Let's go and see him!"

"But your allergy!"

"Oh, I'll keep a tight rein on it. Ha, ha. I love horses! And you know—" She touched her long, tanned fingers to the back of his hand—"I've never seen a Mountie's horse before."

The Healey farm was buzzing in the lazy midmorning heat when Ashenden and Sharon Sharalike wheeled into the yard in her MG. He was relieved to see that no one was around, and led Miss Sharalike quickly to the dark, low-roofed stable. People might get the wrong idea if they saw them going together into a secluded farm building. If Mrs. Boothroyd or Pearl Dumba heard about this, life in Meadowlark would be unbearable. Men had been transferred for less.

"Miss Sharalike," he said, stepping aside at the stable door, "I'd like you to meet my horse, Trooper."

"Ohhhh—what a *beautiful* horse!" she exclaimed, as her eyes strained in the darkness to discern the animal's silhouette. "But you can call me—Sharon."

Ashenden swelled with pride. He had never called a beautiful woman by her first name before. And she liked Trooper! Perhaps—she was—the girl of his dreams.

"He's *gorgeous*," she whispered in his ear, grasping Ashenden's arm in the darkness.

"Actually, Sharon," he said, disengaging her warm hand from his tunic, "*she's* not a he. I mean—she's a mare."

Sharon's eyelids flickered with puzzlement. "Well, why do you call *her*—Trooper?"

"It *seems* a little more, uh, masculine. In keeping with the tradition of the Force."

"Oh! Well, I'm *glad* she's a girl," Sharon said quickly. "Definitely more appropriate. People might think you were a bit—*kinky* otherwise."

"Hmm. I never thought of that."

"Oh, don't pay any attention to me. It's my CBC background. It would blow your mind if you knew what went on there.''

"Like what?''

"Don't get me started! Pederasts, dykes, queens, switch-hitters—''

"Want to feed her an oat-cake?'' Ashenden blurted. Hearing about queer people always gave him the willies.

"No, I'll watch. You're so—masterful with her.'' Sharon lit a cigarette. "What about these dope peddlers and the drug container?''

"Now wait a minute, Sharon. It *was* an old lamp. That's what Gordie Gompers says too. And they're only *alleged* dope peddlers. So far, anyway.''

"No evidence, eh? What will you do next?''

"Well, at the moment I'm awaiting orders from sub-division headquarters in Moose Jaw to go ahead on the investigation. They prefer to be in on top-security stuff.''

"You don't say?''

"Sure. If they knew I was telling you about this now, they'd ship me out to the sticks so fast my hat would spin.''

"What in hell do you call the *sticks*?''

"Oh, there's worse postings than Meadowlark, believe me.''

"Jeez,'' Sharon said, shivering despite the heat inside the barn.

"I don't have to tell you this must be kept in absolute confidence,'' Ashenden said after a moment. "Do I?''

"Oh, absolutely not.''

"I mean, with you working for the CBC and everything, it could be touchy. If word of this operation leaked out to the public.''

"Dismiss it from your mind. I'll tell you what. I'll even *help* you with your investigation!"

"Gee, I'd have to clear that with sub-division HQ."

"No, no, let's keep it informal. Between—" She adjusted his tie snugly around his neck, and a delicious golden scent seemed to envelop him—"you and me."

"It's a deal," Ashenden said, fumbling in the darkness until he found her hand. He shook it vigorously and escorted her back to the sunshine.

Sharon drove him to the detachment office to do a few hours typing on his various reports, summonses, equipment invoices and memos, while she went off to Shakespear to collect more information on Max Christian. They would meet later if one of them had something to report.

In fact, Ashenden didn't see Sharon Sharalike again for two days, although he dreamed about her during the four hours of sleep he managed to get after breaking up a teen-age wiener roast at the park at Monday midnight; there were no arrests, but he issued six warnings for indecent exposure and seized fourteen dozen unopened bottles of beer.

He kept his eyes peeled for Madam Karmakov's Stingray, but it had vanished from the countryside since he had frightened them on Friday. There had been no lights on at Pules-Feltham's suspicious-looking bungalow all weekend, either. Ashenden had the feeling that something was about to happen, that he was being lulled by the very *ordinariness* of life. It was always at this time, his old tutor, Sgt. McLeod had warned, that a major outburst of crime would trap an unprepared Mounted

Policeman.

And Ashenden knew that moment had arrived when Pearl Dumba's phone call woke him at 3:00 a.m. Wednesday morning with an urgent telegram from Regina. He wrote it down and was staring at the stunning message when a wild knocking exploded at the front door of his quarters.

"Jimmy! Hurry! Let me in! We've *got* them *now*!"

It was Sharon Sharalike. Something big had happened.

5 SNAKES AND LADDERS

Ashenden's living quarters were of the modest style afforded single Mounted Policemen stationed in small towns. It was widely held that the prisoner's cell was more luxurious. To squelch such comparisons, Ashenden had placed a straw Welcome mat outside the door and a Happy Face sticker on the end of his bunk. His training manuals were arranged in a neat library along the top of his writing desk. A spectacular photograph of a rearing Palomino stallion (its private parts airbrushed out of existence by the photo retoucher) was pinned on the wall opposite his bunk.

Into this spartan, though homey, room, Sharon Sharalike now burst. Ashenden was struck by how perfectly she harmonized with his simple room. Her stormy red hair set the dull green walls off impeccably. Her pale, excited face was a diamond set in a blaze of colour. Had Ashenden been of a more contemplative nature he might have expressed a passing comment on beauty. But he was a man of action and held his tongue, except to exclaim: "Sharon! What the heck is it?"

"I've got it!" she cried. "*Everything* you need to convict!"

"*Convict*? What are you talking about? Convict who?"

"The dope peddlers!"

A sinking feeling seized his entrails. "It's too late," he said, showing her the telegram he had just received from sub-division, "HQ shut down the investigation. Listen to this:

" 'Constable James Ashenden, RCMP Detachment, Meadowlark, Sask. Re: Jeremy Pules-Feltham and Nadya Karmakov, suspicion of.

" 'Having recd. your report of the nineteenth, I transmit the following instructions: You will not, repeat not, carry out surveillance on the above-named subjects. HQ investigation indicates no possibility of drug offences in your area. You are herewith ordered to cease all activity on the case and resume operation of your radar control unit. Present quota returns are inadequate. Signed, Inspector Angleton J. Heavysides.' "

"But *why*?"

"Well, it says right there! 'HQ investigation indicates no—' "

Sharon seized his arm indignantly. "You sit right down there on the bed and listen to this, Constable Ashenden. I have something you've *got* to listen to. Unless you want to see a perversion of justice!"

"There's nothing I can do about that speeding ticket, you know, Sharon. That's out of my hands now."

"Will you forget the speeding ticket? *Knuckle-head*!"

Stunned into silence, Ashenden sat down on the edge of the bed, his jaw hanging open.

"Oh, I'm sorry," Sharon said, reassuring him. "I didn't mean that. I've already forgotten about the speeding ticket. This is something *big*!"

"What's that?" Ashenden said, pointing to a black leather case Sharon was setting on his desk.

"Reel-to-reel Nagra Three," she murmured, opening the end of the case and revealing a row of dials. Her fingers flicked among them like an airline pilot's; she hit a switch. "Battery operated. Pilot tone for film-sync. It's my tape recorder."

"You don't say?" He got up to look, but was stopped cold by the voice of Jeremy Pules-Feltham.

"Nady!" Pules-Feltham was saying. "How good of you to come around."

"You heff company, Jheremy?" It was the Russian woman. Ashenden could just see her—slinking into the room where the disgusting little pervert waited, hissing with lust.

"No, no, quite alone."

"Iss good. Would not do to arouse suspicions at zhiss stage."

"Yes, with that damned Mountie watching every move, it's going to be bloody difficult."

"*Holy smoke*!" Ashenden exclaimed sharply.

"That's nothing," Sharon breathed, "listen to this!"

There was a silence as Madam Karmakov settled herself on Pules-Feltham's sofa. It had to be in his house. There was the rustling of clothes and the unmistakable sound of a kiss. Ashenden blushed and looked away from Sharon.

"Jheremy," the Russian woman's voice hissed. "*The shipment has arrived in Shakespear*!"

"No! When?"

"Today! Zhis afternoon."

"Finally! After all these weeks!"

"Zhe Chon Chee Diefenbecker School will never be zhe same!" the woman exclaimed.

"Or Meadowlark!"

"Yess. Wonce we have zhe children, zhe whole *town* will be ours!"

Their laughter rose in a demonic giggle that

made Ashenden clench his teeth in fury. He could see them hugging and squeezing each other in fiendish glee.

"This is diabolical!" he said, turning to Sharon in horror. She held her finger up for him to listen.

Pules-Feltham spoke again: "But how shall we ever smuggle the stuff over from Shakespear?"

"Zhere are zeveral possibilities. Myself, I prefer Plan G."

"Ah! Plant it right into the school!"

"Yess. Zen you can distribute zhe shipment to all zhe classrooms! Only question is—when?"

"Let me have a look at the calendar. Right! The annual Meadowlark Sports Day is next Saturday. They'll all be at the park playing baseball."

"Will be *perfect*, Jheremy!"

"There won't be a soul around!"

Again the two villains broke into a cacophony of wild laughter. Ashenden thought they might be doped up. His nerves were stretched like barbedwire. Little had he known that such evil lurked within his jurisdiction.

"Well, darling Nady, shall we retire?"

"Oh yess, Jheremy. We heff all night together!"

"Did you hide your car? We don't want the cretinous Mounted Policeman bursting in on us again."

"Iss okay, Jheremy, I parked behind zhe house."

After a silence came the sound of giggling and running feet. Sharon switched the machine off.

Ashenden turned to her thoughtfully. "What's in the bedroom, a two-way radio?"

"Never mind what's in the bedroom! Let's go and arrest them!"

"But those orders from Moose Jaw! I can't!"

"Surely you're not going to let that stop you! We have to nip this scheme in the bud. Think of all those little school children."

"You're right," he said decisively, striding to his desk. "I'll draft a letter to Inspector Heavysides, asking him to reconsider. With that tape recording, they'll *have* to believe me."

"But we can't wait for that! You have to grab them *now*—while we know where they are. I just left Pules-Feltham's house! They're probably still in bed."

"In bed?" Ashenden's boyish face turned pale.

"Oh fer crissakes!" Sharon snapped her tape recorder shut.

"Wait, Sharon. I can't break into a private home without a warrant. It's against orders. They'd ship me off to Baffin Island so fast I'd just be a blur."

She glared at him. "Well, I don't know about you, King of the Royal Mounted, but I'm sending this item off to my producer in Toronto. If you want to sit around writing speeding tickets while crime runs rampant in Meadowlark, that's up to you." She turned and headed for the door.

"Wait!" Decision-making was painful for Ashenden. "We don't have any evidence. You heard her! We have to get them with the *stuff*!"

"That's Saturday—*three* days away!"

"That gives us time to build an airtight case. We've got to crack Plan G before they get it off the ground! Sharon—will you help me?"

The bright green light in her eyes softened as she stepped back into the room. "Constable Ashenden," she said, extending her hand, "you've got yourself a deal!"

About sixteen hours after Sharon's discovery, Mayor Boothroyd was in the community hall whipping up enthusiastic support for the annual Meadowlark Sports Day and Picnic. It was a meeting to which most of the townspeople went, reluctantly. Everyone knew he or she was expected to contribute time and/or money. In return for this contribution, Mayor Boothroyd would, during the coming year, return small favours from the town office—tax deadline adjustments or pavement repairs, for example. Anyone who did not contribute was politically dead in the town of Meadowlark. Even at the dramatic moment that Mayor Boothroyd declared that the 1973 Sports Day and Picnic was going to make Shakespear's Golden Jubilee look like a hog show, people were craning their necks around the community hall to see who was missing.

"Gordie Gompers is going to organize the baseball tournament," the mayor declared, and a cheer went up for Gompers, who stood on a chair clasping his hands overhead in a victory salute.

"Charlie Cherry is in charge of the gate. And *Mrs.* Charlie Cherry will look after Charlie to make sure all the receipts come in!" The crowd roared their appreciation of the mayor's wit.

"Once again my good wife has volunteered to supervise the refreshment booth." This, too, was a popular decision: the refreshment booth entailed much work. The town was proud to see the Boothroyds setting a good example. It was this diligence that got Phil Boothroyd elected to the mayor's chair every year, "regular as a November blizzard," as Gordie Gompers expressed it. He was planning to run again.

"Now there's the foot-race committee. Fred Kobiak did a dandy job on that last year, and I think it's only fair we should ask him again now. Where's Fred?"

"Where's Fred?" several people said, and the echo died away in embarrassed silence as Fred Kobiak's traitorous absence became apparent.

"Well," Mayor Boothroyd said. "Well, well."

Charlie Cherry edged forward through the crowd and beckoned to the mayor. He announced in a loud whisper: "He's out following Jimmy Ashenden and his girlfriend around!"

"What the heck for?"

"Well, they're following the Limey and the Yewkerainian woman, tryna figger out what *they're up* to."

Mayor Boothroyd glanced around uncomfortably. It looked bad if there was something going on he didn't know about.

"And what *are* they up to?" Mrs. Boothroyd demanded at his side.

"Who knows?" Charlie Cherry shrugged elaborately.

"Well, I notice they didn't put down their names to help with the Sports Day," Mrs. Boothroyd said, and sat back in her chair with a smug glance around.

"Now, Maw," Phil said, but whispers had already begun to hiss through the crowd, concerning the foreign element in Meadowlark, and the decline of morals due to Ottawa's immigration policies. Someone observed that "the Chinaman" had stayed home, too, and several remarks were made on the unsuitability of Orientals for civic responsibility.

Finally Mrs. Boothroyd leaned forward again in her chair and said, "You can talk about foreigners all you like, but it's that—*witch* from Toronto I'm worried about. The one chasing after Jimmy Ashenden."

There was another uproar until Charlie Cherry said, "Have you seen the shorts that girl wears?" and near-bedlam broke out. The mayor was hard put to restrain the clamour for more information. He finally gavelled the hall into silence.

"Getting so you can't tell Meadowlark from Sodom and Gomorrah," Mrs. Boothroyd sniffed loudly. "Poor Jimmy—to fall into the clutches of a —one a them *liberated* types."

Charlie Cherry shook his head sadly. "Sure glad I'm not in his shoes," he mourned. "Bein' tempted like *that* twenty-four hours a day!"

If Ashenden's temptation were real, he was suppressing it with superhuman forbearance. He and Sharon were parked across the street from Pules-Feltham's house in her MG, desultorily engaged in a match of Snakes and Ladders. They had tried Rummoli earlier, but there was not enough room in the front seat of the tiny car to spread the board.

She was on number 37; his counter was on 74. "Your turn," he said, the tension of the game showing in his voice.

"I know," she yawned. "How much longer do we wait out here?"

"This could be my big chance!" If he could just roll a four, he would hit the ladder on 78. His luck was holding. Sharon's marker was still away behind. It was the first real chance of the evening.

was holding. Sharon's marker was still away behind. It was the first real chance of the evening. Already, he had lost three games.

"Why don't we just declare you the winner?"

"Sharon!" he remonstrated. "Don't be a quitter!"

"If it's the *money*, I'll give you your seventy-five cents back."

"That's not the same as winning," he declared crisply.

"Hey!" Sharon pointed out the window. Two figures flitted out of Pules-Feltham's house across the street and disappeared in the darkness around the corner. There was a *vroom* as the engine of the hidden Stingray roared to life.

Ashenden leaped into action, scattering the game in all directions. He pulled his notebook from his pocket.

"They're going in the car!" Sharon yelled. "What in God's name are you doing?"

"Hold on, I have to write this down."

"You *what?*"

"10:20 p.m.," Ashenden inscribed in his precise, square letters, "suspects proceeded from Pules-Feltham residence to the Karmakov vehicle and proceeded in the direction of—"

"Hurry up!" Sharon said, her fist pounding on the dash. "They've disappeared around the corner."

"Holy smoke!" Ashenden threw the notebook down. He started the engine of the little car and, with a clashing of gears, hammered it into reverse, backed out of the driveway, and rocketed off down the street after the fugitive pair.

"Which way did they go?"

"Right at the next corner!"

Ashenden took the corner of McKillop and Elm on two wheels. The weeks of driver training in Depot Division were paying off. He could never have driven his RCMP Pontiac this hard—it would decimate his gasoline budget—but in Sharon's impudent little MG, he could really move. He accelerated down Elm, going past the Legion Hall at seventy m.p.h. "Faster!" Sharon cried. "Faster!" He tried to keep the tail-lights of the Stingray in sight, but at the corner of Buffalo Avenue, the town's second thoroughfare, he screeched to a shuddering halt.

"What's wrong?" Sharon yelled.

"My gosh, Sharon! Don't you see that stop sign? What kind of example would it be if the town's representative of law and order went driving through a stop sign without consideration for life or limb? If you ask me, that's what's wrong with—"

"Never mind," she said. "They've gone." He looked ahead; it was true. The Corvette's sweeping tail-lights had completely vanished from view. "Heck!" he said.

They cruised up and down Meadowlark's side streets, looking for the fugitive car. Crossing Antelope on Poplar Street, Ashenden noticed a pair of headlights suddenly appear in the rear-view mirror. He swung around two corners in quick succession. The lights stuck with them.

"Sharon!" he whispered from the side of his mouth.

"What?"

"Don't look now, but there's somebody following us. *Don't turn around*!"

"Who is it?" she said, staring straight ahead.

"Can't tell. Just a set of headlights."

"Do you think it's them?"

"Might be. Could be accomplices, putting the tail on us. Nothing to do but shake them."

"Right!"

They were still on Poplar, which led straight north out of town to become a trail across the community pasture. Ashenden floored the accelerator, and he could feel the 6.30-13 Michelin radials bite gravel as the car shot forward. For five miles they drove ahead in a cloud of dust. When Ashenden finally stopped, the headlights had vanished from view behind them. A red dial suddenly glowed malignantly on the speedometer dial, and the engine died. They had run out of gas.

6 AN INTERNATIONAL CONSPIRACY

Fortunately, the vehicle following them had not been Madam Karmakov's Stingray, but Fred Kobiak's 1950 Fargo half-ton pick-up truck. It was Fred and his brother-in-law Lowell who came across the frustrated pair fifteen minutes later, arguing over who would walk back to town for a can of gasoline.

Fred stopped a few hundred yards back and killed the lights. He didn't want to interrupt them if they were fooling around, so he and Lowell approached on tip-toe. When they heard it was only an argument, they came forward with jovial assistance.

"Run outa gas, lady? Oh, *hi*, Jimmy. Didn't know you were out here, too! Haw haw haw."

It was two in the morning when they finally returned to town, at the end of Fred's tow-rope. Lowell had kept leering suggestively at them from the back window of the truck. These late nights were starting to get Ashenden down. He remembered he hadn't typed his daily reports yet, either.

"You want to come in to the office for a coffee while I do my reports?" he asked when Fred had driven off.

"Sure. Why not?"

It seemed to take forever to find the key and get the office door unlocked, as Sharon waited impatiently beside him, her hand on her hip. The smell of her perfume (Desiree, she had said during Snakes and Ladders) drifted across his nostrils, making it hard to concentrate.

"I'll bet Trooper's feeling lonely," he said, to spark the conversation.

"Trooper?"

The telephone suddenly jangled inside.

"Give me a light, quick!"

Sharon lit her gold Triggermatic butane lighter and Ashenden twisted the key into the lock. Wrenching the door open, he was at the telephone in three strides, but it had stopped ringing. Strange. Almost as if someone was checking.

"The inspector!" Ashenden exclaimed. Of course! The inspector had phoned, ordering him to go on with the investigation. But now he had missed the message! If it had to come by mail, it could take days.

"What's wrong?" Sharon said. "Your face is pale!"

"I think I—we just missed our big chance. He'll never phone back. He sat down heavily at his desk. the weariness of the past week suddenly bearing down on him.

Sharon moved across the room to him. "Don't worry, Jimmy. We'll do it. You'll see. Things will work out."

"Thanks," he said hopelessly. Her cool hands felt so soothing.

Suddenly the phone rang again, clamouring like a burglar alarm. Sharon yelped, startled. Ashenden snatched the receiver from its cradle and barked:

"Ashenden here!"

It was Pearl Dumba, the telephone operator.

Ashenden liked to think of Pearl as a friend. She knew all the town's secrets. Because he was polite to her, enduring her limited conversation for hours on end, she offered him tidbits of information. On Saturday, Ashenden had phoned her to watch for anything unusual happening on the telephone lines from the Pules-Feltham number. Now his careful cultivation paid off.

"Yes. Uh-huh. I see. Got it, Pearl. Tremendous. Thanks a million, Pearl." He hung up and turned to Sharon, barely able to conceal the excitement in his voice.

"At precisely 9:32 p.m., last evening, that is Wednesday, one Madam Nadya Karmakov, from the telephone number in question, placed a long distance telephone call to—" He paused triumphantly. "*Quebec City*!"

"So?" she said finally.

"Don't you *get* it? The *FLQ*!"

"*FLQ*?"

Ashenden sighed. Sometimes he didn't know if Sharon was pulling his leg or just dumb. "Look," he explained patiently, "supposing *you* were an agent of the Kremlin, trying to infiltrate Canadian society and destroy free enterprise."

"What are you *talking* about?"

Ashenden sat her down gently on the chair. "There are dirty facts of life that you simply do not know, Sharon," Ashenden said sadly. "You might think I'm kind of ignorant about some things. Maybe I am—about opera and hippies and the CBC and stuff like that. But I learned politics and subversion from one of the best men in S.S.!"

"S.S.?"

"Security Services. Top-secret, undercover stuff. Sgt. Fred McLeod. Does that name mean anything to you?"

"Not a thing."

"You see?" Ashenden grinned. "Undercover.

Well, what he doesn't know about terrorism and communism you can just forget about. I'm going to tell you something that will make your hair stand on end. Just pretend for a minute that you're an international Bolshevik. You're happy that your comrades started trouble among the Frenchies in Quebec, right?''

"I suppose."

"It *looked* like they got wiped out in the War Measures Act three years ago. Your red buddies go underground, and where do they surface? *Right here in Meadowlark, Saskatchewan.*"

"Why—Meadowlark?"

"Don't you see?" Ashenden paced back and forth in the confines of his tiny office, striking his hand with his fist. "Where *better*? Some place vulnerable, somewhere right in the heartland of Canada. They think law and order will be a pushover because a rookie constable is on duty! But they haven't reckoned with the training he got from Sgt. Fred McLeod."

"But why the phone call to Quebec?"

"That's what ties it together! They're shipping the drugs in from Quebec to corrupt the innocent youth of Saskatchewan. Striking at the soft underbelly of Canada. A fifth column of dope fiends!"

"I don't know," Sharon said uncertainly. "It sounds far-fetched to me."

"That's because you never studied politics under Sgt. Fred McLeod. Believe me, this is a ruthless bunch."

"Okay, what now?"

"Go into action." Ashenden picked up the telephone and cranked for the operator. It took a few minutes to get Pearl out of bed, but she put through a person-to-person call to Inspector J. Heavysides in Moose Jaw.

"Why didn't you do this before?" Sharon asked.

"I didn't know how desperate the situation was. I mean it's getting *big*. Yes, Pearl," he said into the receiver, "we'll have to call him at home. This is important."

"I hope you know what you're doing," Sharon said.

"Hello, Inspector Heavysides? Good morning, sir! Do you happen to recall a certain report I sent you this week dealing with—beg pardon?" Ashenden's jaw began to tremble and the telephone rattled in his hand. "Oh! Constable Ashenden, sir. Meadowlark detachment. Yes sir, I guess it is after midnight. No sir, I didn't realize you were in the middle of—yes sir. Perfectly, sir." His free hand fumbled for the chair. Sharon put it under him and he sat down. Perspiration broke out on his clean-shaven temples.

"Well, sir, there's new evidence, Inspector. One of the suspects made a phone call to the FLQ. FLQ? It's a terrorist gang in Quebec, sir. One of the suspects in that—long report I sent you on the weekend, Inspector."

Ashenden listened intently. "Right, Inspector. Good night, sir. Sorry about getting you out of bed, sir." He hung up and reached inside his tunic for a handkerchief to wipe his forehead.

"Did you hear that?" he said.

"Hear *what*?"

"Inspector Heavysides is coming! Tomorrow! I mean today!"

"Is that good or bad?"

"I'm not sure. Good, I think. He's going to conduct the investigation himself! 'Get right to the bottom of it,' he said. This could be a promotion. I could get posted to Vancouver!"

"Well, it means we've got a lot of work to do. We better get some sleep." Sharon glanced casually at Ashenden. "What sort of sleeping accommodation have you got next door, Jimmy?"

"Golly, Sharon. I've only got the one room. I better get you home to your motel. Tell you what, I'll drive you in the cruiser."

"Sharon Sharalike gave him an appraising look. "Good thinking," she said. "My room is *much* more comfortable."

Just as they were on their way out the door, the telephone rang again. It was Pearl Dumba on the line. She wanted to know where Inspector Heavysides would be staying when he arrived. As it happened, she had a spare bedroom she had re-wallpapered just that spring, and she was sure that the inspector was the quiet, home-loving sort of *respectable* person who would—

Ashenden cut her off gently. She was, after all, a valuable ally. "Listen, Pearl," he said. "What you are talking about is a top-security subject. Even the inspector and I don't know where he's going to stay. So we won't talk about it. And no one, repeat *no one*, knows that he's coming. Understand?"

Pearl, though miffed, understood. He made a mental reminder to tell her some of the juicy bits from the kids' wiener roast the night before. That would keep her happy.

7 A VERY CLOSE CALL

By nine o'clock Thursday morning, Meadow-
lark was afire with the electrifying news. Jimmy
Ashenden and the liberated woman from Toronto
were sweet on each other. Starting at Gordie Gom-
pers' Garage, Fred and Lowell had made their way
up Main Street, telling of finding the pair five miles
out of town on the prairie trail. "And her with no
more clothes than'ud blind a grasshopper."

"You watch now," Meadowlarkians confided
to each other knowingly. "She's gonna snap him
up, just like that." People would hate to see Jimmy
get married because rookies in the RCMP were not
allowed to both marry and stay in the Force.

"Throwing his whole *future* away just for a bit
of you-know-what," Mayor Boothroyd agreed
when Gordie Gompers told him the story. Still it
was a kind of stupid wind that didn't blow *some-
body* some good, as Gordie pointed out; there were
a hell of a lot fewer speeding tickets being handed
out since the sultry CBC reporter had shown up in
town.

And with Jimmy's boss coming to Meadowlark,
according to Pearl, things might get interesting.
What with all this stuff about the Limey and the
Ukrainian girl from Shakespear, it was a perfect
build-up for the Sports Day and Picnic on Satur-
day. People would be coming from miles around if
Phil Boothroyd could manage to time the big arrest
for some time Saturday night—say during the inter-
mission at the Old-Tyme Dance in the community
hall.

The mayor and Gordie Gompers discussed these matters while standing in front of the gas pumps at Gordie Gompers' Garage, so Gordie could service trucks without interrupting the conversation. It was Gordie's busy time of year. The farmers were spraying and summer-fallowing and haying, as well as getting their equipment together for the harvest. Mid-June was a time of year when Gordie Gompers felt expansive, even philanthropic, and the warm morning sun had lifted his spirits higher than usual. The mayor, looking forward to yet another Sports Day, felt the same.

Thus it was with some delight that they saw young Jimmy Ashenden step out of Ellie Sanders' front door and begin walking toward them up Antelope Street. As Ashenden approached, Gordie could see that he was unusually pale; his eyes were pink around the rims. His customary military stride was slightly off-tempo as though he were suffering from sun-stroke, constipation, or some similar affliction.

"Hiya, Jimmy!" Gordie called.

Ashenden looked up, bleary-eyed. "Morning, Mr. Gompers. Mayor."

"Yer lookin' a little pink around the gills this morning, Jimmy." Gordie elbowed the mayor and chortled. "Up late doin' reports again?"

"Hmm? Oh—yes." Ashenden wondered how to avoid a conversation. If they knew what had really happened the night before, they wouldn't think everything was so funny. His mind shuddered away from the scene at Sharon's motel room; a wave of nausea overwhelmed him. He tried to step around the two men at the gas pumps, but the mayor grasped his arm.

"Say Jimmy, been meaning to talk to you about the Sports Day."

"What is it, Mayor?" Ashenden gasped, suddenly afraid he was going to vomit in front of him.

"Well, it's sort of delicate," the mayor said, still holding Ashenden's sleeve. "Lots of folks around town have been putting a big effort into it, and we were, well, hoping—you wouldn't let the community down."

Ashenden could see a ragged patch of sow-thistle at the corner of the garage, a two foot growth that might hide the contents of his heaving stomach, if he could only get away from the mayor's grip.

"What do you want me to do?"

"It won't take much time. What it is—is we need somebody to judge one of the races during the Sports Day, and we were wondering—if you weren't too busy—"

"Race?" Ashenden said.

"Yeah—the egg-and-spoon race."

"I don't—get it—"

"It's simple, Jimmy," Gordie chimed in. "Yuh get the kids all lined up by age group and yuh got all these spoons, and a buncha hard-boiled eggs, and yuh put one egg in each spoon, yuh see—"

Ashenden uttered a belch. "Excuse me!" he said, lurching to the sow-thistle patch at the corner. He spewed from two yards away, but managed to hit the greenery nevertheless. Not a crumb of Ellie Sanders' scrambled eggs and fried tomatoes stained the sidewalk. He leaned against the corner, retching convulsively till he thought his eyes would pop out, all the time miserably conscious of the mayor and Gordie Gompers staring at the back of his sweat-soaked shirt. That was what came from not following the straight-and-narrow. His mother had warned him about women and carrying on immoral activities. She'd been right; he had only himself to blame. He straightened himself up, surreptitiously flicking two or three globules of scrambled egg from his royal-blue issue tie, and wondered how to save face.

Gompers was standing with the gas nozzle in his hand dripping gasoline, staring in wide-eyed astonishment. Boothroyd himself was as pale as a ghost. Dang it all, Ashenden thought, everybody barfs. Why can't they accept me as *human*? It was hard, being the representative of law and order in a small town.

"Must be flu going around," he said.

"Yeah." Boothroyd nodded, his eyes glazed with shock. "Yeah."

"Now, about this race, Mr. Mayor?"

"Well," Boothroyd cleared his throat. "We figured you'd want to take the opportunity to show your loyalty to the town. Show how you appreciate being part of the community and so on."

Ashenden frowned, the colour flowing back to his cheeks. "Well, I'm pretty busy, you know."

"Yeah, we know that, Jimmy," Gordie said. "But we thought it might be a real big deal for yuh, what with the big cheese comin' up from Moose Jaw and all."

Ashenden was instantly alert. "*What* big cheese?"

Boothroyd tried to warn Gordie with an elbow in the ribs, but the enthusiastic Gompers carried on: "Yer boss—Inspector Fatsides."

The mayor turned away to contemplate the sun, now rising toward its noon-day zenith.

Ashenden was stunned. "You know about the inspector coming?"

"Sure," Gordie grinned amiably, his good spirits frothing like ginger ale. "We got a welcoming committee all set to give him the big howdy-do the minute he steps off thuh bus."

"Oh *no*!"

Gordie stopped in concern. "You're not gonna puke all over my used-car lot again, are yuh, Jimmy?"

"Excuse us, Mr. Gompers." Ashenden seized Boothroyd by the arm and dragged him down the sidewalk towards the Maple Leaf Cafe. "Mayor, how does he know about that?"

"Search me."

"Listen carefully. Inspector Heavysides is coming here on a *top-secret investigation*."

"Inspector Heavysides?"

"Don't play dumb with me, Mayor. You've got to keep Gordie quiet, and not let this get around town. This is highly confidential police material."

"Sure. Whatever you say, Jimmy."

"It wouldn't look too good to have the Orange Lodge band out, when he's supposed to be arriving here on the q.t., would it?"

"Okay, leave it in my hands."

"Thanks, Mayor. Knew I could count on you."

"Oh, just one thing. You won't forget the egg-and-spoon race, will you?"

"Well—all right."

"And how about your girl friend—Miss Sharalike? The missus has her down for serving hot dogs at the booth from three to five. Will you see if that's okay with her?"

"All right, for gosh sakes!" Ashenden turned

and hurried down the street, anxious to leave the petty affairs of the town behind, and get down to his real work, the narcotics-terrorist gang.

"Hey Jimmy!" Phil shouted behind him. "You want to tell Inspector You-know-who he can stay till Saturday fer the Sports Day? Tell him we'd really like to have him!"

Ashenden pretended not to hear. He kept walking down Main Street, past Curley's Barbershop and Burt's Hardware, toward the bus depot. If Phil Boothroyd had things his way, Inspector Heavysides would end up umpiring the baseball tournament.

At the Maple Leaf Cafe and Bus Depot, Ashenden learned that the bus would arrive from Moose Jaw at 3:45 p.m. He had a few precious hours to collect information on Plan G. Or at least Sharon had. He himself had to prepare for the inspector's arrival.

At that very moment, Sharon was in Shakespear, introducing herself to the mysterious Madam Karmakov. They had planned this together the night before, as he had driven her home. Sharon was not known to the drug ring and could use her acting experience ("Queen's University Drama Society, 1964-65," she informed him casually, "*The Three Sisters*.") to infiltrate the group and find out when the shipment of drugs would move from Shakespear into Meadowlark.

In the meantime, Ashenden was rushing to his office to put it into some kind of order before the inspector arrived. He still had three days of reports to do, and had not even started reading the bale of new memos on revised regulations. And now he had to wash out his tie and get it ironed. If only Sharon could find something!

Sharon! The events of the night before slashed into his mind like a nightmare. Had that been *him*, Jimmy Ashenden of Niebelung, Manitoba, doing those things with a woman? His face flushed as he hurried down the street, trying to suppress images crowding into his brain like monstrous phantoms.

While he drove Sharon back to her motel the night before, they planned Thursday's operations. Then she had put her head on his shoulder and begun to hum "My Kind of Guy" in a low, throaty purr. Somehow he managed to clutch the wheel and stare straight ahead for each of the sixteen miles to Shakespear. When Sharon's hand slipped inside his shirt and her slim, elegant fingers began stroking his chest, he didn't know what to do. A force strained in his underwear like his father's big diesel Cockshutt on a rod-weeder. He could only pray Sharon did not notice.

Her hand strayed, descended and finally came to rest on the pyramid in his blue serge breeches.

"Sharon!" he yelled, rigid with distress.

"What? *What*?" She jerked bolt upright. "What is it?"

"Whew! That was close! Big hole in the road. Could have had a blow-out!"

"Try to relax," she sighed.

When they turned into Shakespear finally, Ashenden's knees were trembling from the strain.

"Why don't you come in for a drink?" Sharon whispered, switching off the engine. "I'm sure I can give you—something."

He couldn't think of anything, but her voice made the bristles on the back of his head stiffen.

"Would you have any cold 7-Up?"

"Cool," she said, taking him by the hand to the door of her motel. She pulled him into the darkness inside. Then, while he was innocently waiting for the lights to come on, she suddenly threw herself into his arms, squeezing her bosom against him. Her legs seized him like pythons. Nothing like this had ever happened to him before; he had never even dared *think* of it. It was like a scene from the paperbacks that used to circulate during study period in the Neibelung Collegiate Institute.

Then her mouth was upon his, kissing him wildly. Her tongue forced his lips apart, and she was suddenly inside his mouth, exploring hungrily. He tried to push her away. But she squeezed tighter, forcing him back to the wall. His privates throbbed, and he realized that this could lead to his—wet dream—problem.

He sagged for a moment, nearly succumbing. But somewhere within, purity asserted itself. He tore himself loose from her grasp. "Sharon! You can get *germs* from kissing like that!"

She stepped back in the darkness, momentarily shocked. Then she began giggling. This rose into wild laughter and before Ashenden knew what the heck was going on, she had fallen to the floor, sobbing hysterically. He stepped across her to the door. "Never mind about the 7-Up," he said, finding his Stetson hat. "Now don't forget, you're going to get to know Madam Karmakov tomorrow. I'm counting on you, Sharon."

He drove straight to his living quarters and rinsed his shorts out in the sink. Then he collapsed on his cot, exhausted and drained.

8 MAIN-TEEN LUH DROYT

It was after barely two hours' sleep that Constable Ashenden encountered Ellie Sanders' scrambled-egg-and-fried-tomato breakfast and its horrible aftermath. Well, when he finally cracked the Pules-Feltham case, he would ask for two days' leave to recuperate.

He managed to get the office cleaned up, the prisoner's cell scoured, his hat brushed, and the reports typed before 3:30. But there was no time to clean his vomit-stained tie before going to the Maple Leaf Cafe and Bus Depot to meet the 3:34 bus from Moose Jaw.

As Ashenden briskly marched along Main Street, a black Oldsmobile sedan pulled up behind him so that he saw neither it nor the driver, a heavy man with his jacket collar turned up and his fedora low over his eyes. As the car eased abreast, the window on the passenger's side slid down, and the man's lumpy face scowled through the opening. "Ashenden!" he barked.

The policeman whirled to face the challenge, his hands thrusting forward to deal with any threat, physical or verbal. It was a reaction thrummed into his muscles by months of tough drilling, preparing him instantly to deliver a karate chop or a finger-waving lecture on disrespect for the law.

"Were you talking to *me*?" he said, peering into the dark interior of the Olds, trying to study the face.

"Just get in."

"Do you know who you're talking to, mister?"

"Yes. Constable Ashenden of the RCMP."

"That's right. And I want to see your operator's licence."

The heavy-faced man stared at him, his tiny blue eyes crinkling with distaste. "I am your inspector, you god-damned moron!" he said finally.

Ashenden's training once again served him in good stead. He leaped to attention with instant reflex action, his polished boot heels popping together on the hot sidewalk. His hand snapped into a crisp salute that belied his exhausted condition. "Good afternoon, sir! Pleased to see you, sir!" he snapped, his eyes staring straight ahead across the street, where he could see the green and orange awning of the MacLeod's Store flap in the slight breeze. He hoped his stained tie was not showing.

"For Christ's sake, Ashenden! You'll get sunstroke out there. Climb in!"

Ashenden opened the door and slid into the passenger's seat. The cool, dark interior was a relief on a day like this. He noticed, as the window whirred back into place, that the inspector's car had air-conditioning. Maybe after the Pules-Feltham gang was captured and put in jail, he would get air-conditioning in his car too.

"Now what's all this bullshit about a secret mission?"

"Secret mission, sir?"

"That's all I've heard about for the past two hours. Everybody from Earl's Esso Station to the waiter in the Ponderosa Beverage Room seems to think I'm here on some 'secret' mission."

Ashenden groaned inwardly, but managed to keep his eyes level with Inspector Heavysides'. "Well, isn't that why you're here in Meadowlark, sir?''

"No, that is *not* why I'm here in Meadowlark, sir!" the inspector roared. "I'm up here to kick your ass up Main Street and around the block for you! How come every sonuvabitch and his dog in this town knows I was coming?''

"I think I can explain, sir. There's a manual telephone exchange here and the operator—well, she's a bit of a gossip.''

"Which is *exactly* why we do business by mail in this sub-division, Ashenden!''

"Yes sir. I considered it an emergency under Regulation 352, Clause 17(d).''

"Don't hand me that crap!" the inspector rasped. "Just tell me what I'm doing up here besides booking you for a demotion!''

Ashenden began to perspire again, despite the air-conditioner in the car. "Well, sir, I have reason to suspect there is a drug-trafficking ring being established here, with foreign agents and political connections in Quebec.''

"Foreign agents, eh, Ashenden? That's pretty good.''

"Thank you, sir.''

"*But what the hell are they doing in Podunk, Saskatchewan?*''

"But they could appear *anywhere*, sir. You said so yourself in the Sub-Divisional Memo circulated June 4 of this year. Paragraph 14, Clause (3).''

Inspector Heavysides stared at Ashenden a brief moment, his breath hissing from the corner of his mouth. "This had better be good, Ashenden.''

"I think I can justify your faith in me, Inspector. At this very moment, I have an agent infiltrating the enemy camp. We are going to meet at supper-time to exchange information. I'm pretty confident you'll give me a complete go-ahead after that time."

"An agent, Constable? We do not hire agents in the RCMP."

"Well, she's a volunteer, sir. I could hardly refuse the help."

"*She*?"

"Yes—there she is now, Inspector." Ashenden pointed to the south end of Main Street, a half-mile distant, where it joined Highway No. 15 to Shakespear. There was a bright yellow flash in the sun, and Sharon's MG swerved off the highway onto the gravel road; its familiar plume of dust rose majestically behind as the distant whine of the accelerating engine reached their ears. She must have hit seventy m.p.h. by the time she reached the hotel, when she geared down with a squeal of tires and a series of backfiring explosions. Ashenden leaned over and beeped the inspector's horn, as she zoomed past them. Sharon waved at them prettily, and in the middle of Main Street took a sharp, skidding U-turn with a violent flip of the steering wheel, her lustrous coppery curls swinging free in the faint breeze. She pulled alongside the big Oldsmobile, revving her engine furiously.

"Ashenden," Inspector Heavysides said, gazing at the girl in the MG. "You're starting to worry me, do you know that?"

"Well—sir—"

"Tell her to park that—thing and get in here. I'm going to get to the bottom of this."

Ashenden did as he was told. When Sharon was safely in the back of the car, the inspector drove to Elm Street, where he parked across from the Legion Hall. Ashenden introduced them.

Sharon leaned forward, her winning smile directed at the Inspector's scowling face. "I'm a writer," she said. "For the CBC."

The Inspector's fedora seemed to pop up suddenly off the top of his head, revealing a close-cropped skull with deep fissures running across the forehead. A swollen vessel on the temple pulsed noticeably, and his eyes appeared to bulge from their sockets. He turned his head slowly toward Ashenden, his mouth working, unable to speak.

Ashenden smiled encouragement.

"SHE—WORKS—WHERE?" the inspector bellowed. A couple of faces appeared at the door of the Legion Hall beer parlour across the street to see what all the noise was about.

"Um—CBC, sir." Ashenden knew now that something was definitely wrong. But there had been nothing about the CBC in the memos, and he had just assumed the two federal agencies were working for roughly the same employer: Her Majesty, The Queen.

"Jesus H. Christ! Have you gone right round the *bend*! You're *bushed*, Constable! You must be! CBC!" He shook his head incredulously. "Do you know what I'm going to do to you, Ashenden? Do you know where your next posting's going to be?"

"Baffin Island, sir?"

"Not on your sweet life, Ashenden—Baffin Island's too *cushy* for you. You're going to spend the rest of your life in this police force following the Musical Ride around with a push-broom and dustpan, sweeping up after the horses. That's where *you're* going!"

Ashenden saluted, his face a study in stoicism. "Very good, Inspector. Thank you, sir."

"Shut up!" He turned to Sharon, who was glowering at him with her luminous green eyes. "Now as for you—you goddam *seductress*—you slink back into that Dinky Toy and get out of town. Stop putting lunatic ideas into this kid's head."

"Inspector Heavysides!" Sharon protested. "You have to listen. This is serious. These people are really up to something. We've got a tape recording!"

"Ashenden, I am holding you responsible for shutting this woman up."

Sharon flared. "*Listen, you—fascist pig!*"

"Constable. If she utters another word, I want her arrested for public mischief. Now get her out of here."

Ashenden jumped out of the car to open the rear door for Sharon.

"Never mind!" she said. "I can get out myself." She stepped out, slammed the door, and flounced up the street, turning once, as Ashenden watched in horror, to give the inspector a long, elegant middle finger. Fortunately the inspector was making notes in his small black book. Ashenden stood at attention beside the car.

"See that she's out of Meadowlark by sundown," Inspector Heavysides said, not looking up from his jotting.

"Today, sir?"

The inspector glared at him. "Every day, Ashenden. Is that understood?"

"Yes, sir."

"I'm giving you one last chance." The inspector looked up at the young officer, his bushy eyebrows nearly concealing his tiny blue eyes. "Let's say you're entitled to a couple of mistakes. But this is conditional upon your clearing up this mess. You have to redeem yourself, Ashenden."

"Thank you, sir."

The inspector's chilly smile was intended to convey compassion. "I was a raw rookie just like you once, Ashenden. I know what it's like. Especially when women get involved."

"But, sir—"

The inspector held up a hand. "Your superior officers have confidence in you, Ashenden. They *have* to have. Or they wouldn't have given you that uniform. And now—good luck." Inspector Heavysides extended his enormous hand to Ashenden, then pumped the accelerator, apparently anxious to begin the long drive back to Moose Jaw.

"Thank you, sir. Now—about these red FLQ types bringing in the shipment of drugs?"

"Ashenden."

"Yes, sir?"

"There are no reds here. There is no FLQ here. There aren't any drugs *for a hundred miles*! I am hereby issuing you an order—on threat of dismissal from the Force—to get rid of this crazy obsession of yours about a drug conspiracy!"

Ashenden tried to locate the inspector's ice-blue eyes under the shaggy brows. An order had been given; it had to be carried out. A direct order from a superior countermanded all previous orders, all the regulations in the book. It superseded individual discretion. "Yes, sir," he said smartly.

"We know what we're doing in Moose Jaw, Constable. And now, I'm keeping you from your highway patrol duties. So long."

Ashenden stepped away from the car, forsaking its cool interior for the mind-numbing heat waves beating upward from the sidewalk.

"Oh, and get that goddam tie dry-cleaned," the inspector said, slamming the door shut. Then the black Oldsmobile was gone, purring down the street and out of Ashenden's life as ominously as it had entered. He was left on the sidewalk, gazing after it. His headache was getting worse. He needed sleep desperately, and he wanted to visit Trooper. The companionship of his horse always lifted his spirits. He glanced at his watch. Nearly supper-time. Maybe he could slip out for half an hour before Ellie Sanders rang the little hand-bell in her dining room.

As though in answer to his yearning for sympathy, a loud racket burst out behind him, and Sharon's speedy little roadster screeched to a halt at his elbow.

"I thought the old fart would never go!" Sharon yelled above the roar of her engine, waving at him gaily.

He moved toward the car, facing one of the most painful tasks of his life. He gestured to Sharon to switch off the engine. "Well, I guess that's it, Sharon. It's all over."

Her dark green eyes stared at him incredulously. "You don't mean it!" she breathed. "After all we've gone through to crack this case?"

"I'm afraid so. An order is an order."

"Well, it might be for you, Constable. But I don't take orders from some brass-hatted ape."

"Duty comes first, Sharon."

She gazed at him, her beautiful face intense with conviction. "Does it, Jimmy?" she said quietly. "Is duty always first? How about initiative, and responsibility?"

"Let's not get started talking about *principles*,"

he replied shortly.

"Listen to me, Jimmy. Listen to me as you've never listened to anything I've said before! Those—persons are going to execute Plan G on Saturday. In this *town*, which you have sworn to protect to the best of your ability! Are you going to abandon *that* duty?"

"Sharon, please!"

"I'll tell you what. You won't even have to dirty your hands looking after it. Go back out and *run* your radar trap. I'll do the investigation for you, unofficially. We won't even *tell* them in Moose Jaw."

"No, no, no!"

"And then, when we crack the ring—you'll be a bigger hero than ever—because you did it all yourself. You persisted in your sworn oath in the face of all obstacles!"

"But an order," he groaned. "From Inspector Heavysides!"

"Hah! Inspector Heavysides! What does *he* know, sitting in his plush office in Moose Jaw? I bet it even has an air-conditioner—so he won't get contaminated by the rich, clean dust of the prairies! Why do your superiors want to suppress this investigation?"

"My duty—!"

"Your duty is to the law! To justice! Jimmy, tell me, what is the motto of the Force?"

He could not suppress a quaver of emotion from his voice, as he declaimed the oath he had memorized for the graduation exercises: "Main-teen luh droyt!"

"Yes! *Maintien le droit!* Let it ring, Constable Jimmy Ashenden! Let it ring through the length and breadth of Meadowlark! Don't surrender now!''

Sharon stood on the seat of her MG, her right hand raised in a fist. Her rings glittered in the late afternoon sun. She seemed, silhouetted against the outline of the Legion Hall, like an avenging angel of the law. For the first time in his career, RCMP Constable James Ashenden faltered in the execution of a direct order.

"Sharon, do you know what's going to happen to me if this doesn't work?'' He paused, white-faced. "Horse latrine detail with the Musical Ride.''

She looked at him with pride. "I knew you wouldn't give up, Jimmy.'' Her tanned thighs flashed alarmingly as she vaulted out of the car. She took him by the arm and breathed in his ear, "Do you know what I found out today? Do you know the Wheat Pool elevator agent?''

"Well, not personally.'' The grain buyer at the Wheat Pool elevator was the only Oriental in town, a man by the name of Yu Ching with a reputation for quietness. He smiled a lot and nodded, but had never spoken to Ashenden.

"Do you know why he's so quiet? Why he never talks to *anybody*?''

"Well, he's only been here a couple of months, Sharon. Maybe he's very shy. These things take time, you know.''

Sharon shook her head triumphantly, her copper hair swinging from side to side. "Not even close. It's because he doesn't speak English! Just Chinese!''

Ashenden stood rooted to the spot. It was as though a blindfold had been ripped from his eyes.

The yellow hordes of China were at the gates of Meadowlark!

9 FIREWORKS AT MIDNIGHT

The revelation that Yu Ching did not speak English was the electrifying spark Ashenden needed to shake off his fatigue and prepare to battle the forces of darkness which threatened the Rural Municipality of Meadowlark.

"That's it, Sharon!" His voice had a ring of iron firmness. "We'll bust this case wide open! To heck with Inspector Heavysides and his air-conditioner."

"What next?" Sharon, too, was vibrant with excitement.

"Hm. Good question! What did you find in Shakespear?"

"Madam Karmakov works in the Shakespear United Church Nursery School."

"I don't like that." Ashenden shook his head. "I don't like the sound of that at all."

"A good cover. She comes to Meadowlark every day to get the children books from the public library. There is no library in Shakespear."

"Did you find out about Jeremy Pules-Feltham?"

"She came right out and admitted she was having an affair with him."

Ashenden blushed. "Well, she'd have to admit it, wouldn't she? Everybody knows about it now. They might as well be social outcasts."

"I think Yu Ching might be worth checking out, Jimmy. He *has* to be part of the whole operation."

"How did you find out about him?"

"Stumbled into it by accident. I went into the Shakespear Post Office to find out where Madam

Karmakov lived and the postmaster started telling me about this Chinese guy from Meadowlark, who *collects his mail in Shakespear.*"

"Wow!"

"And if that isn't enough, it comes from all over the world."

"An international agent!"

"And get this. He never speaks a word of English, or anything else, either. Showed up for the first time about four months ago, and started gesturing for mail. Of course, the postmaster was holding all these letters for somebody named Yu Ching and right away he knew it was him."

"Anything else?"

"Just that he has this big smile all the time. The postmaster says he's the happiest-looking guy he's ever seen."

"It must have been him following us through town last night." Ashenden lapsed into silent concentration.

"Look, Sharon," he said finally. "Seeing Yu Ching is in Meadowlark, I'll do the stake-out on him. You stay here and keep Madam Karmakov under surveillance."

"Oh?" Sharon bristled with defiance. "How come *I* get stuck in Shakespear?"

Ashenden thought for a minute. He couldn't tell her about Inspector Heavysides' order; he didn't feel up to another argument.

"Well, um, what about your documentary on Max Christian and the Pitcairn Islanders. Don't you have work to do on that?"

"Hah!" she replied. "I dropped it, what with working night and day on your case, wearing myself into a frazzle."

Ashenden decided to try the stern approach. "Darn it all, woman!" he thundered. "I'm issuing an order! Tonight you *stay* in Shakespear. We'll rendezvous in the morning."

Sharon gazed at him for a moment, and goose-stepped back to her car, twitching her rear-end at him as she got in. "*Ja, Herr Commandant*! I shall report—later." She saluted sarcastically and the MG sped off down the street toward the highway.

Ashenden turned to the job at hand. At least he could follow the letter of Inspector Heavysides' order, if not the spirit. Sharon would be out of town by sundown; he would make sure she was out every night. It would also help her resist temptation. His power over women was positively frightening. He pushed the thought from his mind. That kind of stuff, if allowed, would rot his moral fibre like a plague of wheat rust. To fight this battle he had to keep himself strong.

Nourished by Ellie's superb supper of cheese-and-macaroni casserole, Ashenden walked over to the mayor's house. If Mrs. Boothroyd didn't have something on Yu Ching, nobody in town would.

The Boothroyds were finishing their supper when he knocked. "It's important, Mayor," Ashenden began, "or I wouldn't bother you at home."

Boothroyd lowered his voice. "Need a place for the inspector, Jimmy? We got a spare bedroom upstairs, just needs a little dusting and—"

"No, no. Inspector Heavysides has already gone back to Moose Jaw."

"Couldn't stay for the Sports Day, eh?"

"Well, he—asked me to pass on his regrets."

"Well, step right in and I'll get the missus to put

out some coffee and pie for you. Look who's here, maw!''

Mrs. Boothroyd grinned at Ashenden. ''Where's yer lady friend, Jimmy? Thought yuh'd be bringin' her around one of these days. Heard you and her were up till the small hours last night.''

''This is a very confidential matter,'' Ashenden said, his face turning hot. ''I hope you both understand that.''

''Sure, sure,'' the mayor agreed.

''Um, it's about the—Wheat Pool elevator agent.''

Mrs. Boothroyd grinned at Ashenden. ''Where's yer lady friend, Jimmy? Thought yuh'd be bringin' her around one of these days. Heard you and her were up till the small hours last night.''

''Did you ever wonder *why* he's so quiet?''

''Well, I never pry into other folks' personal affairs—''

Mrs. Boothroyd shrieked with laughter. Ashenden gave them both a level stare and said evenly:

''It's because he doesn't speak English.''

''You don't say?'' Boothroyd said thoughtfully.

''Don't you see what that *means?*''

''No,'' the mayor said slowly, ''I can't honestly say I do.''

Ashenden restrained his impatience. Civilians had to be coaxed. ''It *could* mean,'' he said tightly, ''that Yu Ching is a Chinese Communist spy sent to subvert the town of Meadowlark!''

''You don't say!''

''*Look!*'' Ashenden's patience snapped. ''If the Chinese Reds are infiltrating a community, what better place to start than the Wheat Pool, the very heart and soul of democratic institutions in this town?''

"Just a dang minute! If you're suggesting I don't run a democratic council, I'll—!''

"No, no. Mayor, we have to *do* something. He's a dangerous character!''

"He seems like a nice man to me, Jimmy,'' Mrs. Boothroyd interjected. "Smilin' all the time.''

"Have you noticed anything unusual about him, Mayor?''

"Can't say as I have, except for the rhubarb with the Wheat Pool farmers.''

"What rhubarb?''

"Well, he makes out their grain cheques, see. Only he writes them in Chinese. And they can't cash them anywhere! Hasn't been a grain cheque cashed in town since he got here. None of the banks can honour them. Oh, it's causing an awful row. Wheat Pool committee's in a sweat about it.''

"Why doesn't somebody *tell* me these things?'' Ashenden groaned.

"Well, it isn't against the law to write Chinese, you know. Why don't you talk to Gordie Gompers? He was supposed to ask You Chink about helping at the Sports Day. He might tell you something.''

"How about you, Mrs. Boothroyd? Any—information?''

"Well, I hardly ever see him, Jimmy. He spends all his time in that little shack he lives in beside the elevator. The only place he ever goes is the public library.''

Ashenden's face turned pale.

"What is it, Jimmy?'' the mayor said, impressed. "He took over the library, too?''

"No, no. I think we're onto something, Mayor.

At last." Ashenden put his hat on and ran out the door.

"I just can't believe it," Mrs. Boothroyd sighed. "That You Chink's got one a thuh nicest smiles I ever seen in Meadowlark."

By the time Ashenden reached Gordie Gompers' Garage, Gordie had closed for the night and driven to Sand Valley for the weekly meeting of the Masonic Lodge, as he did every Thursday.

With a few moments of free time, the Mounted Policeman decided to drive out and visit Trooper before setting up the long stake-out on Yu Ching. He felt a need to find solace in the intimate silence between true friends. He had considered visiting Sharon in Shakespear, but she might misunderstand his intentions and force him to take advantage of her. Despite Sharon's forwardness and occasional vulgarity, he felt attracted to the willowy CBC reporter. If they could keep their friendship pure, perhaps someday, when this ugly business was finished...

Trooper nickered in recognition as Ashenden stepped inside the stable door. Although it was pitch-black, he walked straight to the bay mare's stall and patted her flank. "Hiya Trooper."

He allowed himself fifteen minutes, letting her munch on honey-dipped oatcakes and nuzzle his chest. This was hard on his tie, but it had to be cleaned, anyway. On the way out, he stopped at the farm-house to pay Mr. Bryant, the caretaker, stable fees for the month.

He drove to the Wheat Pool elevator to take up scrutiny of Yu Ching's two-room shack, nestled beside the towering grain-storage building. The sheet metal walls housed the traditional bachelor quarters and office. Ashenden was struck by the similarity to his own quarters. He parked the cruiser a few hundred feet away, near the abandoned railway station, and settled down to watch. There was a car parked beside the shack: a 1967 Ford hardtop. The light was on inside the office.

Ashenden decided he would keep watch until Yu Ching turned off the office light. It was only when the sun began to rise again, about 4:00 a.m., that he realized Yu Ching must have gone to bed and left his light on all night. Irritable and nearly dead with fatigue, he dragged himself home to bed for a few hours' sleep.

A hammering on his door woke him up. "Just a minute." He struggled to his feet, reached the basin, and threw cold water on his face. He was stiff from sitting up half the night. He still had a stack of typing to do, and hadn't issued a speeding summons for a week. Today was Friday. At two o'clock, he had to be in court to prosecute an impaired driving charge. And his tie, he noticed as he slipped it over his head, was still an awful mess. He opened the door.

Sharon burst in, radiating warmth and energy. Ashenden realized how crucial her enthusiasm was going to be in this operation.

"What did you find?" she asked eagerly.

Ashenden went over the details he had uncovered. "How about you?"

"Not much. I followed her here to Meadowlark last night. She went into Pules-Feltham's house and stayed till midnight. Then I followed her back."

"Did you tape them again?"

"Nothing new." She glanced at him. "Want to

hear it?''

"No, no, I'll take your word for it."

After breakfast, he took her to Gompers' Garage. Gordie was working on a tractor engine with a socket wrench. His was an old, dilapidated garage with a dirt floor and the comforting smell of boards that had been soaked in oil for decades. Nails studded the walls on every side, and on each hung a different object—a cork gasket, a carburetor from a '53 Studebaker, piston rings for a John Deere tractor. Only Gordie knew which of the many thousand parts in stock would fit a given motor at a given time; he could put his hand on it without looking.

"Morning, Mr. Gompers," Ashenden said.

Gordie looked up, back at his engine, and did a violent double-take at the sight of Sharon Sharalike standing two feet away under the dangling light bulb, the neckline of her clinging white jersey dress plunging to the waist, and the deep shadows of her cleavage moving back and forth in front of his eyes as the bulb swayed. She smiled at him.

"Morning, ma'am. Kin I help yuh? Need some gas?"

"No, no," Ashenden said. "This is police business."

"Police!" Gordie's grease-blackened fingers pushed the stained Motolube skull-cap to the back of his head. "Somebody usin' purple gas in their car again?" he asked, glancing nervously at Sharon.

"No, nothing like that. Can you tell us something about the Wheat Pool agent?"

"You Chink? What'd he do?" Gordie stared at Sharon with renewed interest.

"That's classified information. Have you talked

to him recently?"

"Oh yeah. Real great guy, too. Grins tuh beat thuh band, yuh know. Course it's hard tuh tell with a Jap."

"What did you talk *about*?"

"Oh, lessee. Giss I was askin' him tuh umpire thuh ladies' softball tournament tomorruh."

"*And what did he say*?"

"Nuthin', now yuh mention it. Juss stood there, grinnin' away. But I think he unnerstood me."

"Mr. Gompers, he didn't talk because he doesn't know English."

"Izzattafact?" Gordie's eyes were still locked on Sharon's neckline. "Well, I'd like to stand here and jaw it over with yuh all day, Jimmy, but the truth is Charlie Cherry's gonna be comin' in here any minnit fer his tractor."

"Just one more thing. Is Jeremy Pules-Feltham doing anything for the Sports Day and Picnic?"

"He didn't offer, neither him nor his girl friend."

"They want to keep the day clear," Ashenden murmured to Sharon.

"Queer ducks, them foreigners," Gompers offered.

"If I told you what was going on around here, Mr. Gompers, it would blow the top of your head right off."

"Izzattafact?"

"Come on, Sharon. We've got a lot to do."

They agreed Sharon should take the first shift on the Yu Ching stake-out, from 10:00 until 4:00 p.m. After synchronizing his Timex with Sharon's watch, he took her to the Pool elevator. Across the tracks from the elevator was the old Canadian National

Railway station, now a shell of decaying yellow stucco. It remained in the town as a hollow reminder of the one-time importance of railroads in Saskatchewan. But at least it hid their cars from the viewpoint of the elevator. It had an upper storey that looked over the whole Wheat Pool operation. They would rendezvous at four, leaving Sharon plenty of time to get back to Shakespear by sundown.

Ashenden spent the afternoon catching up on his work, which included picking up his mail at the Post Office, returning to his desk to study all the new memos, typing a few dozen reports, and doing laundry at the Coin-o-matic Wash. He also dropped his tie off at Shirley's Jiffy Dry Cleaners.

When Ashenden returned to the CNR station down Buffalo Street, he pulled up behind Sharon's dust-covered MG. The upstairs room of the station was bare and dusty with fallen plaster, but Sharon had managed to cozy one corner of it with cushions from an old sofa. She had fixed up a table on an old soft-drink crate; she passed him a thermos of coffee.

"Coffee?" he laughed. By golly, he thought, what luck to have a partner like this. He forced himself back to grim reality. "You go for supper now and get some rest. I picked up some sandwiches at Ellie's. If you can come early tomorrow morning to relieve me, I'll get some sleep then."

"How early do you want me?" Sharon said, leaning toward him and tracing his marksman badge with her fingernail.

"Well, I'll be pretty tired by four a.m. That'll be about sunup. Didn't get much sleep last night."

"Four a.m.," she murmured. "Right on."

"You'd better go, if you want supper."

She pouted. "Don't you want to hear my report?"

"Oh, sure. What happened?"

Sharon dug a note-pad from her purse. "At 2:42 p.m., Yu Ching walked out of his office, down Buffalo Street to the public library and entered. He didn't communicate with anyone. He left ten minutes later, carrying two books."

Ashenden's eyes narrowed. "It's a dropping place for messages."

"Neither Madam Karmakov nor the Englishman showed up."

"That doesn't matter. They could be concealing the messages in the books."

"Anyway, the books he checked out were Chinese. I got the titles." She handed him the note-pad. *The Way of Lao Tzu* and *The Four Virtues of Confucius.*

He didn't recognize the names. Probably henchmen of Mao's. He put the paper in his pocket. "You sure he didn't notice you trailing him?"

"I don't think so. I stayed away back."

"Anything else?"

Her pleased smile told Ashenden she had been keeping the best till last. "Just this." She handed him a carbon copy of a telegram. "I hurried back to Yu Ching's office before he returned from the library, and found this."

Ashenden was appalled. "Sharon! What a heck of a chance to take!"

He tried to ignore the scent of musk rising from Sharon. His hands shook as he read:

"Watch for fireworks. Saturday. Midnight." It was signed, "Ching." It had been transmitted four days before from Shakespear.

10 INTO THE ELEVATOR

After Ashenden had sent Sharon off for supper, he settled down with the binoculars. When Pules-Feltham or Madam Karmakov showed up to make contact, he would move in closer with Sharon's tape recorder. He needed definite proof of conspiracy. Through the binoculars, he could see Yu Ching moving around in his office.

He began sifting through the clues, trying to fit the pattern together. "Fireworks at midnight." "Plan G." It was all tied in with the Sports Day tomorrow, he knew that; the town would be defenseless and unsuspecting. Everyone would be at the dance when midnight came; the bar would have been open for four hours and no one would be in any condition to offer resistance.

All day the townspeople had been busy putting the final touches to the preparations. A cotton banner was strung across Main Street, from the flagpole of the Post Office to the neon sign on the hotel. "Come one, come all!" it said. "Meadowlark Sports Day and Picnic! June 23. Baseball, Exhibits, Races, Dance, Prizes. Ladies' softball." The hall had been cleaned and polished; the baseball diamonds limed; two whole truck-loads of soft drinks had arrived from Moose Jaw.

By 8:30, nothing had happened. Ashenden wished he had brought the High-Q game his mother had sent on his birthday. He poured himself a cup of coffee from Sharon's thermos. *Fireworks at midnight*. What could it mean?

And suddenly he saw it had been staring him in

the face all along. Yu Ching could not have sent that message—unless he knew English! He had been lulling people into a false sense of security so he could carry on his evil subterfuge. Ashenden began considering him with new respect. He peered through his binoculars at Yu Ching's window, a frame of light in the growing dusk. He could see the Chinese occasionally move across the room.

Suddenly, a set of car headlights stabbed out of the darkness to his left. Instead of going to the elevator, it swung into the vacant lot behind the station, where his car was parked, with its RCMP coat of arms emblazoned on the door. It was a dead give-away to Pules-Feltham or Madam Karmakov.

A car door slammed. Ashenden held his breath. Someone entered the station on the floor below. Footsteps crunched across the scattered broken glass; they advanced to the staircase, paused, and began the ascent. The flare from a flashlight suddenly lit up the stairwell. Slowly, Ashenden stood up and eased his Smith & Wesson from the holster. The light went out as the footsteps reached the top of the stairs.

"Hold it right there!" Ashenden roared, switching on his powerful flashlight.

It was Sharon, blinking in the harsh light, a box under her arm. She had put on a trench coat.

"What are you doing here?" Ashenden demanded.

"I couldn't sleep in that lousy motel room. I decided to come and keep you company. I got a Rummoli game at the drug-store and a lantern. I brought some sandwiches and chocolate bars."

He gazed at her in admiration. Well, at least she had been out of town at sundown. The inspector couldn't blame him if she returned. "All right," he said. "But let's keep our minds on business."

"You're on!" Sharon pulled the blind over the window to black out the light and put the camp lantern on the table. She set up the Rummoli game while Ashenden kept watch on Yu Ching. Then they played to pass the time, looking out the window on alternate turns. For an Eastern girl, Sharon played well. Somewhere she had mastered the rudiments of Rummoli.

"Still there," he said, checking on Yu Ching. "Nothing happening."

"I wonder what he does with his time?"

Ashenden thought for a minute. "Chinese checkers."

"By *himself*?"

"Oh, I don't know," Ashenden said cautiously. *He* had played Chinese checkers by himself. "By the way," he said, changing the subject, "you're supposed to sell ice cream in the refreshment booth tomorrow."

"I'm *what*?"

"Well, I volunteered for you."

"What kind of sexist trick was that? Why didn't *you* volunteer? Or do you have to organize the *egg-and-spoon race*?" she asked sarcastically.

"All right," he said. "Don't get upset. I'll tell them you're busy."

"Better check on Yu Ching," Sharon said shortly.

Ashenden no sooner had located the lighted window in his binoculars than the light suddenly went out.

"Sharon!" he hissed. "Kill the lantern. This might be it."

She joined him at the window. "There he goes," she said. "Into the elevator."

Ashenden located Yu Ching in the binoculars, walking up the cindered driveway to the big doors that opened onto the platform scales of the grain elevator. He slid open one of the enormous doors and disappeared inside.

"That's strange. I didn't see any trucks pull up."

"There aren't any trucks this time of night, you dummy. He's *up* to something!"

Before they could slip out and follow him inside, the Chinese came out the door, closed it, and went back to his office. The light turned on again.

Ashenden made a sudden decision. "I'm going to see what's in that elevator! You stay here and cover me. If he comes out of the office, run down to my car and blow the horn. That'll be my signal to get out the other door."

"Don't go, Jimmy. Let's stay here and watch."

"There's nothing to be afraid of."

"No? What about that big hole in the middle of the floor where they dump the wheat out of the trucks? We'd never see it in the dark. You'll fall in!"

"The hopper? Don't be silly. There's a metal grill over it." He gave her an encouraging grin and was gone.

Three hours later, when he had not emerged from the elevator, Sharon knew a rescue operation had to be mounted. It was 2:30 a.m., and it was getting cold in the unheated old railway station. The light was still on in Yu Ching's shack, and she could see him moving around. But there had been no sign of accomplices.

She wrapped the trench coat around her as she stumbled across the tracks toward the black tower looming over her in the darkness. With a mighty effort, she levered the door open.

The interior of the building was pitch dark. But it was not silent; everywhere there was the rustle of grain falling in trickles. Thousands of mice scurried to and fro in the cracks and crannies. Cables creaked in the elevating device, an endless belted circle of buckets that scooped wheat out of the deep hopper below the floor and carried it eighty feet to the top, where the spouts were located. There was the moan of the night wind through the chinks and crevices of the dozen tall vertical bins in the building. The air was thick with grain dust.

"Jimmy?" she whispered tentatively. "*Jimmy?*"

A loud rattle echoed through the building. She nearly fainted with terror. It seemed to come from all around.

"*Jimmy!*" she yelled.

"Shussh!"

"*Where are you?*"

"Down here! Don't move any closer!"

"Where?"

After a silence, his voice rose from somewhere beneath her: "Down in the hopper."

Sharon switched on her flashlight. Three paces in front of her was a deep black hole in the floor. She peered over the edge.

Jimmy was about six feet below, looking up at her with a red face. "He must have took the grill off," he said.

Sharon stifled a giggle.

"It isn't funny," he snapped. "I could have hurt

myself. See if you can find a rope."

She went to the weigh scales at one side and poked around until she found a thick rope coiled on the floor. Returning to the hopper, she threw one end down to Ashenden and tied the other around a timber on the other side of the platform. In a few seconds, Ashenden had climbed out of the hopper, his uniform looking as though he'd been dunked in asbestos.

"I got worried when you didn't come back," Sharon said.

"Thanks for coming. Is Yu Ching still in his shack?"

"Yes. Did you find anything?"

"One very important thing," Ashenden said, beating the dust off his clothes. "There hasn't been a bushel of wheat delivered to this elevator for at least a week. That hopper is empty! It hasn't been used for days."

"That must be why he had the grill off!"

"Precisely. Well, we better get some sleep. To-morrow's going to be a forty-hour day."

"Maybe we can come back and have a look around in the daylight," Sharon suggested.

"Good thinking. If I could only convince the brass in Moose Jaw, we could get reinforcements."

"Don't you *dare* say a word to them, after the way that Inspector Heavysides treated you. There's something wrong with that man. It isn't right to stop an investigation before it gets started."

Before Ashenden could protest, a tremendous sound like a gigantic gong reverberated through the building—more like a violent, ghostly shudder than a noise. The floor trembled under their feet. Ashenden seized Sharon's hand, pulling her across the scales and out the far door of the elevator.

"What was *that*?" she gasped, as they ran down the drive and across the railway tracks.

"Don't know! Keep running!"

They reached the station before looking back. The dark elevator had not changed. Neither of them mentioned the noise; they both feared there was no answer, no explanation for it. They resumed their vigil on Yu Ching's lit-up window. Suddenly, it went black.

"He's finally going to bed," Ashenden said.

"Speaking of bed, Jimmy, I think I'll find a place in Meadowlark tonight. I'm too tired to drive all the way back to the motel."

Ashenden remembered his O.C.'s order. "It's okay," he sighed. "I'll drive you back."

"No. Not in your condition! You're absolutely wiped out. I'll get a room at the Meadowlark Hotel. If they're still open."

He gazed at her, torn between the regulations and sleep. "Well, Sharon, if you don't mind the discomfort of an old bachelor's quarters—"

"Yes?"

"Maybe you could sleep at my place."

She jumped at him before he could leap aside, and hugged him so tightly he could feel her bosom pressing against his tunic buttons, her warm thighs cleaving to his yellow-striped breeches.

"Hey!" Ashenden gasped, escorting her firmly to her car. "Now, you take your car and I'll meet you over there. And for gosh sakes, park it around behind the back where nobody can see it."

The MG took off in a fury of flying gravel. By the time he reached his building on Antelope Avenue, she was standing at the door of his living quarters, her trench coat already removed and folded on her arm.

She made Ashenden so nervous that his key hammered all around the lock like a woodpecker. He couldn't seem to find the hole. It was as though he had lost control of his hands.

"Hurry up," Sharon moaned. "I'm cold."

"For gosh sakes, put your coat back on, if you're cold."

When he finally switched on the lights, Sharon ran to his cot and lay down. Ashenden approached slowly. Her green eyes blazed with appeal. "*Now*, Jimmy! Take me now!"

"Gol*darn* it, Sharon! Take you where? Where do you want to go?" Ashenden reached below the bed and pulled out his locker. "I have to get some blankets."

She stared at him, her eyes glowing feverishly. "Blankets? What for?"

He opened the locker and lifted out a pair of khaki blankets. "I always keep extras for emergencies."

"*Emergencies*?"

"Yeah," he said, carrying them to the door and glancing once around the room. "I think you'll find everything you need. Latrine's through that door beside the sink." He pointed.

"You aren't *staying*?"

Ashenden smiled bashfully. "Gosh, no! I'm going to bunk down with Trooper. Good night— Sharon."

As he closed the door behind him Ashenden heard one of his plaster horse-head bookends—the pair his mother sent him for a graduation present— shatter into a million pieces against the inside of the door. He sighed. It would be a long time before he understood women.

11 THE MYSTERIOUS HORSEMAN

As the sun rose over Trooper's stable, a thin shaft of sunbeam pierced the darkness and illuminated Ashenden's blond cropped head, propped up on the black RCMP issue saddle he had bought in a second-hand store in Sand Valley a few weeks before. He stirred under the khaki blankets, yawned and glanced at his Timex. Seven a.m. Seventeen hours until midnight. Seventeen hours to crack Plan G.

He took Trooper out to the water trough for a drink, and splashed his own neck and ears with the cold water. He could feel the sun on his back already; it was going to be another scorcher. He searched the skies. If it didn't rain soon, the crops were going to burn.

He put Trooper back into the stable, leaving oats and hay. Then he ran to his car and drove back to town. He had to waken Sharon before the townspeople discovered her sleeping in his quarters. If word ever got back to Moose Jaw, Ashenden would be up on an orderly room charge, no matter how successful this investigation.

He managed to slip into town the back way, avoiding Main Street, where Mayor Boothroyd already had his workers out, putting up signs to direct traffic, hanging bunting on the store fronts, stocking the refreshment booth with ice, and doing the hundreds of jobs that have to be done on Sports Day.

He roused Sharon with a knock at the door; then, while she made herself respectable, he took his cruiser through the 25¢ car-wash. It would have to be shined up in case the editor of the *World-Spectator and Times* took pictures of the arrest.

Sharon seemed tired and cranky when he came to collect her for breakfast. He hoped she wasn't getting sick. He was counting on her vigour to help them through a very heavy day.

After breakfast Sharon agreed to take the morning watch on Yu Ching, where there probably wouldn't be much happening. Ashenden would stake out the Pules-Feltham place, waiting for the connection to show up with the drug shipment. After lunch they could switch places. The only problem was the egg-and-spoon race, which Ashenden had unfortunately agreed to supervise.

"Maybe if you asked nicely, they'd find somebody else to do it," Sharon suggested. "And while you're at it, look for a pinch-hitter at the ice cream counter."

She stepped into her car with a flick of her hips, and zoomed off to her vigil at the railway station.

Ashenden stopped on his way to the Pules-Feltham surveillance to ask Mayor Boothroyd about a replacement for the egg-and-spoon race.

"This is important, Mayor! Top-security. I *can't* take time off for a kids' race."

"Still chasing poor old You Chink around, Jimmy? And those depraved foreigners?" The mayor paused in the middle of hosing down the sidewalk in front of the town office.

"This case is so big, I can't even tell you about it."

"Is that so?" the mayor said shortly. "Well, for *me* the biggest thing is a Sports Day so good it'll make them stubble-jumpers over in Shakespear look like undertakers. And *that* means an egg-and-spoon race!"

"But Mayor—!"

"In this part of Canada, Jimmy, a man's word is as good as a contract. Now, did you give your word or not?"

Ashenden was trapped, and they both knew it. Mrs. Boothroyd sidled up, her face sour. "The refreshment booth's all set to go, Philip," she said, ignoring Ashenden.

"Morning, Mrs. Boothroyd."

"Well," she sniffed. "Where's your—*friend*?"

"Friend?"

"Miss Sharalike. The one who stayed at your place *all* night."

Ashenden was stunned. His face blushed blood-red. The woman's intelligence network was incredible. "Mrs. Boothroyd, she was—that is, I didn't stay there myself! I let her use my bed. I slept in the stable!"

Mrs. Boothroyd was not to be mollified. "Where there's smoke, there's fire," she announced smugly. "One night she's sleeping in your bed, and the next night *you're* in it, too."

"Mrs. Boothroyd!" Ashenden said firmly. "Ours is a professional relationship. Anything you say about Miss Sharalike's character only reflects on your own."

"Professional—hah!"

"At this very moment, Miss Sharalike has the suspect Yu Ching under surveillance at my request. She's assisting my investigation."

"You still tormentin' that poor little guy?"

"Poor little guy!" Ashenden exploded. "If you people had *any* idea of the criminal activity going on under your noses, you wouldn't be so complacent! Anybody who'd think an egg-and-spoon race was more important than preserving the free-enterprise system of Meadowlark doesn't even *deserve* to be saved."

"What kind of a bee have you got in your bonnet now?"

Ashenden whipped the tattered telegram carbon from his shirt pocket. "Just cast your eyes on this."

"What is it?" the mayor said, wrinkling his nose.

"A message. From Yu Ching's office."

"'Watch for fireworks at midnight—Saturday'?" The mayor looked puzzled.

"Their scheme is due to go off at midnight—tonight!"

"Yeah," the mayor said thoughtfully, "then on the other hand, maybe he's only going to watch the fireworks."

"Fireworks?"

Mrs. Boothroyd hooted. "The fireworks display goin' off at midnight, yuh dumb-head!"

"*Real* fireworks?"

"Fraid so, Jimmy," the mayor said. "Had them specially imported for the occasion."

"Where from?"

Boothroyd looked surprised. "China. Only place they make 'em."

Before Ashenden could pursue this stupefying piece of information, Gordie Gompers' tow-truck appeared, speeding down Main Street toward them. It screeched to a stop and Gordie leaped out.

"Where's You Chink?" he demanded.

"Don't know, Gomp. Better ask the Mountie here. He's been following him around for two days.''

"Where is he?''

"What do you want him for?'' Ashenden inquired.

"He's supposed to be umpirin' thuh ladies' softball, that's what for! We can't get started till he shows up. I got twenty wimmen over at the ball di'mond ready tuh chew the covers offa softballs.''

"You see, Mayor?'' Ashenden said. "There *is* something funny going on. And I'm going to find out what it is, even if you aren't interested in the safety of this community.''

"Now, let's not be hasty, Jimmy.''

"I want one favour, Mayor. Postpone the race till four-thirty. By then, I should have it all cleared up.''

"Ashenden, you can't run a Sports Day the way you run your detachment office. How do I know you aren't going to sneak off for a little smooching?''

"Yeah!'' Mrs. Boothroyd said.

"Mayor! The future of Meadowlark is at stake!''

"Okay, I'll postpone her till four-thirty. But if you're not back, I'll cut off the water to the RCMP office.''

"Thank you. Now I've got to go and check on Pules-Feltham, and then make sure Sharon is okay.''

"Hah!'' Mrs. Boothroyd said. "It's You Chink I'd be worryin' about. Prob'ly gettin' led astray by that Jezebel!''

A car horn suddenly began blowing in the distance.

"What the heck's that?'' Gordie Gompers said.

A battered old IHC truck pounded down Main Street toward them. It was Peter Danchuk, who farmed a few miles north of town.

"Hey you guys!" Danchuk shouted, leaning on the horn, his head out the truck window. "There's some crazy sonuvabitch riding into town on a *horse!*"

"A horse!" Ashenden repeated.

Peter's words seemed to have a magical effect. Crowds of people began gathering in the middle of the street, shouting: "A horse! Somebody on a horse! There's a guy on a horse!" Soon a hundred faces were searching the northern horizon for the horseman. Even Ashenden's eyes strained for a glimpse of the approaching steed. Except for Trooper, whom no one knew about, there hadn't been a horse in the district since the Sand Valley Rodeo the previous year.

"Who is it?" someone asked Peter Danchuk.

"Dunno, but he's travelling cross country. When he came past my place, I went running out and he said which way tuh Meadowlark, so I tole him, and off he went. Funny-looking guy. All dressed up in a cowboy outfit. Looks like Roy Rogers er somebody!"

A sudden thought flashed into Ashenden's mind. "Did he look—Chinese?"

"Nope." Peter shook his head. "You looking for a Chinese cowboy, Jimmy?"

Mrs. Boothroyd snorted. "He's looking for Chinese everythin'! That floozy from Toronto scrambled his brains."

"Look!" somebody yelled and pointed to the north end of Main Street, past the railway crossing.

The mysterious horseman had appeared. A

strange hush fell over the crowd. As they watched, he spurred his black stallion into a gallop straight toward them. In the split second before charging into the crowd and perhaps killing several, the horseman hauled back on the reins and the stallion reared high in the air. It rose majestically over Peter Danchuk's truck, its white-stockinged feet pawing the air with a grace Ashenden envied. The horseman sat back in the saddle, the reins gathered in one gloved hand. With the other hand, he lifted the wide-brimmed plainsman's hat and waved it over his head in a salute to the crowd. The "Oooooooos" and "Aaaawwws" swelled into an outburst of applause as the horse settled down on all fours again. Ashenden felt a twinge of envy. It might be years before he could train Trooper to do that.

The horseman stood up in the stirrups to speak. There was a jagged scar slashing across the right side of the rider's face like an angry red flag, from his ear to the corner of his mouth.

"My fren's." the horseman began in a deep voice. " 'Ave I foun' de touwn of Meadowlark?"

There was no mistaking the accent. The French connection had arrived! Ashenden unfastened the holster of his Smith & Wesson, and began edging forward in the crowd. The time for action had come.

12 A HEROIN REFINERY

Ashenden elbowed his way through the crowd milling around the stirrups of the French horseman.

"RCMP," Ashenden announced, looking steadily into the horseman's eyes. "Identify yourself and what you're doing here."

The horseman glanced at him, a smile playing on his lips, below a thin, black moustache.

"I am 'appy you 'ave asked that question. I 'ave ridden many miles to entertain de good people of Meadowlark at deir celebration, wit' my famous riding, roping and Wild West tricks."

The crowd murmured its gratitude.

"Wait a minute," Ashenden said. "Where did you come from? Who told you there was a Sports Day here?"

But his questions were swept aside in the torrent of excitement as more citizens flocked to the scene, trying to touch the black stallion. Others clamoured for the horseman's autograph.

"Show me where the arena is!" he shouted, ignoring Ashenden's questions.

"At the park!" someone yelled. "That way!" With a happy roar the crowd began rushing down Buffalo Avenue toward the campgrounds, where bleachers had been erected for the baseball games.

Ashenden ran to the front of the multitude, trying to stem the flow. "Don't listen to him!" he roared. "This man is a Communist agent. He's been sent by the FLQ to infiltrate Meadowlark!" But no one paid the slightest attention; they were

blown along like wheat chaff in a prairie wind. The
fools, Ashenden thought, selling their birthright for
cheap entertainment. He could see Mayor Booth-
royd and Gordie Gompers running along in the
mob, excited as schoolkids. Was there no one left
with common sense?

Sharon Sharalike! He had almost forgotten her.
Beautiful, loyal Sharon who at this dark moment in
the history of Meadowlark was maintaining her
dangerous vigil at the CNR station. And now that
Yu Ching hadn't shown up for the ladies' softball,
it could mean she was in deep trouble. Ashenden
sprinted for the cruiser.

But before he could go to the elevator, he had to
check on the Pules-Feltham place to see if anything
was happening. As he drove up to the tiny bunga-
low, he noticed a flash of sunlight in the trees be-
side the house. He backed up, looked again.
Madam Karmakov's Stingray. They were assemb-
ling their forces for Plan G.

Ashenden leaped from his car and ran to the
front step of the house. It was time for a confron-
tation. Pules-Feltham and Madam Karmakov
would break under his relentless questioning. Yu
Ching and the mysterious horseman would be
tougher nuts to crack.

He rapped smartly on the front door. No an-
swer. Once again he knocked, more insistently. Fin-
ally Pules-Feltham swung the door open and stood
there, yawning in his yellow, silk-textured pyjamas.
Ashenden's glance flicked rapidly about, looking
for a concealed weapon. He observed a gap in the
man's p.j.'s, where his drawstrings were loose.
Limey pervert.

"What the bloody hell is it this time?" Pules-

Feltham said, as his bleary red eyes recognized the policeman standing at ramrod attention in his doorway.

"Constable James Ashenden. Meadowlark detachment of the Royal Canadian Mounted Police. Open up in the name of the Queen."

"The door is open."

"I mean I'd like to enter."

"Perhaps you'd better tell me what you want."

"What is it, Jheremy?" the yoghurt-sounding voice of Madam Karmakov floated from the dim inner recesses of the Englishman's house. "Who is at zhe door?"

"No one, darling. Go back to bed."

Ashenden made a mental note of this exchange. It was all a ruse, of course. They wouldn't really be in bed on the day they were planning to execute Plan G. As Ashenden's eyes grew accustomed to the darkness inside the room, he noticed that the walls of the living-room were lined with books. He was itching to compare the titles with the list of subversive literature which Security Services issued periodically from Regina. He sniffed deeply, trying to identify the tell-tale odour of drugs. His keen nostrils confirmed the suspicion. The case was fitting together as neatly as the pieces in his Phil Esposito jig-saw puzzle.

Madam Karmakov suddenly appeared at Pules-Feltham's elbow, clad in a black negligee which highlighted her voluptuous curves.

"Oh!" she said, yawning. "Is polisman who found my lamp. When can we get zhe lamp, polisman?"

"It'll be ready soon enough," he said. "Mr. Gompers is fixing it at his garage."

"It's all right, darling." Pules-Feltham chucked her under the chin. "I'll look after this gentleman. You go back and get your beauty sleep."

"Now, Jheremy, don't be nasty. He is *good* polisman."

"Let me get right to the point, Pules-Feltham." Ashenden whipped his notebook out of his pocket and stood, Bic poised. "Why aren't you taking part in the Meadowlark Sports Day and Picnic today?"

"Very simple, old sport," the Englishman yawned. "No one asked me."

Ashenden tried another gambit. "Why didn't you volunteer?"

"Well, in case you haven't noticed, I seem to be a social pariah in this town."

Ashenden wrote down "social pariah." "And what's a social pariah?" he asked.

"Outcast, old bean. Alien. Foreigner. *D.P.*!"

"I see."

"As a matter of fact, I would have liked to take part. I'm quite partial to celebrations."

"I too, polisman. I also like parties."

Ashenden impaled Pules-Feltham with a stare, and sprung the trap. "Especially with fireworks, eh? At midnight?"

Pules-Feltham didn't betray a twinge of emotion. "Oh, will there be fireworks, too?" he said, looking innocent.

"So you're going to be around all day?"

"Absolutely, old man."

Ashenden suddenly had an inspiration. He would kill two birds with one stone. He could keep Pules-Feltham out of action for the afternoon, and free himself to keep an eye on the horseman, as well as relieve Sharon.

"How'd you like to be a good community sport and organize the egg-and-spoon race at four thirty?" he asked.

"Egg-and-spoon race?"

"Nothing to it. I would do it myself, but something has come up—and I thought you and—the lady might like to take part. If you want to."

"Love to," Pules-Feltham said. "Four thirty."

"Chust a moment, Jheremy, I sink you heff forgotten somesing." Madam Karmakov pulled the Englishman back into the shadows toward the bedroom hallway. Ashenden's trained ears identified the words "Plan G!" in her syrupy voice.

Pules-Feltham returned, red-faced and agitated. "I'm sorry, old bean. Seems I'll have to turn down your generous invitation. I'd forgotten a very pressing prior engagement."

"Prior engagement, eh?" Ashenden wrote it down.

"Yes. Terribly stupid of me."

It was time to take off the kid gloves. "What prior engagement?"

"I say—it *is* a personal matter."

"Okay, Limey. If you want to play tough, we'll play tough!"

"No need to get vitriolic, old sport."

"I'll get as virile as I darn well like! I'm the law in this town, and no social parrot's going to tell me I'm not."

"Jheremy, make him go away. He is suddenly onplasant."

"There you are. Buzz off like a good fellow, Ashenden."

"Okay, but I'm warning you, Limey! I'm onto your rotten game, and if you step out of this *opium-*

den you'd better watch your step."

He turned on his heel, slammed the door, and stood on the porch, listening carefully. He was rewarded by Madam Karmakov's voice filtering through the closed door.

"Jheremy!" she hissed. "He *knows*!"

"Don't be absurd. How could he know?"

"Maybe zhe agent talked?"

"He'd never talk."

Their voices died away as they retreated into the interior of the house. He couldn't waste any more time. Sharon might be in danger. He dashed to the car and took off for the Pool elevator. He had to rely on her more than ever. She was the only other person in town whose judgement hadn't been completely subverted. Oh, the fools! Not lifting a *hand* to protect themselves from disaster!

He floored the accelerator, hitting sixty-five by the corner of Elm and Sagegrouse. He switched on the siren to warn pedestrians he was coming through. In two minutes, he had swerved in behind the CNR station, where Sharon's car sat like a yellow grasshopper. He ran up the stairs three at a time, yelling "Sharon! Are you here, Sharon?"

His faithful companion almost clubbed him over the head with her thermos bottle. "Fer crissakes," she hissed, "can't you be *quieter?*"

"I was worried about you," he said.

"Why? Nothing's happened."

"Yu Ching was supposed to go to the park for the ladies' softball, and he didn't show up."

"Hm. He might be getting suspicious. He went into the elevator an hour ago, and I think he saw my car behind the station."

"I warned you to be careful."

Sharon's green eyes lit up with indignation. "At least I didn't drive down the street, blowing a siren like a demented asshole!"

"There's a whole new development," he said, changing the subject. "A mysterious French connection has shown up in town, riding a horse."

"Holy Jeeze!" Sharon said, collapsing on a seat and shaking her head. "This is getting un*real*!"

He allowed her a moment to regain her composure. "What have you got to report?"

"Well, there's definitely something going on. There hasn't been a single truck come in to the elevator all morning to unload wheat."

"On account of the Sports Day."

"I thought of that, but they've been lined up ten deep at the United Grain Growers elevator farther along the tracks."

"Hmm. That must be why he's been making out the grain tickets in Chinese! Trying to drive the farmers over to the opposition, so he could keep the elevator empty! Sharon, we've got to go in there and find out what's going on!"

"Well, there's a long string of boxcars behind the elevator. When he went inside, I sneaked over to check them out."

"They always keep some there. This time of the year, the wheat quotas are increased."

"Well, I don't know about quotas. But I do know this." Her face glowed with excitement. "Those boxcars have never carried wheat!"

"*What*?"

"Look." She lifted the tattered window blind and pointed to the railway cars stretched along the elevator spur. There were about ten of them, all the same reddish-brown colour, covered with grime. He couldn't detect anything unusual.

"See those pipes coming up at each end of the cars?"

Ashenden nodded.

"Now look at those two beside the UGG elevator."

He looked. No pipes. His eyes glanced sharply back and forth. These boxcars looked slightly bigger than regular boxcars.

"All right," he said quietly. "What does it mean? What's in them?"

"They're empty. But two of them are refrigerator cars. You can see by the frost on the rivets. Three of them have windows at one end and they're fixed up inside like house trailers—stereos, TV, Teflon frying pans, the whole lot."

"Holy smoke!"

"And the other five are full of crates of machinery and parts. It looks as though something is being assembled *inside the grain elevator*."

The answer came to Ashenden in a blinding flash. "My gosh!" he exclaimed. "A heroin refinery!"

13 THE INSCRUTABLE ORIENTAL

Ashenden concluded there was only one thing to do: find out what was going on inside.

"You wait here, Sharon!" he said, removing his Stetson. "This might be too dangerous for you."

"For *me*? It wasn't me that fell into the hopper. Besides, I want material for my story."

"That was an order."

"I'll scream." She pouted.

"Oh, all right," he said. "But try to stay out of trouble."

They slipped from the building into the searing high-noon sunshine. The Sports Day was another blast furnace of a day, the kind of heat to sap one's strength. Yet there was a hint of mugginess in the air. Ashenden would not be surprised if there was a thunder storm before sunset.

They waited in the shadow at the east end of the station, looking for the Chinese agent. He didn't seem to be watching. Seizing Sharon's hand and dragging her behind him, Ashenden sprinted the hundred yards across the tracks. They paused for breath, huddled against the blind side of the elevator. The sour smell of rotting wheat hung in the hot, still air. The hum of grasshoppers began buzzing unpleasantly inside Ashenden's head. They waited there, listening intently, but could hear no sound at all inside the building. Either Yu Ching had sound-proofed his operation, or there was nothing in there but mice and wheat screenings.

On Ashenden's signal, they moved toward the shed which housed the weigh scales and hopper, running up the sloping cinder driveway on the side hidden from Yu Ching's shack.

The big door was locked this time, but Ashenden's training had prepared him for such emergencies. He searched in the pigweed around the door until he found a foot-long piece of lath. Forcing it through the crack, he managed to catch the hook in the door sill. It fell back with a clink. Holding their breaths, they opened the door and quickly slid it shut again.

Ashenden slipped the hook back into place and looked around. But the Meadowlark Wheat Pool elevator had become eerie with disuse. It seemed foreboding and silent in the mid-day sunshine. Sparrow manure was splashed whitely all over the walls and floor. In front of them, the empty hopper yawned darkly. Its large metal grill had been removed and leaned against a wall. It had not moved for at least a week, or so Ashenden calculated by the layer of dust around it. The dust was two inches thick everywhere, a boon to a trained daylight tracker like Ashenden. He pointed silently to a faint pathway in the dust which ran from the door nearest Yu Ching's shack across the big platform scale, then into the catwalk toward the grain bins.

No word between Ashenden and his companion was needed. They stole along the trail into the gloomy darkness of the walkway, until the light grew too dim for them to see the walls. Ashenden realized he had forgotten to bring his flashlight.

"We'll have to feel our way," he whispered in Sharon's ear.

"Sounds like fun," she said, gripping his hand. "Can't you light a match?"

"No!" Ashenden shuddered. "The grain dust

around these bins is like gunpowder. If I lit a match, we'd be incinerated in an instant!''

"Hmm. Never mind. Lead on."

The catwalk rounded a corner of the timbered bins and disappeared into complete blackness. Ashenden advanced a few inches at a time, feeling with outstretched hand. Normally a few shafts of light descended from cupola windows high on the building, but Yu Ching had sealed them off. Perhaps he had anticipated casual visitors roaming around inside the building.

Ashenden suddenly reached a dead end. They could advance no farther. There seemed to be an open space on the left where he could sense a slight waft of dusty air. Yet at his feet the wall was solid.

Then he remembered that every grain elevator has a narrow, rickety staircase to the top. He remembered going up a few steps in the elevator in Niebelung when he had helped his father haul wheat. The elevator agent used the stairs to climb to the top of the building and examine the spouts.

"It's a staircase," he whispered. "It must be where the trail leads."

"Just a minute!"

"What is it?"

"I think—I'm going to—sneeze!"

"For gosh sakes, hold your finger under your nose!"

"I ab—but it's still—" a dainty muffled sneeze burst at him from the darkness.

"Here, take my handkerchief. Put it over your face."

"It's by hay fever," Sharon said miserably. "I *dew* whed I saw all this dust—!"

"Never mind, it can't be helped. Let's keep going. It won't be so bad higher up."

Step by painful step they climbed in the darkness, their ascent punctuated with the moist *whooshes* of Sharon's sneezing. Ashenden knew the pretty reporter must be experiencing terrible fears, but she stayed right behind him. She was the most courageous girl he had ever met. He gave her hand a squeeze of encouragement.

As they climbed, the darkness above began to grow lighter, and they could see the stairs once again. But, Ashenden noted, the steps were thick with dust! They had lost Yu Ching's trail. But there was no point in going back now. At the top, they could get their breath.

As they climbed higher toward the light, the hum of electronic machinery—from the heroin refinery, Ashenden supposed—reached their ears. Then came a metallic gonging, like the sound that had shocked them the night before. Occasionally, they could hear a man shouting, but so muffled as to be unrecognizable. And there was something strange about the light, a bright flourescent light which flickered eerily. There were also abrupt hissing flares, as from an electric arc welder. The noise grew louder and harsher, a mixture of shouting and whirring motors. Over all came the banging of metal against metal. Ashenden's sinews began to tighten. It was a big operation, much bigger than he had suspected.

With a final sharp turn on the stairs and two steps upward, Ashenden emerged onto a platform overlooking the interior of the grain elevator. The platform was so small that he could easily have overshot it and gone hurtling into the tall bins below.

But to Ashenden's astonishment, there *were* no bins below! The thick, two-by-four partitions that had once separated barley from oats, and Durum wheat from No. 2 Northern, had been completely dismantled! In their place, the inside of the elevator had been hollowed out like a gigantic feed silo.

And within it was a scene that he could never have described in his report to sub-division. It would have strained the imagination of a sci-fi addict. There was a vast jumble of wires and pipes; men ran feverishly around, checking dials and gauges. In the centre, like an enormous steel idol among its perspiring worshippers, was a long, gleaming cylinder, so tall that the top of it vanished into the rafters far over the heads of Ashenden and Sharon. Its base was deep below ground level. It must have been a hundred feet tall.

"It looks like a—boiler—or something!" Sharon whispered in an awe-struck tone.

"Boiler!" Ashenden exclaimed. "Do you know *what this is*?"

Sharon looked up dubiously. "The heroin refinery?"

"Heck, no! It's a rocket! Some kind of missile. And they're getting ready to fire it somewhere!"

Ashenden felt something touch the back of his shaved neck, and he lost his temper. "For cripe's sake, Sharon, do you always have to be stroking—"

He stopped. If that was Sharon's index finger, it had turned very cold and metallic. When he heard the voice, he knew it was a gun.

"Aren't *you* a clever skin-head!" the voice said in a sing-song Oriental accent.

It was Yu Ching, the "friendly" Wheat Pool agent—and the agent of Peking.

14 SPACE TRAVEL

Ashenden reflected for a moment. Nothing in basic training had prepared him for this. Except for Sgt. McLeod's constant dictum—resourcefulness! In a stern voice, he said, "You'd better hand over that gun right away and give yourself up, Yu Ching. If you know what's good for you."

"You must be out of your *gourd*, Mountie! Why would I give *you* my perfectly serviceable automatic pistol?"

"Because," Ashenden replied after another moment's reflection, "it's illegal to carry a loaded sidearm in public. Bylaw 39 of the Town of Meadowlark."

Behind him, the Chinese broke into a wild laughter that pealed throughout the building. Several of the men working below looked up in surprise. White men, Ashenden noted. Probably Albanians.

"Bylaw 39!" Yu Ching shrieked hysterically. "Of the Town of Meadowlark! Hahahahahahah!" His maniacal laughter subsided into giggles.

"Stay calm, Sharon," Ashenden assured the pale girl beside him. If she slipped and fell over the edge, she was a goner. "We're dealing with a madman."

"Careful with the epithets, onion-head!" The Oriental's voice turned cruel. "Now lift your hands above your head."

Ashenden felt the agent's hand unfasten his holster cover and remove the heavy .38.

"You need not say anything," Ashenden

warned him in a clear voice. "You have nothing to hope from any promise or favour and nothing to fear from any threat whether or not you say anything. Anything you do say may be used as evidence against you."

The reply was a crude snicker.

"All right, Yu Ching. I warned you. Start writing this down, Sharon."

"What do you mean, start writing?" Sharon snapped. "You start writing. I'm not your secretary."

"Okay," Yu Ching snarled, "cut the idle chatter. Now turn around slowly, both of you, and start walking downstairs."

Ashenden turned and encountered his adversary face-to-face for the first time. The smile had disappeared, as he knew it would have. The pleasant face Ashenden associated with You Chink, the Wheat Pool grain buyer, had become the cruel visage of Yu Ching, arch-enemy of Meadowlark. His black eyes glittered in the harsh glare of the missile silo's lights.

"So you speak English after all, eh?" Ashenden said, stalling for precious time. He was waiting for a fatal lapse in the concentration of the Chinese. In a split second he would be upon him, delivering the karate blows he had mastered during training.

But Yu Ching had been well instructed by his mentors behind the Bamboo Curtain. He remained in the shadows, his automatic pistol at the policeman's head. "You guys never learn, do you, Whitey? An Oriental comes along with a flashy set of teeth, and everybody thinks he's incapable of learning the rudiments of the English language."

"The what?"

"Let it go, let it go." Yu Ching gestured with the pistol. "Now let's start the long haul down."

They descended the dusty stairs in single file, illuminated by the beam from Yu Ching's flashlight.

"How did you know we were in here?" Sharon asked.

"Microphones, sweetie-pie. Planted every six feet apart all through the building. Your sneezes were coming through to the control panel like megaton bombs."

"Then you must have known we were here last night!" Ashenden exclaimed.

"Yeah, but I hoped we might have scared you off. Too bad for you we didn't. Okay, stop there."

They were at the bottom of the stairs. Ashenden could see that the dust trail had ended at the wall of one of the bins. Yu Ching pressed a nail in a timber, and a buzzer sounded. A section of the heavy planking—what seemed to be the wall of a wheatbin—swung inwards. The intense light from inside flooded the gloomy passage they stood in. There was a rustle of mice scurrying in search of darkness.

"Through here," Yu Ching motioned with his gun. "Mind your heads. Wouldn't want you getting a bump on the noggin and complaining to the Wheat Pool committee! Hahahaha!"

Inside the silo, Ashenden and Sharon were taken to a glassed-in control room set into the surrounding wall. Moving past the frenzy of activity around the missile, Ashenden realized that these men must have been there for weeks, going out at night to sleep in the boxcars. They moved like automatons, not speaking to one another, or to Yu Ching.

"I just have one question, Mr. Yu," Sharon said

as they entered the cubicle. "Are you free-lancing or do you report directly to Chairman Mao?"

The Oriental turned to her with a wide grin. "Not bad, sugarface. Shows you're thinking. Tell me, why's a swinger like you hanging around with this Trudeau cowboy? Show me a little more leg and I'll, um, give you the grand tour."

Sharon spat at his feet. "Sexist pig!"

Yu Ching shrugged. "Well, I'd like to hang around all afternoon rapping with you two, but I have a lot of things to do before midnight."

"Midnight!" The significance suddenly bashed Ashenden's brain like a sledgehammer. "*Fireworks at midnight!*"

"That's right, banana-head! All those yahoos from the town are going to be at the Sports Day gawking at the fireworks I got shipped in."

"The fireworks will cover the firing of this—this monstrous weapon!"

Yu Ching eyed him appraisingly. "You're quicker on the uptake than you look, Mountie. A pity they have to scrub your name off the graduation roll."

"There's only one flaw in your insane plan, Yu Ching."

"Oh?"

"Yes. I've sent a report to sub-division HQ, outlining my discoveries. If anything happens to me, the wrath of the entire Royal Canadian Mounted Police will descend on your head."

Yu Ching stared. "You must think," he said quietly, "that I got my credentials out of a Crispy Critters cereal-box, Baldy. If you had any backing, they would be in here now, tearing the place apart. I happen to know Inspector Heavysides doesn't believe a word you say. So what's he going to think about you discovering an intercontinental missile in *Meadowlark*, huh?''

Ashenden had to concede that one. There must be a leak in town somewhere. If he ever got out of this, he vowed, he would track it down.

Yu Ching glanced at his Bulova Accuquartz. "It's five to two. We were *going* to fire it immediately, in case you snitched on us. Now we have to recompute the flight pattern."

"Meaning what, Yu Ching?"

"Meaning the Wheat Pool Express will depart at midnight after all, but with a heavier load than expected." He flicked a series of buttons high on the panel.

"This is a pretty small missile, but it's no toy. It is a miniature ICBM powered with solid fuel. No dangerous fluids to set the grain elevator on fire."

"You call that *small*?" Sharon said.

"Just a baby," the Chinese agent smiled. "Like the pay-load. Another Tonka Toy."

"What's the pay-load?" Ashenden hardly dared to ask.

"A thermonuclear fusion device no bigger than your lunch-bucket, flat-top. A hundred times as powerful as Hiroshima."

"You'll never get away with this!" Ashenden growled.

Yu Ching chuckled. "What's going to stop me? Wait, don't tell me! I got it! Meadowlark Bylaw Number 41! Hahaha! No firing nuclear warheads inside the town limits! Hahahahaha!" He staggered against the wall and fell to the floor, rolling around in a fit of hysterical merriment.

Ashenden had been waiting. One leap and he

had the Chinese in a headlock, squeezing Yu Ching's neck. But his hand gripped the weapon like a vise.

"Grab the gun, Sharon!" Ashenden yelled.

That did it.

Half a dozen of Yu Ching's underlings ran into the room—alerted through the omnipresent microphones the policeman had forgotten about. They pounced on Sharon and clubbed Ashenden over the head with crescent wrenches and ball-peen hammers, forcing him to let go of Yu Ching. Then they backed the two of them against the wall of the silo, while the wily Chinese staggered to his feet.

"Well!" he gasped. "I'm going to have to control my sense of humour. Some people never enjoy a good laugh, do they? Now you force me to become ultra-serious, Mountie. So here's the secret. We're going to treat you and your little poppet to a free ride. Economy class!"

Two of the "mechanics" appeared with lengths of heavy chain.

"Now, if you'll oblige me by backing up to the base of the rocket there, we'll fasten your seat belts for you."

Sharon screamed and fainted.

15 A MATTER OF TIME

Yu Ching grinned his sinister grin. "What's with her? Afraid of flying?"

"You mad dog!" Ashenden had barely managed to catch Sharon before she smashed her exquisite nose into a jellied pulp on the concrete floor.

"Maybe it's the heat," Yu Ching shrugged. "It's getting so hot you could fry eggs in here. I'm glad we didn't schedule this shoot for July."

His two stooges hustled Ashenden out of the control cubicle to the base of the gleaming rocket. They began chaining him to one of the fins. Then they did the same to Sharon. Yu Ching's lieutenant appeared and announced that the rocket was ready for firing. He spoke English like an American, Ashenden observed. Could he be a brain-washed dupe?

"Good." The Oriental's dark eyes gleamed sadistically. "Clear the men into the railway cars. The locomotive will arrive at eleven o'clock to move the train. I'll stay behind and do the calculations."

"Yes sir!" The assistant saluted and motioned the men to carry equipment out of the building.

Ashenden glanced at the clock through the glass front of the control room. Two thirty.

"One last question, Yu Ching," he said as the Chinese clamped a lock onto Sharon's chain.

"Listen, Fuzzy. If I had a dollar for every 'last question' I've been asked, I would've retired from this game years ago."

"What's going to happen to Pules-Feltham and Madam Karmakov?"

"Who?"

"Jeremy Pules-Feltham and the Russian woman."

"Never heard of them," said Yu Ching. "Now, if that's all—"

"What about Plan G? Ever heard of *that*?"

Yu Ching scratched his head. "Isn't that a rock band?"

"Oh my gosh!" Ashenden said. "Have I done those people a terrible wrong?"

"That's your fourth 'last question,' Mountie. I've really got to go. I have to clear out my office." He stepped to the main door of the missile silo. "Don't worry about your luggage, Redcoat," he snickered, throwing one last jibe. "We'll send it on the next flight."

"You'll be punished for this, Yu Ching!"

"Yeah, I know," the Chinese chortled. "Bylaw 43 of the Town of Meadowlark!" His maniacal laughter was cut short by the slamming of the door.

All around Ashenden and the unconscious form of Sharon there was silence, except for an eerie humming from inside the rocket, and an occasional bleep from the control panels as the minutes ticked toward oblivion for Constable James Ashenden.

"Sharon!" he shouted. "Wake up!" But her enchanting smile was fixed, as though she were thinking happy thoughts far removed from rockets and Communists.

The minutes slid away under the second hand sweeping the dial of the control room clock. Ashenden knew despair for the first time. He shuddered to think what would happen if he didn't free them from the rocket before it was launched.

Suddenly his face broke into a relieved grin. Of

course—the egg-and-spoon race! When he didn't show up for the egg-and-spoon race at 4:30, Mayor Boothroyd and the other citizens would come looking for him! They knew he was trailing Yu Ching, and would connect his disappearance with foul play. They knew Constable Ashenden would not shirk his civic duty. He sat back, breathing easier. It was a matter of waiting patiently until 4:30, and then help would come.

But at that moment, the mysterious French horseman had the entire populace of Meadowlark in thrall with an incredible display of riding and roping. He and the gorgeous black stallion had made pass after pass in front of the stacked rows of fairground bleachers. He had swirled around barrels in figure-eights, ridden standing up in the saddle backwards, even sideways. He had volunteered to put on a calf-roping demonstration but no one had any calves to rope. Charlie Cherry saved the afternoon by volunteering his wife's Airedale Terrier. The horseman also roped a few fence pickets, Mayor Boothroyd's hat, and young Eleanor Campbell. It was the best show Meadowlark had seen since Laffin' Jack and The Prairie Podners had hit town with their Western Family Entertainment Show. The citizens responded with a standing ovation and waves of applause. The stranger with the scar and his magnificent horse had totally eclipsed the baseball tournament, and would probably have forced the cancellation of the egg-and-spoon race, if that event had not already been re-scheduled to 4:30.

At 4:15, following the riding show, the crowd moved from the park to the finish line of the race, a half-mile distant at the corner of Main and Buffalo. Constable James Ashenden was nowhere to be seen.

"That pea-brained numbskull!" the mayor exploded. He hated to see the day spoiled by incompetence after such a terrific beginning.

"Aw Phil," Gordie Gompers said. "Don't be hard on thuh kid. He hasn't bin at this Mountiein' trade too long, and what with that redhead with the big knockers draggin' him off to thuh bushes twice a day, it woulden suprize me none if his *memory* was startin' to go."

"A promise is a danged promise," the mayor insisted.

"Yeah, but look—we did without You Chink for thuh ladies' softball. We kin make do here."

"Wat seems to be de problem?" The horseman moved toward the knot of worried officials.

"Aw, same old thing. Jimmy Ashenden, the local Mountie, was suppose tuh be here for the egg-and-spoon race and he didden show up."

"Where is de problem? I will step into his place. It cannot be said that I 'ave shirked my duty, wen it comes to 'elping de law."

"Say, that's darned decent of you, Mister—?" Mayor Boothroyd had been waiting for this opportunity to discover the horseman's name.

"Levesque. Jean Levesque."

"Sounds familiar, awright. You weren't ever on Ed Sullivan, were you?"

"Unfortunately, no."

"Lissen, John, that was a terrific display of horseback riding. Just fantastic!"

"Was nutting."

"No, no. I mean that. We don't get a chance to

see much horse-riding around here now.''

"No 'orses?"

"Jimmy Ashenden's got a horse. Keeps it out at the Healey place.''

"De Mounted Policeman, 'e 'as a horse?''

"Yup. Oh, he's real keen.''

"Hm. I fin' dat very interesting.''

"Well, I'll leave you in charge of the race then, John. Thanks a million! I have to skedaddle over to the community hall to make sure everything's ready for the dance.''

Sweat was coursing down Ashenden's handsome features when the clock ticked past 6:00 p.m. He had strained mightily against the chains, but could not force a quarter-inch of slackness out of them. In an attempt to ward off despair he began to sing "God Save the Queen'' in his shaky baritone.

The clock read 6:17 when Sharon Sharalike finally returned to consciousness. "What is it?'' she mumbled. "Is the movie over?''

"Sharon! Wake up, Sharon!''

"Where are we, Jimmy? My bed or yours?''

"For gosh sakes, Sharon! Wake up. *We're in trouble*.''

She bolted upright with a clanking of chains. "Oh, my God!'' she exclaimed, a look of terror on her elegant features. "The pill. I forgot my pill!''

"Pill? What are you talking about? Don't you remember the rocket?''

"Rocket?''

"Look at us! We're chained to the bottom of a missile timed to go off at midnight! Now start thinking!''

"Rocket?'' Sharon gazed in stupefaction at the

chains. "What have you *done*, you stupid ass?"

"Darn it all, Sharon. Stop that. Remember, you had to be in on *everything*. So listen to me and be sensible. Sooner or later, the people in town will miss us and come looking, right? Don't forget, I was supposed to look after the egg-and-spoon race."

"When was that?"

"Four thirty."

Sharon looked at the clock. 6:25. She burst into tears.

Ashenden vowed to himself that he would not let *anything* happen to this brave CBC reporter. "Don't worry, Sharon. At this very minute, I bet they're starting a search party. You'll see—we can *depend* on the people of Meadowlark."

At that very minute, Jean Levesque was being treated to a corn-on-the-cob by Mayor Boothroyd in gratitude for all he had done to make the Meadowlark Sports Day a success.

"By de way, Mayor. Did your Mounted Policeman ever show up? If 'e doesn't come soon, 'e will miss all of de celebratings. Especially de dance."

"Don't worry about him, John. He's probably off somewheres tied up with that sexy girlfriend of his."

"Girl? W'at girl?"

"Oh, you didn't meet her, eh? Miss Sharalike— the CBC reporter. They're always stirring up some kind of trouble. She's *supposed* to be doing a documentary over in Shakespear."

"Did 'e tell you where 'e was going, Mayor?"

"Let's see. He said something about the Englishman and the Russian lady."

"And who are dey?"

"Hmm? Oh, Jimmy's got this crazy idea they're involved in a plot with the Wheat Pool agent. He's a nice kid, but he's got a real *wild* imagination."

"Is de Wheat Pool man a Chinese by de name of —Yu Ching?"

"Yeah. You Chink. How did you know?"

Levesque took the mayor by the arm and pulled him around the corner of the refreshment booth, where a group of children were collecting bottle caps. He threw the corn-cob away. "Mayor, I must reveal my identity to you."

"You're not John Levesque?"

"No, I am not." The horseman reached into a shirt pocket studded with pink mother-of-pearl snap buttons and pulled out a badge. "Sgt. Fred McLeod, Security Services." The French accent and the bravado manner had disappeared.

"RCMP!" Boothroyd gasped. "You're working with Jimmy? There's something going on, after all?"

"More than you suspect, Mayor. Constable Ashenden doesn't know it, but for months I've been tracking Yu Ching, the international agent."

"You're talking about You Chink, over at the *Wheat Pool?*"

"He is capable of anything, Mayor. A genius of disguises."

"Well, your disguise isn't so bad either, Sergeant. Riding around in those Western duds. How'd you think of that?"

Sgt. McLeod shrugged modestly. "It's a long story. I used to instruct Horsemanship Training at Depot Division. When they ceased to use the horse, to put it bluntly, I was out of the saddle. I took up spy work."

"Spies, eh? Hot damn! This is going to make them look *sick* over in Shakespear!" A thought struck the mayor. "But why spies in *Meadowlark*? It doesn't make sense."

"I don't have time to explain, Mayor. Constable Ashenden and this girl could be in danger. But Yu Ching and his backers have perfected a miniature ICBM. They plan to fire it from Canadian soil. To be specific, somewhere near or in the town of Meadowlark."

"I don't get it. Why *here*?"

McLeod shrugged. "Who knows? They wanted it somewhere away from RCMP observation. They obviously did not take into account Constable Ashenden's acute perceptions."

"But how did *you* find out?"

"We know they ran a train-load of equipment in from the U.S. earlier this month. It was a special shipment of boxcars for the Wheat Pool. Those boxcars carried all the equipment and personnel necessary to construct the missile. Now, we *must* find out where this is being done. And we don't have much time."

"Holy peel-heel!" The mayor staggered against the side of the refreshment booth. Inside, the Ladies' Auxiliary chatted away about community scandals and romances. Around them, children continued to collect bottle caps and popsicle sticks, their innocent hearts unaware of the cataclysm about to explode from the brown elevator basking in the sun just a short distance to the northeast.

16 THE RESCUE SQUAD

At that moment, Yu Ching was in his office, carefully shredding his papers and manuals. He had completed the launch calculations and fed them into the rocket's computer. He had settled all the technicians into the "boxcars"; the locomotive was due at 11 p.m. to pick them up. Now all he had to do was clean up and wait for the fireworks. He whistled "Next Train Blues." Yu Ching had a right to be cheerful. His plan was going off without a hitch. That is, except for the dumb Mountie and his broad. He shook his head and chuckled.

Inside the missile silo, Ashenden was trying to keep Sharon calm. If she went hysterical, they'd never get free.

"I'm *starving*, too!" she pointed out. "You didn't even give me lunch!"

"Oh, for gosh sakes. I brought you a couple of chocolate bars. They're in my tunic pocket."

"Maybe I can reach them."

She manoeuvred and twisted for fifteen minutes, trying to reach his pocket, but without success. She threw herself back in bitter frustration— and discovered that one of the loops in her chain was loose. It must have happened when they were tying her up. Ashenden tried to get her to concentrate on freeing her hands, but she seemed to be interested only in the chocolate bars.

"Good gosh, Sharon," he pleaded. "I can understand *hungry*, but this is stupid! If we don't get loose, you'll never eat another chocolate bar again.''

"I can't concentrate when I'm hungry!'' she snapped.

At the Community Hall on Maple Street, the band had arrived and begun tuning their instruments: piano, guitar, drums and accordion. The children played Auntie-Auntie-Aye-Over with a softball over the roof of the hall. Life went on in its ordinary Meadowlark way.

But Sgt. Fred McLeod had gathered some key citizens around him in the hall foyer, and was questioning them on Ashenden's whereabouts. He and the mayor had waited hours for the Mountie to show up, and they now had to act.

Mayor Boothroyd mentioned Ashenden's suspicions of Jeremy Pules-Feltham and Madam Karmakov. "There's something funny going on, Sergeant,'' he said. "Those two are as slippery as a chamber pail full of earthworms.''

Gordie Gompers said he had seen Ashenden drive off toward Pules-Feltham's house.

"Right. That's where we'll go. Now Mayor, I'll take these men with me to the Pules-Feltham place. You stay here and warn the townspeople what is happening. Then assemble a group of men to wait here at the dance hall, ready to move at a minute's notice. But no weapons!''

"Right, Sergeant.''

"Okay, you men come with me.'' McLeod walked out into the gloomy evening, flanked by Gordie Gompers, Charlie Cherry, Fred Kobiak and his brother-in-law Lowell. They advanced down Maple Street, now growing dark as storm clouds obliterated the evening sun. Tension crackled around them. Even the grasshoppers were silent with foreboding. Each man knew that before the evening was over he would smell the blood of conflict, and each was searching his heart, wondering how he would face the test. They were welded together by a mystical bond, like Arctic musk-oxen defending the weak and helpless of the herd. As they approached Pules-Feltham's house, each felt a secret desire to be at home watching "Hee-Haw" on television, but the bond held firm. A sudden breeze smelled of thunder.

They reached the overgrown caragana hedge surrounding the house, where McLeod signalled to wait. He ran to the front porch and waved them on to the building. They galloped together like a herd of musk-oxen.

"It's too quiet," he whispered. "They've either holed up inside or they've taken him somewhere else." He glanced around at the men. "Either way, we have to go in," he said, slipping his gun from a holster inside his shirt.

He tried the door. It was locked. Heaving his massive shoulder against the door, once, then twice, then a third time, McLeod burst into the house in an explosion of wooden splinters.

"This is the RCMP!" he shouted. "Come out with your hands where we can see them!"

But the only answer was an echo in the darkness. He switched on the light and waved his men in.

"They've gone," he said. "I'll have a quick look around the rooms. Check outside. See if there's any sign where they might have gone."

McLeod looked at the long shelves, overflowing with books. The place stank of subversion. Some day he would return and rip it apart. Then he heard a strange sound growing in the distance, like a rising wind, or the distant mutter of thunder. But now he could identify it as a human sound. It was a crowd of people, getting closer.

He stepped to the front door, where Fred Kobiak stood nervously. "What's that noise?" he said.

"Sounds like the gang from the dance! Don't know what's got into 'em. Sounds like they all gone rangy-tang."

McLeod could make out the gravelly-voiced shouts of the mayor. There was violence in the air as at least a hundred Meadowlarkians turned the corner at Maple and McKillop, two blocks away. Angry beams from flashlights and lanterns darted in every direction.

"There they are! Let's get 'em!" The crowd roared and surged toward McLeod in a wild stampede.

"What's happening?" McLeod gasped. Was the mayor a traitor? The mob plunged through the caragana hedge and up the sidewalk to the porch, where McLeod stood, gun in his hand, watching with detachment. He lowered the gun until it pointed at the leaders of the crowd. Without moving his arm he squeezed the trigger. A bullet whistled over the heads of the mob. The townspeople stopped in their tracks.

"Hold it right there," McLeod said quietly. "What's going on here?"

Mayor Boothroyd jostled to the front of the crowd. "Couldn't stop them, Sergeant!" he wheezed. "I was just whipping up support for

Jimmy Ashenden at the dance, and they went buzzerk! They think he's in danger, and that the Englishman and Madam Karmakov are behind it.''

McLeod stepped forward two precise paces. "And what if they are?" he said. "This is a matter for the law to decide.''

"Not if they hurt Jimmy Ashenden!" someone shouted from the back of the mob. They shifted weapons in their hands angrily. For the first time, McLeod could clearly see the array of wheel wrenches, jack handles, lengths of two-by-four, an odd shotgun.

"We don't know what has happened," he said. "And we'll *never* find out with a mob trampling all the clues. Go back to the hall and wait until we call you. And leave your weapons behind.''

They murmured angrily, but no one moved a step backwards. McLeod realized there could be trouble here, if there was a single wrong move. It was Gordie Gompers who made it.

"Hey you guys!" he shouted, appearing around the corner of the house. "I found that Yewkerainian lady's tire tracks! And they lead straight toward the school!''

"The school!" Mayor Boothroyd shouted. "That's where they're pullin' off Plan G!''

"Hey!" someone shouted from the crowd. "Over there! The school! It's all lit up!''

They all craned their necks toward the school. It was true. Even through the thick caragana hedge, lights could be seen blazing from every window in the John G. Diefenbaker Composite School.

An incomprehensible roar burst from the throats of the crowd, like a cry of rage from a wounded beast.

"Stop!" McLeod shouted. He fired his gun over their heads again. The mayor made a semi-valiant effort to stand, but he was knocked aside like a fly, getting a nasty scrape as he was sent skidding on his face along the cinder path.

McLeod ran after them, but they were already stampeding toward the school, screaming for revenge. The bloodlust was upon them, and McLeod knew they would have to be stopped or they would rip the spies apart with their bare hands. Then he would never find Ashenden and the girl!

"You fool!" he hissed at Boothroyd, jerking him to his feet. "What did you tell them?"

"Well, I just said Jimmy'd been captured by the Communists, and they took off. Nothing I could do."

McLeod stared at the mayor. His eyes blinked in astonishment. "Yu Ching isn't a Communist, you bloody idiot! He's a Nationalist Chinese—one of Chiang Kai-shek's top men—and he's working hand in glove with *U.S. Army Intelligence*."

17 PLAN G

As Sgt. McLeod and his band of deputies took off running after the crowd, they heard a siren in the distance. Maybe, McLeod thought as he sprinted toward the school, Regina was sending reinforcements. Maybe it was Ashenden. But he didn't have time to ponder the question because the schoolyard was like an obstacle course, full of high-jump bars and sandpits for track and field spring training. All around him people were smashing into poles and falling into the pits. But he, superbly conditioned, was gaining on the leaders of the mob.

The siren he had heard was on Ashenden's cruiser, which was hurtling toward the community hall on the other side of town, with Sharon Sharalike at the wheel. She had finally freed herself from the shackles. As the car screeched to a stop in front of the hall, she leaned frantically on the horn to attract attention inside. But there was no response except for the drops of rain spattering in the dust around her. Sharon felt complete hopelessness.

Then one of the musicians, who had been stationed to guard the instruments from vandalism, ventured out the door to see what the racket was about.

"*Help*!" Sharon shrieked at him, and crumpled forward onto the steering wheel.

"What's wrong, lady? Horn stuck?"

Sharon bravely raised her exhausted face as the man approached the window. "Help Jimmy!" she whispered. "Get help!"

"Jimmy Ashenden, yuh mean?"

Sharon nodded dramatically, and collapsed again on the steering wheel.

"Well, they all went over to thuh Englishman's place, figgerin' Jimmy was held prisoner over there. I'd like to help you out, but I gotta stay and look after the insterments. Last time we had excitement like this, somebody put their foot through thuh base drum."

But Sharon was no longer listening. Rallying her failing energy, she wheeled the cruiser into a power-turn in the street and headed for Pules-Feltham's house, pounding on the horn with her hand and maintaining the siren at full blast.

She braked to a stop at the front gate and collapsed against the steering wheel again. The blaring horn this time attracted the attention of a rioter who had surreptitiously returned to the Englishman's house. He now halted in the process of evacuating the stack of empty soft-drink bottles from the back porch, and stepped into the glare of the headlights of the cruiser, his hands in the air.

"Help Jimmy!" Sharon moaned.

"Everybody's gone to the school, lady. To rescue Jimmy Ashenden. I'm just guardin' this—"

"Rescue Jimmy Ashenden?"

"Yeah. Thuh Commies got him over at the school, torturin' thuh hell outta him and his girl friend. Hey—aren't you—?"

But he was left standing in the yard among the soft-drink bottles. Sharon was accelerating straight through the school's playing-field, leaning on the horn and squeezing the siren switch. Smashing through the goal-posts at one end of the field, the Pontiac abruptly disappeared into the sand dunes behind the pole-vault and hurtled into the air from the other side. Then it crunched onto the ground again, splitting the shock absorbers from top to bottom. Sharon kept the gas pedal jammed to the floor. As she crossed the 25-yard line, she saw a heavy wire fence suddenly appear in front of the headlights. She held the pedal to the floor, gritting her teeth.

With a terrific rending of metal, the cruiser ripped out three sections of fence and carried them up to the bicycle racks beside the front door of the school. The demolished car groaned to a stop. Sharon leaped out and ran into the building, her exhaustion forgotten.

"It's her! It's the Mountie's girl friend!" people were saying as she pushed through the crowd. The citizens of Meadowlark fell back in awe as she dashed past, half her clothes ripped away from her by her frantic efforts to reach help.

The mob rampaged up and down the corridors, breaking through locked doors and closets. Sharon followed the charge toward the staircase, where an even wilder commotion was going on. She had to find help. Someone had to waken her from this nightmare of absurd destruction. Everyone was going in the wrong direction.

At the far end of the hall, near the stairs, a mass of people boiled madly in front of a classroom, clamouring to smash the door down. "Rip the place apart!" they shrieked. "Let us at 'em!"

The mayor and a scar-faced man Sharon did not recognize were standing before the door as though protecting it, their faces pale with tension and fear. The stranger's scar was like an angry red slash across the side of his face.

"Stand back, Phil!" roared a man in the crowd. "Git that goddam Mountie outa thuh way!"

"Listen to me!" the stranger cried. "We know they're in there, but they probably have guns at the heads of Ashenden and the girl! If we go in, they'll shoot. We'll never find out where the missile is!"

Sharon ran and threw herself at the feet of the two men. "Help Jimmy!" she gasped. "You have to help him!" Then she fainted dead away.

The sergeant stared at her half-naked form in astonishment. "Get this hysterical bitch out of here," he ordered. "And the rest of you stand back. I'll shoot the first man who advances."

McLeod may have been an expert on international nuclear criminals, but it was clear he knew nothing about the natives of Saskatchewan. He had issued an irresistible challenge. With a garlic-scented roar, they swept aside the last bastion of constitutional law. Four men threw McLeod down and sat on him. The rest fought for handholds on the prostrate Sharon and lifted her out of the doorway. Then they attacked the locked door with fire axes and two-by-fours.

"Wait a minute!" Boothroyd yelled. "It's her! That's Sharon Sharalike!"

But no one heard. With a howl that obliterated even the sudden crack of thunder outside, the gang burst through the door and into the classroom. Against the blackboards at the far end stood Jeremy Pules-Feltham and Madam Nadya Karmakov, huddled in each other's arms, livid with terror. Scattered around the room were a dozen opened packing-cases.

"There they are! Get 'em!"

Sharon pulled herself to her feet and staggered

to the door. "Stop!" Her piercing cry halted the mob where it stood. "They're innocent! They're not the kidnappers!"

"What?"

"What did she say?"

"Innocent?"

"They're innocent. It's Yu Ching—the Wheat Pool agent! He's got Jimmy locked up in the elevator. Rocket going off at midnight! They're innocent."

Jeremy Pules-Feltham stepped forward, his face a trembling mass. "No, *no*!" he said. "We are guilty. Take us away! Madam Karmakov and I planned the whole thing together."

"Then you'd better come with me quietly," said a voice at the door. In the confusion McLeod had freed himself and recovered his gun. "I promise you a fair trial."

"You don't understand!" Sharon pleaded. "These people have nothing to do with it. We've only got—" Sharon looked frantically at the clock above the teacher's desk, "*thirty minutes* to save Jimmy Ashenden from being launched into the stratosphere!"

Pules-Feltham walked slowly toward McLeod with his arms thrust forward. "Put the handcuffs on, copper. We will give you a full confession. Come, Nadya."

"But, Jheremy!" the dark-eyed woman pleaded.

"We will make our defence in an open court, when the press is present to hear my statement."

Sharon ran to McLeod. "If you're a Mountie, you've got to stop this! Jimmy Ashenden's going to be killed. I am his assistant on the case!"

McLeod stared at her. "Miss Sharalike?" He

hesitated. "Do you have any identification?"

"No! Please believe me!"

"If these people aren't part of it, why does Pules-Feltham want to turn himself in?"

"Is true," Madam Karmakov sobbed. "We planned it!"

"Planned *what*?" Sharon cried, at her wits' end.

"We brought the books in!" Pules-Feltham admitted. "We were going to sneak them into the schoolrooms when the teachers weren't here."

"Books? What books?"

Pules-Feltham waved his limp wrist around the room, indicating the jumble of packing-cases—the "shipment" from Shakespear. McLeod wrenched the lid off one of them. It was full of books. He plucked one from the top of the stack. *Songs of Innocence. Tristram Shandy. Fruits of the Earth. The Little Prince. The Cherry Orchard. Great Expectations. The Canterbury Tales.* Communist books, he was willing to bet.

"What *is* all this crap?"

"The great literature of the world!" Pules-Feltham's eyes blazed fervently. "The children of Meadowlark have never known it, will never experience it! We—Madam Karmakov and I—were going to—turn them on to the classics!"

"Eh?" McLeod stared in disbelief. The crowd began to mutter.

"Don't you see?" the Englishman cried. "They grow up believing Louisa May Alcott was a good novelist, that Rudyard Kipling and Pauline Johnson were great poets! We came to save them!"

Sharon almost tore her hair out. "Please!" she pleaded. "These people are harmless nuts. We have to save Jimmy!"

"Maybe you're right," the sergeant said, eyeing the Englishman with deep suspicion. "Charlie Cherry. You keep these two here, while we head for the grain elevator. Don't let them out of this room. And write down every title in these boxes. I want to check them with a list I've got back in Regina."

"Hurry!" Sharon cried, urging the scar-faced horseman out of the room. The clock at the far end of the hall showed 11:40. Twenty minutes left. The drive would take five minutes. And the chains had to be cut. It would be close.

"Who are you?" Sharon asked as they hurried out the door to the RCMP cruiser. The rain was pelting down.

"Sergeant Fred McLeod, Security Services. RCMP." He paused in front of the car, whistling a short burst of appreciation for Sharon's navigational ability. The cruiser looked as if it had been driven through a hammer mill. "Delighted to meet you, Miss Sharalike."

"Hop in. I know the way."

They lurched around the yard in a wide turn. One of the front tires had blown out, making the car almost impossible to steer, but it was too late to do anything else. She hit the siren switch as the car bounced onto the street, caroming off the hedges along the driveway, and neatly decapitating the flagstaff in the schoolyard.

In the rear-view mirror Sharon saw the mayor and a couple of other men leap into Gordie Gompers' tow-truck to follow them.

"Where's Yu Ching?" McLeod said.

"Don't know. He's around the elevator somewhere. Probably in his shack. You won't believe this, Sergeant, but he's got a *rocket* inside that grain elevator. He's going to fire it!"

"Yes. I know. At the People's Republic of China."

"*What*?"

"I know this sounds strange, Miss Sharalike. But world politics are changing so fast it's hard to know *where* the rockets are aimed at any more. You see, the American Pentagon and Joint Chiefs of Staff are determined to wreck détente with China. So they turned to Taiwan—who would like nothing better than the destruction of Peking."

"I don't know," Sharon said dubiously, veering across a lawn at the corner of Gardiner Avenue and Main Street. "I don't see what that's got to do with Canada."

"That's the interesting part. Look out for those flamingoes!"

Sharon swerved, narrowly missing several pink lawn ornaments.

"You see, Canada is lobbying to end the NORAD defence treaty with the U.S."

"Which upsets the Americans."

"Precisely! The nuclear warhead will destroy the Chinese capital. China will immediately retaliate by unleashing its entire arsenal straight at Canada. And the U.S., under the NORAD treaty, would be compelled to mount massive counter-attacks against China. The Russians stand back—making angry noises, naturally, but secretly pleased at the turn of events. And the Pentagon will be able to concentrate on their main enemies, the Soviets."

"This is crazy!" Sharon exclaimed. "The world has gone mad!"

"Such is politics, Miss Sharalike. Only thirty years ago we were fighting Germans and Japanese!

Now look at them.''

They were bouncing north on Main Street toward the railroad. A burst of chain lightning flashed through the sky and silhouetted the row of elevators standing in the distance. The rain was a downpour; gutters which had been bone-dry for days were now rivers of rainwater.

"Can't you get more speed out of this thing?" McLeod said.

Sharon already had the pedal pressed to the floor and the police car swerved madly from one side of the street to the other.

"A chain-cutter!" Sharon suddenly cried. "I forgot the bloody chain-cutter! We have to get him free of those chains!''

"Pull over—*there*!" McLeod ordered, pointing at the hardware store opposite the town office. Sharon veered across to the left-hand side of the street, bouncing off a fire hydrant and opening a foot-deep gash along the entire length of the car as it screeched to a stop.

McLeod leaped out with Ashenden's heavy-duty RCMP lantern in his hand. He hurled the lantern through the plate-glass window. There was a splintering crash as the glass fell away in big shards. McLeod kicked out some jagged remnants and jumped into the hardware store through its gaping front.

Sharon felt the engine cough and sputter; she pumped the accelerator. The throttle must have got bent in one of the collisions. She kept pumping and fiddling with the choke, determined to keep the engine going. Once, she glanced into the rear-view mirror and saw Gompers' tow-truck flash into view, its yellow light winking in the distance. She peered ahead in the rain toward the elevators, two blocks away. Her mouth opened in horror.

At the level railway crossing, two hundred yards from where she sat, the red signal light suddenly flashed on and off, then on again. A train was approaching the crossing. The elevator was on the far side of the tracks!

18 A VALIANT EFFORT

Sharon blasted the horn to alert McLeod. "Get out!" she shrieked, rolling down the window. "There's a train coming. We'll be cut off from the elevator!"

In the hardware store, the light suddenly flashed off. "Got it!" McLeod's voice bellowed.

He dived out the window, clutching the chain-cutter, and landed running. Sharon had the car moving as he wrenched open the left rear door and piled into the back seat. The Pontiac's tires squealed in agony as she tramped the pedal to the floor, praying the throttle would hold till they accelerated past the flashing red lights. If only it was a slow freight!

They picked up speed, though the cruiser swayed violently from side to side, and the acrid smoke of burning rubber from the tires filled the car. Fifty yards to go! The headlight of the freight diesel stabbed toward them from the darkness on the left.

"Stop!" McLeod roared. "You'll never make it!"

"Shut up! We're going through. Get in the front!" she yelled, ignoring the horrifying proximity of the diesel pounding closer and closer. Its flat, mournful horn blatted through the rain.

Unable to force another ounce of speed from the battered Pontiac, Sharon cursed it violently. A sudden bolt of lightning split the Meadowlark sky, lighting up the town, the elevators in the distance, and the road. It was like the light of Creation; illuminated in it, the willowy CBC reporter contemplated for a split second all of eternity. What was she doing here? Why was she driving through a torrential rain, famished and dehydrated, her clothes torn and ragged, trying to reach a Wheat Pool grain elevator that contained a rocket aimed at the capital of China? But there was no answer. On her left, barely five feet from the crossing, the CNR locomotive clanked its monstrous way toward her destruction. She hit the brakes with a cry of desperation.

The car spun on the wet pavement as darkness mercifully descended again. Her eyes saw a jagged whirl of flashing red lights, the looming iron juggernaut, the mercury lamps spiraling overhead. With a splintering crash of metal and glass, the locomotive smashed into the car. Sparks flew everywhere as the engine mauled and clawed at them like a prehistoric monster.

Then it was over. There was a sound of boxcars clunking past. Sharon opened her eyes slowly. There was no pain. She wondered if she was dead. She looked around. McLeod sat beside her, staring straight into the windshield, now laced with so many cracks it was nearly opaque.

"Look!" he said. They were facing in the opposite direction. Gordie Gompers' tow-truck was chugging toward them, its yellow light blinking in the gloom. A sudden gust of wind from behind drenched them with rain. They turned together to stare at the back seat. The entire rear half of Ashenden's cruiser had disappeared. The train was rolling past two feet from their faces. The back of the car had been hacked off behind the front seat like a shear-pin. Sharon's knees began trembling violently. Her eyes rolled up in her head as though she might faint.

"Hold on!" McLeod yelled above the monotonous *clunk-clunk* of the wheels rolling by. "We've got no time for that! Only ten minutes left!"

Sharon's mind fluttered frantically. Save Jimmy. Get to the elevator. She wrenched open a door and scrambled out into the driving rain. The train seemed to be a hundred cars long. It would take half an hour to roll past. Sharon stamped her foot in frustration.

"Come on!" she shouted. "We have to climb over!"

"Where?"

"Over the train. Elevator's across the tracks. No time to wait!"

She ran to the nearest boxcar, trying not to think of the massive heavy wheels clunking below, wheels that could sever a leg instantly. McLeod helped push her foot up to the first rung of the ladder on the end of the car. She grabbed at the second rung and was jerked off her feet as the boxcar trundled past. Running alongside, McLeod boosted her other foot up. Slowly, she pulled herself up the iron ladder. Twice, her numb fingers nearly slipped and let her drop past the couplings of the boxcars, where certain death clanked menacingly past. She finally hauled herself to the top of the car and lay there for a moment, exhausted, recovering her breath and her nerve. She felt like a salmon at the top of a waterfall—and just as wet. The rain was pouring down. But where was the sergeant? His head appeared above the top of the car.

"Come on!" she croaked. "No time!"

They ran, feet skidding dangerously on the soaked wooden walkway atop the boxcar, to the far end where a ladder descended on the other side. Sharon tried to avoid looking at the gravelled rail-bed grumbling along beneath them. One misstep and her exquisite profile would be as crumpled as the front end of Jimmy's cruiser. Jimmy! She thought of him chained to the bottom of that rocket. Even stronger than his fear of death would be his disappointment that Meadowlark had failed him in his hour of need.

"Hurry!" she cried, passing a pipe on the roof that looked strangely out of place, and at the same time vaguely familiar.

She slid over the edge at the end of the boxcar, her new D'Amico shoes beating a useless tattoo on the side as they searched for the top rung. Sharon kicked the shoes off, and the tips of her sensitive toes finally found the step. She clambered downward on the ladder, abandoning all caution. If Jimmy Ashenden disappeared into the depths of China, life for her was ended.

Then, as one plum-coloured panty-hosed foot reached for another rung below and felt only the rushing wet air below the train, she knew she had to jump. The ditch beside the tracks seemed to lie twenty feet away.

"Jump!" McLeod yelled from above.

She took a deep breath, closed her eyes tightly, and flung herself off into the dark, rushing empti-ness. There was a sensation of rising through water, straining to break the surface and to suck in the first lungful of air. Then her feet struck the gravelled roadbed and she was running crazily alongside the train, whipped along as though she'd been expelled from a wind tunnel. A sudden pain shot upwards through her leg, and she sprawled forward into the stones, barely managing to get her arms out to break the fall. Even so, her patrician nose came to rest a scant half-inch from the surface of crushed rock.

Before she could think about her near-mutilation, or the rending pain in her ankle, McLeod was pulling her roughly to her feet.

"Come on," he ordered. "Which elevator?"

Sharon looked around in a daze. The train had carried them nearly a hundred yards down the track past the Wheat Pool elevator. In a sudden blaze of lightning, she saw the familiar POOL logo towering above, bright yellow on the building's dark side. Too shaken to speak, she pointed.

McLeod took off running along the railbed, waving the chain-cutter like a broadsword. Forcing the pain from her mind, she hobbled after him. She dared not look at her watch. Ashenden's time was measured in seconds.

"Wait!" she yelled. "We won't have time! We'll have to stop Yu Ching from firing the rocket!"

"Where?"

Sharon pointed at the lighted window of the shed where the Chinese agent was co-ordinating his engine of destruction. Another flash of savage electricity zagged across the skies, illuminating the elevator above them like an obelisk.

"My God," she wailed. "*Look*!"

McLeod's eyes followed her arm upward. On the top of the building, one side of the cupola was lifting, folding back like the top of a package of cigarettes, giving the missile access to the skies.

They redoubled their efforts, straining against the mud sucking at their feet. As they reached the driveway, the lights in Yu Ching's office flickered and went out. There was a noise like the tearing of silk from the inside of the building. A cloud of smoke suddenly billowed from its base.

They were too late.

19 THE HERO'S EPITAPH

"Get back!" McLeod yelled. "Too late!" He lifted Sharon from the muck and flung her across the embankment to protect her from the blast.

In that instant, the whisper became a rumble and then an ear-shattering roar. The lower half of the elevator suddenly burst into four sheets of fire, lighting the town like the noon sun. Out of the flaming fury rose the slim needle-point of Yu Ching's rocket. Emblazoned on its side was the Canadian flag, a final touch of the Chinese agent's sardonic wit.

Sharon shrieked once and flung herself full-length in the sodden gravel, sobbing incoherently. "Jimmy!" she cried over and over again. "Jimmy!"

McLeod stared at the rocket as it shuddered upward to the heaving thunderclouds. But he could not see Ashenden hitched to its tail. The glare was too bright. The elevator was burning like a torch, flames shooting up in an uncanny display.

"He was a fine and a brave man," McLeod said, saluting the fiery missile angling toward the west. "It was a death worthy of a Mounted Policeman."

"I would have quit the CBC, Jimmy!" Sharon wailed. "I would have stayed in Meadowlark!"

The missile's roar faded into the distance. With one final, malignant flare it disappeared into the clouds, on its way to China. McLeod shook himself into action.

"Come on, Miss Sharalike," he said. "We have to get to a telephone and call S.S. headquarters. If it's not too late, they can alert the Chinese and have it shot down.''

''Oh jimmyjimmyjimmyjimmy!'' Sharon moaned, jabbing her fingers into the cruel gravel. McLeod lifted her gently, removing his velvet cowboy vest to cover her heaving, nearly naked bosom. She was trembling violently.

''What about Yu Ching?'' she said, looking at him with dull eyes. ''Shouldn't we try to catch him?''

''Too late. Look at his office. He didn't get out in time.''

There was nothing left of the agent's shack but a mound of glowing embers. The once-proud Wheat Pool elevator, tallest edifice in town, was a shattered landscape of timbers, burning fitfully in the pouring rain. A pungent smell of burning grain hung in the air.

As they stepped onto the road, the last car of the freight train clanked past. Gordie Gompers' truck crossed the tracks and coughed toward them, yellow light flashing. It pulled up beside the pair, both so bedraggled from rain and mud as to be barely recognizable. The colours in McLeod's gaudy Western costume had run from top to bottom and side to side, so that he looked—in Gordie's headlights—like a fingerpainting. And the erstwhile toast of Toronto's Four Seasons restaurant had become a pitiful, bedraggled sorrow as she limped along the road.

''*What* in the name of holy prophets was *that*!'' Gordie Gompers shouted, pointing at the burning ruins.

''Yu Ching's rocket. We were too late. Train got in the way.''

"And—Jimmy Ashenden?" Gompers inquired hesitantly.

McLeod shook his head stoically; Sharon burst into tears.

Mayor Boothroyd lifted his Western hat, exposing his bald spot to the chill rain. "He was a good kid, even if he was goofy."

McLeod threw the mayor a furious glare. Contempt for civilian authority glinted in his eyes. "He was a brave and dedicated policeman, who died to save his community and his country."

"He was a crackerjack," Gompers offered emphatically. "No two ways about it!"

By now, the roads of Meadowlark were coming to life, as the people rushed from the school in cars and trucks to see the fire. Within minutes, dozens of vehicles had congregated at Gordie Gompers' tow-truck, attracted by its flashing beacon.

McLeod approached the mayor to ask for a telephone so he could sound the international alarm. But before he could reach him, Mayor Boothroyd had climbed into the back of the truck and spread his arms out to calm the citizens.

"This has been a sad night in the history of Meadowlark," he began, striking a dignified pose in the rain. "First, the fireworks, through no fault of the Sports Day Committee, were completely rained out..."

The Mounted Policeman's eyes flicked through the crowd, looking for a familiar face. Even Gompers had disappeared. Then he spied Jeremy Pules-Feltham and ran to him. "Have you got a car here?" he whispered urgently. "We have to alert Ottawa about this missile, fast!"

"Just a moment." The Englishman turned to

Madam Karmakov. "Nady darling, this policeman wants to borrow the Corvette. May he?"

The dark-eyed Ukrainian glanced at the policeman, her face a mask of contempt.

"Please!" McLeod said. "The free world depends on this."

"Okay," she said finally, tossing him the keys. "Save us the free world." She walked away in the darkness.

McLeod grabbed Sharon and ran to the Stingray, parked up the road. Behind them, Mayor Boothroyd was telling the townspeople about Ashenden's bravery. "I think I can say without fear of contradiction that the town of Meadowlark is going to miss Constable Jimmy Ashenden!" he shouted. There was an answering chorus of cheers.

"Some day, there will be a monument constructed to the memory of—Ashenden of the Royal Mounted!"

Someone in the crowd broke into "O Canada," and within two bars the assembled throng was bellowing the national anthem at full volume, tears trickling down their faces and mingling with the rain.

"Come on, let's get out of here!" McLeod started the big Corvette and powered it down the road, slewing around the corner onto Main Street.

"What can we do?" Sharon asked in a low voice.

"The first thing is to find a telephone and alert Ottawa. Then we've got to get every detachment for forty miles to send in reinforcements. We'll empty the whole Moose Jaw sub-division."

"Oh! Inspector Heavysides!"

"What about him?"

"Well, I mean, he was against Jimmy's investigation in the first place. If he finds out I'm still here—!"

"Don't worry. He's going to be booted upstairs for incompetence anyway." The car slid to a stop in front of the RCMP detachment office, and McLeod ran to the door. Sharon, limping behind, noticed the chain-cutter in his hand.

"What are you going to do?"

"Stand back!"

With a single stroke, McLeod smashed the lock cleanly out of the door. He heaved it open and stepped in, already reaching for the telephone, when a baseball bat swung out of nowhere and smashed McLeod in the head. He slumped onto the step. A man leaped out the door, gun in hand. Sharon opened her mouth to scream.

"Sharon! What the heck happened to *you*? And what are you doing with *him*?"

20 CONCLUSION... MORE OR LESS

"Constable Ashenden!" McLeod said, trying to rise to his hands and knees.

"Not so fast!" the constable retorted. Whipping a pair of handcuffs from his tunic, he snapped one onto the horseman's wrist. "Now just step into the cell there and you can keep your buddy company."

He yanked McLeod toward the barred metal door at the rear of his office.

"Jimmy!" Sharon exclaimed, flinging wet strands of hair back from her face. "You're making a horrible mistake. This man is a Mountie!"

"Oh yeah? Like *him,* I suppose! The friendly Wheat Pool agent!" Ashenden pointed through the cell bars to the cot, where Yu Ching stared gloomily at the calendar on his wall. Ashenden had decorated the tiny cell himself; the calendar featured a full-colour photograph of Queen Elizabeth inspecting the RCMP on Parliament Hill.

"It's Yu Ching!" McLeod cried. "But how did you get him—?And how did the rocket—? *Oh my God!* Get Ottawa on the phone! We have to stop the warhead from reaching China!"

Ashenden held his hand up. There was something disturbing about this man's voice, something familiar. "Don't worry about that. Security Services are going to be asking you a *lot* of questions."

"But I *am* Security Services! Ashenden, I'm Fred McLeod. In disguise!"

"It's true, Jimmy! He is!"

"Look. I've got my I.D." He showed Ashenden his credentials.

"Holy smoke! Sergeant, it's really you! Sharon, this is the guy who taught me everything!"

"For God's sake, unlock the handcuffs!"

Ashenden did.

McLeod ran to the telephone. "Get me national RCMP headquarters in Ottawa," he barked. "And make it snappy. This is a national emergency."

"Oh, if it's the missile you're phoning about, don't worry," Ashenden said. "It's harmless."

McLeod turned to him, mouth open. "Harmless?"

"Yes. I defused the warhead before it took off. With Yu Ching's help, of course. Right, Yu Ching?"

A growl issued from the cell.

"But *how*?" McLeod replaced the telephone receiver.

"Never mind that!" Sharon said. "How did you get free from the rocket? We thought you'd be halfway to China!"

"Oh, that." Ashenden grinned a small, shy grin. "When I realized you'd never make it back before midnight, I took out my hacksaw blade and cut the chain off."

Sharon stared, her bright eyes nearly popping from their elegant sockets. "You had a *goddamn hacksaw blade*?"

"Oh—yes."

"You had it—*all the time*?"

"Well, I always keep one taped inside my boot, you see. It's in case I ever get overpowered by a prisoner and he locks me inside my cell. Sergeant McLeod taught us that little trick," he said proudly, nodding at the sergeant.

"But why in God's name didn't you use it when

Yu Ching first chained you to the rocket?'' McLeod demanded.

A puzzled look crossed Ashenden's face. ''Well —Yu Ching didn't lock me in a cell. Otherwise, I would have remembered it in a flash!''

''But what *happened*, Jimmy?''

When Ashenden had finally remembered the hacksaw blade in his left boot, the minute hand on the clock had just reached 11:30 and he knew he had to act quickly.

Cutting through the chain was easy. His fingers —strengthened by years of milking cows at Niebelung—sawed the blade through the soft iron as though it was butter. In less than five minutes he was free and running to the door in the wall of the silo.

It was locked, of course. He had expected that. He glanced quickly around. There was no way he could get into the control room to jam the firing mechanism.

Without pausing to think, he leaped to the wall of the silo. There was no ladder, but there were toeholds on the wooden wall where a trained climber could advance to the uppermost reaches of the building. Ashenden started up quickly, knowing the urgency of his task. He had to stop the rocket. He scrambled upwards, muscles cracking with the strain of hauling his two-hundred-pound frame up the sheer surface.

At one point, he nearly gave up. His frantic fingers could not find a single sliver or crack to grasp. He tried to look up, but the briny sweat running into his eyes blinded him. He took a deep breath, and with a single reckless thrust he threw himself upward, praying there would be something up there to grab onto—and the fingers of his right hand closed on the edge of the platform he and Sharon had stood on nearly twelve hours before!

With the last dregs of his power, Ashenden pulled himself onto the platform and kneeled for a moment, recuperating.

When he stood up and saw the gleaming rocket in front of him, he felt overwhelmed. What could one man do, alone, against a machine like that, the end-product of the technological revolution?

The clock far below said 11:40. He stared at the rocket. There was an open space on its surface, just over his head. It was through that hole—about the size of a man—that the thermonuclear device had been armed.

Ashenden quickly climbed onto the wooden ladder above the platform. At the top was the hopper and the big gerber spout which fed grain into the elevator's bins. The gerber was wired to the wall—and still intact. He unfastened the wire on the gerber and lowered it until the lip of the spout was opposite the opening on the missile.

He descended to the platform again, then turned and ran down the stairs, stumbling against the walls at every turn. But there was no time for caution. Hitting the floor at the bottom, he stumbled and ripped the knees out of his breeches. Another thing to worry about. Sub-division always raised heck about issuing uniform replacements. He got up and ran across the platform scales, carefully skirting the open hopper. He ran out the door and down the drive.

Yu Ching's light was still on! Ripping a board off the staircase to the Wheat Pool office, Ashenden smashed through the door—just in time to came face-to-face with the Chinese stepping out the door, carrying his black Samsonite brief case.

"We meet again, Yu Ching!"

The smile on the Oriental's lips vanished in a snarl of contempt. "Maybe we meet again, skin-head—but it isn't going to do *you* much good. Within an hour, Peking will be one big crater."

"*Peking*? I don't get it!"

"No, I don't expect you *would*, baby blue-eyes! Well, when Peking goes, they're going to blow your precious Meadowlark off the map, too. And by then, I'll be back in the good old U.S. of A."

"Not so fast, Yu Ching. I don't know what this is about, but we're going to end it right now. Step back inside and cut the power."

"There's nothing you can do, stupid! I've already fired it. The mechanism is completely auto-mated. The propellant is going to ignite in"—he glanced at his watch—"eleven minutes."

"Get moving!" Ashenden barked.

He prodded Yu Ching up the drive and into the elevator scales-shed, turning on the light.

"This is crazy, Mountie! We have to split! This place is going to blow!"

"Is there any grain left in this building?"

Yu Ching shrugged. "Might be some left in one of the annex bins."

"Good. Now, start the belt drive and let's get that wheat up into the gerber."

"But if we don't get out—!"

"Move!" Ashenden snapped, lifting the board over his head for emphasis.

"What do you plan to do?"

"I moved the gerber to that opening at the top

of the rocket. We're going to run a few bushels of wheat into it and see what happens."

The Chinese turned pale. "But the warhead! That'll stop the—!"

"*Aha*!" Ashenden cried.

They stuffed the armed warhead of the rocket with a boxcarful of No. 2 Northern and, with three minutes to spare before the blast-off, made the escape. They were driving to Ashenden's office in Yu Ching's car as Sharon and McLeod made their frantic dash to save him.

"Oh Jimmy!" Sharon sighed. "You'll get the Order of Canada!"

"And a promotion," Sgt. McLeod added. "Maybe even a posting to Parliament Hill."

"And it's my story!" Sharon cried, jubilant despite her bedraggled appearance. "I've got the scoop of the century. Finished with Minority Group documentaries forever!"

Yu Ching's maniacal laugh rattled in his cell. "It sounds neat," he chortled. "But who's going to believe you? Who's going to believe there was even a rocket here in the first place?"

"The train!" Sharon squealed, suddenly remembering the pipes on the boxcars. "All his workers! They were in those cars we climbed over! They're Americans!"

"Too late!" Yu Ching cackled. "They'll be across the U.S. border by now."

"Not likely," Ashenden said, picking up a blank report sheet and inserting it into his typewriter. He faced a long night catching up on the paperwork caused by Yu Ching and his insidious crew. "I opened the switch to the siding into the livestock yards. They'll still be down there with the sheep and hogs, trying to get back onto the main line. I called the CNR section gang and they locked the train onto the siding for me. I also phoned Regina. Security Services is on the way to arrest them.''

21 EPILOGUE

By dawn, CBC Radio News had spread the story across the nation. Telegrams of congratulation poured in for Constable James Ashenden. Meadowlark was crawling with Mounted Policemen hauling spies to Ottawa for investigation.

During the night, Sharon had written her story and telephoned it to "The National" in Toronto. She had only three hours' sleep before waking up and finding herself a celebrity—and she looked delectable.

Mayor Boothroyd, having eulogized Ashenden's memory for an hour and a half in the pelting rain, until his audience had finally dwindled to Gordie Gompers, was confined to bed with a bad chill. He was even unable to rise and make a press statement about Meadowlark's oustanding constabulary.

By eight o'clock, Ashenden finished typing his report—which had assumed the length of a fair-sized book. Sharon had returned from her motel in Shakespear, decked out in her most alluring halter. Together, they sat at Ellie Sanders' breakfast table, tired but giddy with triumph. The breakfast was not one of Ellie's best—she had been up late herself the night before with all the excitement—but it was cheerily laid out: enormous bowls of Prairie Maid Wheat Puffs swimming in fresh milk; steaming cups of instant Nabob; a stack of toast with her incomparable crabapple jam.

"Well—Constable," Sharon smiled. "I guess congratulations are in order."

"Gosh. I never could have done it without your

help, Sharon! You convinced me to keep going when everything seemed hopeless. You deserve half the credit.''

Sharon shrugged demurely. ''It was my job. The CBC says they might even promote me to London. If I want to go.''

''Gee, that's great, Sharon!''

''I'll be around for a while, though. I have to finish my documentary on the Pitcairn Islander. Max Christian's been waiting for a week now.'' She lifted a spoonful of puffed wheat to her ruby lips. ''I might stay in Meadowlark a while longer, too.''

''How come?''

Sharon put down her spoon and sighed. ''They'll want somebody to sell ice cream at the Sports Day and Picnic next year.''

''Yeah, they might.''

''So we might see each other, once in a while.''

''Gee whiz. I don't know, Sharon. I've got a lot on my hands just looking after Trooper. Do you realize that I've spent hardly *any* time with her for a week now?''

A crystalline tear appeared in the corner of one of Sharon's emerald-green eyes. ''Jimmy, does that horse mean more to you than I do?''

''Now that isn't fair, Sharon. It's two different things! I respect you and you're really good-looking and I like you a lot—but—Trooper *needs* me!'' He did not notice the tear fall from Sharon's cheek into her milk; he could only see a vision of the glorious future, man and horse together in the world's most famous Mounted Police force. His eyes shone.

''Do you know what Sgt. McLeod said, Sharon? He told me to keep training with Trooper! Because of my work on this case, he's going to recommend me for—*The Musical Ride*!"

Sharon stood at the door, gazing one last time at Constable James Ashenden's starry blue eyes.

"Good-bye, Jimmy," she said, and hurried out the door to the yellow MG waiting at the curb. Behind her, she could hear Ashenden call to Ellie Sanders. "Do you have any more of those honey-soaked oatcakes, Ellie?" he said. "I'm going visiting this morning."

And before she could start the engine and roar out of Meadowlark, obliterating the sound of his voice forever, he burst out humming the overture of "Rose Marie."

ODE ON THE OCCASION OF THE VISIT OF H.M. ELIZABETH REGINA TO THE QUEEN CITY DURING THE RCMP CENTENARY

You pause on the ramp
of the Royal Jet
bravely smiling at a dozen
Old Spice-scented Mounties
a hundred Legionnaires with red wet noses
a thousand kiddies with
maple leaf flags in one hand
a popsicle in the other.
God save the Queen!

You survey the sticky throngs,
the Royal Mask now slightly wrinkled
but still adored by twenty million
Canadians more or less.

Then taking one sharp breath
You leave behind the sculpted
gardens of Windsor and Balmoral,
plunge once again
into the tide of hands
and stupefied hosannas.

Your Majesty, there must
be easier ways to earn
Your room and board.

GILLY AND BOSS MORGAN
(from THE CON MAN)

In the morning, Gilly woke up in a state of shock. It was not his attic room in Brochet. It was not his cell in the P.A. Pen. In fact, to his stunned eyes, it looked like the set from a Fred Astaire musical, with white rococo furniture and elaborate gilt mirrors. Somehow the stench of stale beer rising through the floor was mixed into it. Gilly crawled out of bed and explored the two-room suite, his mouth a raw mélange of plaque and pepperoni. Looking out the window, he was cruelly struck back to reality. The main street of Willson was being lashed by an icy wind; he shivered and turned away from the window. On the writing desk, he found a couple of postcards featuring the hotel restaurant. A waitress stood beside the cash register holding a Terminal Hotel menu, smiling saucily at the camera. He decided on the spur of the moment to send a funny message to his friend Clint Malach, but before he began, there was a tap at the door.

Gilly walked to the door in his underwear and opened it. He blinked in amazement. It was the waitress from the postcard, smiling the same smile; the same little green cap perched atop her honey blonde hair. Her delicately sculptured jaw was punishing a wad of bubble gum, he noticed. His gaze descended down the bursting bodice of her clean white dress, past the exquisitely narrow waist, to the most perfectly dimpled pair of knees he had ever seen. Or could ever remember seeing.

"You," he breathed.

She laughed, a tiny pink tongue showing through her bright teeth. "Seen the pitcher, ay?" she said in an adenoidal grate which sobered Gilly instantly. She handed him a menu, the one she was holding in the postcard. "Stan says it's gonna make me famous, but I think he's pullin' my leg, so's he don't hafta pay me a model's fee. Whutcha like fer breakfast?"

"Fried eggs and coffee."

"Okay. You better get dressed before yuh freeze yer toes off," she said, backing down the hallway.

"And juice," Gilly said, closing the door as she disappeared. By the time he had shaved and dressed, she was back with his breakfast tray. She sat down on the bed to watch as he ate.

"Whatcher name?"

"Gillman Savard."

"Mine's Georgia, but everybody calls me Marilyn. Know why?" she said, her cheeks dimpling as her jaw cranked on the wad of gum like a hammermill.

"No. Why?"

"You dummy! Cuz I look like Marilyn Monroe! Know why?"

This was dangerous territory. Gilly concentrated on his eggs, keeping his eyes averted from the long curve of thigh that disappeared under the white dress. He stuffed his mouth to capacity.

"Stan sez you're buying the hotel, so I thought I should interduce myself. I sorta go with it. I mean, along with the rest of the staff. Stan sez you're a bigshot."

"Maybe so, maybe not." He started on the toast and jam. "Anyway, I'm leaving for Regina today."

She gazed at him and sighed. "Ya know, that's why I kinda like you? You're cute and modest. Most guys try to play the bigshot. I don't even give 'em the time of day."

"That's very wise," Gilly agreed.

"I only been working here since I left school in March. It's a stepping stone on the road of life."

"I see."

"Well, I gotta get back to work before Stan flips his lid. See ya." She bounced out of the room, her firm young body springing as she walked, her blonde curls bouncing on her shoulders, her thighs winking at him through her white uniform. Gilly turned to his coffee. He was perspiring freely, despite the cold.

Stan was waiting for him at the bottom of the stairs a half hour later. "Well, what do you think?"

"Nice room."

"No! The broad! Nice little country girl, eh? She goes with the hotel."

"She's something, okay."

"Well, you ready to inspect the hotel? We have a little while before Mom gets here."

"Mom?"

"My mother, Mrs. Parnell. She has a half-interest in the property."

"Oh—well, I really should be—"

"Come on." Parnell showed him into the restaurant, an expanse of chrome and vinyl, where Georgia bustled from the milkshake machine to the coffee counter and back before an admiring row of farmers and truck drivers who were perched on stools.

"The reason I'm selling now," Parnell was explaining, "is for reasons of health. I haven't been well for years. And now business is so heavy, I have to find something less strenuous."

Gilly looked out the window. The main street of Willson ran for half a mile, parallel to the railway and the inevitable row of grain elevators. There was not a tree to be seen, except for a ragged fringe of caragana bushes near the railway station. Icy grit whirled through the air, blasting everything it struck. There was not a pedestrian in sight, although several large dumptrucks rumbled past in both directions.

"See that?" Parnell cried triumphantly. "All those trucks are working on the South Saskatchewan Dam—about twenty miles down the road. Know what happens when *that's* finished? Willson becomes the tourist capital of Saskatchewan!"

A white Cadillac with a set of enormous tailfins suddenly pulled up in front of the hotel. Its horn blared. At the wheel of the car was a stylish-looking woman with marcelled silver hair, a cigarette dangling from her lips.

"There's Mom," Parnell said, pulling Gilly outside. He placed him in the front seat of the car and climbed into the back. "Mom, this is Mr. Savard."

Mrs. Parnell power-turned in front of the hotel,

spraying gravel and snow in a circle before rocketing down the street in the opposite direction. She turned to Gilly with a cruel grin that somehow contradicted her swirling blue-rinsed hair and flashy spectacles.

"Delighted to make your acquaintance, ma'am," he said, smiling his most charming smile.

Her lips pulled back to show a set of brilliant white false teeth. They barely moved when she spoke. "So you're the son of a bitch who thinks he's got us by the short and curlies, eh? Well, we'll see about that!"

Gilly sat the rest of the way in reflective silence, completely unnerved. The car pulled up in front of a large brown house, one of Willson's most impressive mansions. It was buttressed with sunporches all around and crowned with a network of lightning rods. Mrs. Parnell made Gilly wipe his shoes before entering the hall. The front parlour was an extravaganza of paisley curtains and Gainsborough prints. Mom Parnell placed a straight-backed chair squarely in front of her old rocker and gestured Gilly into the chair for interrogation.

"Now," she said, her false teeth clattering over every consonant, "What's all this bullshit about a hundred grand for the hotel?"

"Well—I'm really not in the market for a hotel. We were just engaged in idle conversation."

"Oh yeah? Idle conversation, eh? You must think you got a couple of smalltown hicks to fleece out of their life's savings! Well let me tell you something, you smarmy-faced swindler, I've had this hotel appraised independently at a hundred and thirty thousand!"

"Hm," Gilly said. This was getting serious. He

had to find a means of escape.

"Well?" she snapped. "Are you going to just sit there like a pile of chicken-shit?"

"Now, Mom," Stan said.

"Stay out of this, Stanley. You've already buggered up enough."

Mrs. Parnell held Gilly captive for two hours, insulting, exhorting and threatening him, not once listening to his pleas of innocence. He finally agreed to buy not only the hotel and café with all their furnishings, but also the Avalon movie theatre, the Willson Arms apartment block and an anonymous building mysteriously leased to the government. He was then allowed to leave. They did not agree on a price, although Mom Parnell's final figure was $190,000.00

Stan walked him back to the hotel. "There she is!" he cried ecstatically, pointing to the neon sign. "This time tomorrow, she'll be all yours."

"We'll see," Gilly said, thinking he had to be far away by this time tomorrow. "Is Georgia still at work?"

Parnell leered at him knowingly. "Naw. She works the early shift and goes out to her dad's farm for the rest of the day. But I got something what'll take your mind off that. There's a big Liberal meeting tonight in the town hall!" Parnell's nose glowed with enthusiasm. "Boss Morgan's giving a speech!"

"Gee, I don't have any good clothes with me, Stan. You know how it is when you're travelling." Gilly preferred the beer parlour to politics.

"No problem! Come on, it's not six o'clock yet. I'll introduce you to my friend Huppe at the Clothes Rack, just down the street."

"I don't have enough money with me, Stan."

"Quit worrying. He's a friend of mine."

As it turned out, any friend of Parnell's was a friend of Huppe's; credit wouldn't cost a dime. If Gilly admired that new narrow-lapelled suitjacket, it was his. So was a handful of button-down shirts and a rich assortment of the needle-thin ties that were just going out of fashion.

"By God, you even look like a politician," Parnell cried, as Gilly stood before the mirror.

As they approached the town hall after supper, Gilly could sense the growing rumble of politics. There would be a provincial election in a few months and Boss Morgan was determined to lick the Socialists this time. The entrance to the hall was emblazoned with slogans: "Time for a Change!" and "Save Us All from Socialism!"

Inside the door, a large beefy man was pumping the hand of all who entered. He was Boston Morgan, a man who had spent ten years fighting his way to the top of the Liberal party. He had been a Socialist before that and had been converted after losing out in a power struggle. Now his crusade was to rally the soldiers of private enterprise.

"Hiya, Boss," Parnell said. "This is the new owner of the Terminal Hotel, Gillman Savard."

"Good to see you again!" Morgan boomed.

"I don't think we've met before," Gilly murmured.

"Well, well—but I've heard of you, of course!"

"Of course," Gilly admitted.

"News travels fast in these parts when you keep your ear to the ground like I do. Anyway, I'm pleased to hear you're a Liberal!"

"Actually," Gilly pointed out, "I'm not."

Morgan's eyes narrowed to suspicious slits behind his glasses. He turned to Parnell, questioning him.

"He's going to join, Boss. Gilly has great plans for Willson."

"Well, that's what we need, Gary. Men of action! It's guys like you who will halt the tide of creeping Communism. Take Medicare, now."

"Gilly's in oil, Boss."

"Ah—a man with the nation's economy in his grasp! Are you aware of the secret Socialist plan to expropriate every drop of oil, every gallon of gasoline in this province?"

"No," Gilly admitted.

"But we are going to smash this totalitarian regime, if they ever dare to announce the date of a general election. You and me and every other ordinary working joe in the province—we'll crush them!"

The crowd standing around them went wild. Boss Morgan knew that in politics, rhetoric was everything. If Boss Morgan could restore decency and free enterprise to this bastion of North American Socialism, he was a god and benefits would accrue to all who kept the faith.

"I think you made an impression, Gilly," Parnell said, as they hurried to find seats. The hall was filling rapidly. The chill of the unheated building had disappeared.

"My fellow sufferers under Socialism!" Morgan began. "I come to you tonight with a message. We in this *great* Liberal party are about to lift the heavy yoke from your shoulders!" The crowd roared. "The task we face is not an easy task. Nor is it a simple one. It is nothing less than the total pulverization of creeping Socialism!" The crowd surged to its feet and cheered mightily.

For an hour and a half, Morgan ripped apart public transportation, free school texts, the failure of the Socialist cheese factory and the sinister designs of every Bolshevik in the government. He promised to cut taxes, liberate business and provide untaxed purple gasoline to farmers. When Boss Morgan rode the wave of approval to his conclusion, the whole audience pressed toward the stage to congratulate the politician.

Later, Morgan and his aides somehow ended up in Gilly's Deluxe Suite. Parnell had invited them back to the hotel for a few drinks and Gilly's was the only decent room he had to offer.

"Well, we really had 'em moving tonight, eh?" Morgan said, a glass in one hand and a cigar in the other.

"You can say that again, Boss," Parnell cried.

"Great speech, Boss," said one of his young sidekicks, manoeuvering Gilly out of the way.

"Whuddaya mean—*great speech*? It was the same goddam speech!"

"I mean, great delivery," the assistant said, thinking fast.

"Thanks," Morgan said, reaching for his rye and Seven-Up. "Well, Gary, what do you think? Ready to join the forces of free enterprise now?"

"I'm thinking about it."

"Don't think too long, my boy. There's going to be a nominating convention in this constituency before Easter. I want you to think about it."

"But I don't have any experience."

"Experience!" Morgan laughed. "You don't need experience! You got the greatest face for politics I ever seen." He leaned close and jabbed him with one blunt finger. "You got a sincere face, Gary. I don't know where you got it from, but I'll tell you it's worth a million bucks in this game! As long as you believe!"

"In what?"

"Anything you like! The party! Money! Taxes, freedom. Even Socialism! I can never remember all the stuff I'm supposed to believe in. That's why I hire these assholes." He jerked his thumb at his assistants who were milling around the liquor bottles in their Ivy League suits.

"Let's look at your assets. You got a wife and family, eh?"

"No, I'm afraid not," Gilly admitted.

"Hm. Let's see. How about a war record? You ever in the armed services?"

"No-o-o-o—but my brother was a hero in the Second World War."

"That's it! Play it for all you can get. And one word of advice. Honest exaggeration! That is the art of politics. I'll look for you at the nominating meeting." With that, Boss Morgan swept out of the hotel with his flock of aides to return to the capital and the arena of bigger politics.

THE HOUNDS OF NOTRE DAME

When I was first asked by producer Fil Fraser to write a screenplay about Father Athol Murray of Notre Dame—one of Saskatchewan's most enduring legends—I turned him down. "Frankly," I said, "I never cared much for him." I believed he was a religious charlatan, and a foul-mouthed little drunk.

However, nothing is ever final, and after a couple of other writers had failed to come up with an effective treatment, Mr. Fraser came back with an offer and a deal: "Just write him as he was— warts and all. Try and bring the real Murray to life."

The result was *The Hounds of Notre Dame*, which won international acclaim and, of course, a Genie award for actor Tom Peacocke in 1981. (Needless to say, the film was panned by local Saskatchewan reviewers.) The film caught most of Pere Murray's many contradictions, and I hope it finally reveals some of the respect and affection I developed for the man in the course of research. The film is set on Feb. 12, 1940, one day in the life of Notre Dame College, Wilcox. They play a hockey game against the Moose Jaw Junior Canucks, take in a new adolescent rebel, get caught in a blizzard on the open prairie.

In Murray's later years, when he became a parody of his own Depression legend, he was taken with a paranoid obsession, I am told. He believed that he was going to die, "assassinated by some son of a bitch from Moose Jaw." He died in bed, as it turned out, still haranguing the public for more support for his beloved "Hounds."

The assassin from Moose Jaw came too late, and offered an elegy instead.

Pere's pep talk

There is a painful silence. All the players are slumped against the wall, exhausted. MURRAY paces before them. He makes two false starts on his pep talk.

MURRAY: Gang, the problem is obvious. You're not skating hard enough. *(Pause)* I know some of you aren't feeling so hot, and we're short-handed, but you can't just up and run out of steam! You're not skating like Hounds—more like a flock of puppy-dogs!

ANOTHER ANGLE: Camera pans around the room. The players obviously feel bad and are beginning to get angry at MURRAY's unfair comments. A couple spit on the floor. He eyes them, and goes on.

MURRAY: In fact, this is the most weak-kneed, hollow-chested, simpering bunch of weak sisters I've ever had the bad luck to watch!

FRYER: Hey, take it easy! Half the team's sick.

There is a murmur of agreement. CORMACK glances at FRYER in gratitude and apprehension? After all he knows PERE. However, MURRAY turns on him in a fury.

MURRAY: Sick! What a lame excuse! Dammit-all gang, this is *Notre Dame*! You can't just lie down and die because of an outbreak of measles! *German* measles!

He pauses for breath, lights another smoke.

MURRAY: And even with half of you sick, you're still a better team of hockey-players than those pansies from Moose Jaw. They look worse than you guys! What are we going to tell the gang at home if you let *these* muckers beat you? You owe it to your sick friends, gang! They're counting on you to defend your reputation. We need it to bring people out to these games! You're playing for Notre Dame! God is fighting on our side—and he's asking for more effort from *you*!

The warning buzzer sounds. The Hounds surge to their feet with new spirit.

MURRAY: You have to skate hard! You have to back-check! You have to get the lead out—and whip these city slickers!

The players march out, and he claps each one on the back. As the last player disappears, Murray shouts after them toward the arena.

MURRAY: And if you can't beat them, at least give them the goddam measles!

WHEAT CITY

CHARACTERS

BILLY: The postmaster of Wheat City. He is 35-40, rather obese, not the brightest in the world.

ROSE: Wife of the Wheat City railway agent. She is probably younger than Billy, but could be fifty. A chain-smoker.

TIME: It is a hot sunny July day, about 1:00 p.m.

PLACE: The platform of the railway station in the small Saskatchewan town of Wheat City.

The station is drab and weather-beaten, in a serious state of decay. At rear is the outer wall of the station house, with a pair of dirty windows looking onto the platform. There is a door with torn screens, and a bench below one of the windows. Upstage are four cream cans awaiting shipment. At left rear is a slight ramp and a path leading to the street. There is a large red platform wagon. Downstage right is a signal arm and lever. The station sign "Wheat City" hangs tenuously from the eave. There is the sound of a baby crying sporadically;

also the sound of children playing and shouting in the distance. Rose enters from the station door, looking hungover and harassed. She wears a shabby housecoat and men's shoes. She goes left, peers down the path, and apparently sees something. She runs into the station, fixing her appearance.

ROSE *(off)*: Brenda! Bren-n-n-n-da! *(Sound of children stops.)* Come and look after thuh baby!

CHILD'S VOICE *(off)*: Wha-a-a-at?

ROSE *(off)*: You get in here and watch her before I come and *tan your hide! (Billy appears at left, pulling a small coaster wagon. There is a nearly empty mail sack in it. He wears a plaid flannel shirt and a bright tie.)*

CHILD'S VOICE *(off)*: Awwwwww!

ROSE *(off)*: There, there now, don't cry, sweetie-pie. Mommy's got a ni-i-ice bottle a milk for yuh. There! *(The crying stops.)* Isn't that yummy? *(pause)* Brenda!

CHILD'S VOICE *(off)*: Co-ming!

Billy places his wagon in a precise location near the bench. He goes to a window and peers in. He taps on it, waves.

BILLY: Hi!

ROSE *(off)*: Hi, Billy!

BILLY: Hi!

ROSE *(off)*: Be right out!

Billy goes back to his wagon, adjusts it a couple of degrees. Rose re-enters, still trying to put herself to-

gether.

BILLY: Hi!

ROSE: Hadda feed thuh baby.

BILLY: Oh.

ROSE: Hadda fix thuh kids' lunch, too.

BILLY: Yeah.

Rose sits on bench.

ROSE: Can't wait till school starts again!

BILLY: Yeah, it must be—tough... *(pause)*

ROSE: Whatsa time?

Billy removes from his watch pocket an old watch on a leather thong.

BILLY: Thirty-two minnits tuh go.

ROSE: Ahhh—lotsa time.

BILLY: Fer sure.

ROSE *(pause)*:   Anybody come intuh town today?

BILLY: Nope. Not a soul. *(pause)* Not a single soul all morning.

ROSE: Didden *git* any myself.

BILLY: Eh?

ROSE: Lunch.

BILLY *(pause)*:   *You* gotta eat too, yuh know.

ROSE *(deprecating)*:   Aaah!

BILLY: Yuh *gotta* eat tuh stay healthy!

ROSE *(grinning)*: Like you.

BILLY: Yeah, I giss—so.

ROSE: But who wants tuh be a *fatso*?

Billy turns and moves down right.

(pause) Hey, sit down!

BILLY: Naw. Train be in soon.

ROSE: So whud *you* have for dinner?

BILLY: Doughnuts.

ROSE: Thuh kids like doughnuts.

BILLY: A whole box a glazed doughnuts. *(Pause. Billy adjusts wagon.)*

ROSE: Enny mail this week?

BILLY: Naw. Couple a letters.

ROSE: Sell many stamps?

BILLY: Six.

ROSE: Well, 'at's better'n none! Eh, Billy?

BILLY: Giss so. *(Pause. He looks out left.)* Train on time?

ROSE *(shrugs)*: Far's *I* know.

BILLY: Never late these days. Must be the diesels.

ROSE: Makes a differnce when you got a good station agent.

BILLY: Yuh mean Merv?

ROSE *(defensive)*: Yeah, *Merv!* He works at it

real hard, yuh know!

BILLY (*enthusiastically*): Oh, you're dang tootin'!

ROSE: Thuh C.N.R. was goddamn *lucky* to get him!

BILLY: Boy, yuh can say that again!

ROSE: Ain't *every*body'd live in a rotten ole shack like this.

BILLY: Nope.

ROSE (*gesturing*): Half the goddamn *windows* broken.

BILLY: Yeah. (*long pause*) So—Merv not here today?

ROSE (*pause*): Gone tuh Meaduhlark.

BILLY: Oh. The—beer—?

ROSE: *No, not the beer parlour!*

BILLY: Oh—good.

ROSE: There's more in Meaduhlark than a beer parlour, yuh know!

BILLY (*weakly*): I know.

ROSE: And is it *yer* bizness if he *does* have the odd beer? Huh?

BILLY: I didn't say...

ROSE: *Fatso!*

BILLY: ...he was...

ROSE (*pause*): Anyways, I kin look after everythin' needs doin' 'round here!

BILLY: You don't have tuh tell *me*, Rose! I seen yuh do it!

ROSE: Yer damn right yuh did! Right here! *(pause)* They ever have a beer parlour here?

BILLY *(confused)*: *Here?*

ROSE: In town, yuh dumb-head!

BILLY: Oh, yeah—back in the forties, I think. Hotel. Burned down, though.

ROSE: Bet it was nice then, eh?

BILLY: Wheat City?

ROSE: Thuh *beer* parlour.

BILLY: I was only a kid then.

ROSE: Forties? *(Calculates on her fingers.)* You were a kid in the forties? Time sure flies, don't it?

BILLY: Kin say that again.

ROSE: Seems just like—yesterday, we came here. Must be. . .

BILLY: Two years!

ROSE: No!

BILLY: Yup.

ROSE: Well, I be-go-tuh-hell!

BILLY: Two years ago last month.

ROSE *(stunned)*: Two-*years*!

BILLY *(modestly)*: I got a head for dates. *(Pause.*

Rose is preoccupied.) Fer instance. Did you know— *today* is thuh hottest day a thuh year?

ROSE: Eh?

BILLY: July the twentieth. Hottest day a thuh year.

ROSE *(vaguely)*:   Think it was hotter on Monday.

BILLY *(earnestly)*:   No, I mean on the long term! Since they started takin' tempatures in the guv-viment! Today's the hottest.

ROSE: Yuh don't say.

BILLY: They kin *prove* it with—*(carefully)*—statistics.

ROSE *(conclusively)*:   It was hotter on Monday!

BILLY: I *know*, but *I'm* talkin' about the *aver-age . . .*

ROSE *(deliberately interrupting)*:   Dodgers won yestiday.

BILLY: . . . temperature—huh?

ROSE: What the radio said.

BILLY: Oh. *(pause)* Ya hear thuh weather report?

ROSE: Didden lissen.

BILLY: High pressure movin' in.

ROSE: Six tuh three.

BILLY: Huh?

ROSE: Over thuh Giants.

BILLY: 'Zatso? Good game?

ROSE: Yup. *(pause)* Pirates won, too.

The baby wails once, off.

BILLY: What was that?

ROSE *(cocking her head)*: Coulda bin thuh baby.

BILLY *(checking his watch—a joke)*: Musta bin. Train ain't due fer another twenty-six minutes and —four seconds.

The baby yells again.

ROSE: It's thuh baby, awright.

Pause. Billy clears his throat.

BILLY: How is—she?

ROSE: Gettin' better.

BILLY: That's nice.

ROSE: Finally got Merv tuh drive me tuh Mea-duhlark, yestiday, so's thuh doctor could see her. Gave me some gunk fer her face.

BILLY: How about thuh cough?

ROSE: Gave me some stuff fer that, too. Fer free! Don't seem tuh do much good, though.

BILLY: Awwwww.

ROSE: Damn colds. Person gets tireda wipin' noses!

BILLY: Dang tootin'.

ROSE: Yer sure lucky, not havin' kids.

BILLY: Oh, I dunno.

ROSE: Take my advice, boy. Stay a bachelor!

BILLY: Oh, I dunno.

ROSE: That's what I shoulda done—stayed single. Coulda had my own life. *(pause)* No kids whinin' alla time! No fightin' with yer husband.

BILLY: Aw, cummon Rose! It izzen *that*...

ROSE: Whadda*you* know?

BILLY: Well. Dave and me—fight.

ROSE *(interested)*: Yeah?

BILLY: Sometimes.

ROSE: What about?

BILLY: Oh—differnt things.

ROSE: Well, like what?

BILLY: Differnt things.

ROSE *(pause)*: Hey! Ya wanna switch thuh signal?

BILLY: Me?

ROSE: Yeah!

BILLY *(points right)*: Switch thuh signal? By *myself*?

ROSE: *If*—yuh tell me.

BILLY: Oh, I dunno, Rose.

ROSE: Come on! *(Billy goes to the corner of the station and looks to make sure they are alone: He comes back.)* Yeah?

BILLY: Well, I like to keep thuh house clean. I mean, it's thuh least I kin do if Dave's away all day workin', izzen it? Mom used tuh keep thuh place shiny as a pin.

ROSE: Jus' like me.

BILLY: Uh—yeah. *(pause)* So Dave comes home, and thuh first thing yuh know, he butts his cigarette in the middla thuh floor! The floor I jus' swept!

ROSE: Tch, tch, tch.

The platform by now is littered with butts Rose has stepped on.

BILLY: Well, nacherly I get a little hot under thuh collar. Can't stand messiness, yuh see.

ROSE: Me neither!

Billy finally sits, at the far end of the bench.

BILLY: And sometimes—he don't like the suppers I cook.

ROSE: Ha! You should hear Merv about *my* suppers!

BILLY: Says he's gettin' sicka weiners and fried putatuhs.

ROSE: Well, that's just plain *stoopid*!

BILLY: Sure it is!

ROSE: *Fulla* vitamins and stuff!

BILLY: But he won't lissen.

ROSE: Juss like Merv!

BILLY: Dave won't even eat Kraft Dinner any more!

ROSE: Tch, tch, tch. *(pause)* So—who wins?

BILLY: Eh?

ROSE: Thuh *fights*.

BILLY: Oh—nobody, I giss.

ROSE: Didja ever—*(she makes a fist.)*—poke him in the *chops*?

BILLY *(horrified)*: I coulden hit Dave! *(Rose giggles).* He's my brother!

ROSE: Some fight.

BILLY *(reluctantly)*: Sometimes we—rassle a bit. *(Rose shrieks with laughter. Billy rising)* What's so dang funny?

ROSE *(almost in hysterics)*: Rassling! Two big fatsoes—that tiny house—ahahahaha! *(It takes her a while to subside.)*

BILLY *(finally)*: Dave izzen fat, yuh know.

ROSE: Eh?

BILLY: He ain't fat!

ROSE: Tuh *hell*! He's fatter'n *you* are! That's how fat *he* is!

BILLY: He isn't!

ROSE: I'll never figger out how a tubba lard like him *got* a job on thuh section gang!

BILLY: *Dave is not fat!*

ROSE: Okay. *(shrugs)* He ain't fat.

BILLY: Anyways, we sure in heck don't fight like you and Merv!

ROSE: What?

BILLY *(retreating already)*: We kin hear, y'know. All thuh way over to our house.

ROSE: *Whaddaya hear?*

BILLY *(turns away)*: Aww—nothin'.

ROSE: *What?*

BILLY: Nothing!

ROSE: Yer god-damn *right*, nuthin'. *(long, tense pause)* I better get the cream cans checked. *(She goes to the four cans stacked against the station wall at left. She checks the labels wired to the handles.)*

BILLY *(too cheerily)*: Not too many today, eh Rose? *(no answer)* Less farmers shippin' cream every week.

ROSE *(exploding)*: Willyuh lookit *that!*

BILLY: What?

ROSE: Charlie Burnses' *cream can!*

BILLY: Charlie Burnses'... ?

ROSE: No god-damn *label* again!

BILLY: How about that?

ROSE: They expect *me* to do all the work! *(She flounces angrily into the station. She is heard off stage.)* As if I got nuthin' better tuh do all night and day than fixin' *cream can labels!* Just 'cause they're too goddamn *lazy* to get their fat asses off a tractor and do it themselves!

BILLY: Yeah—same with stamps!

Rose re-enters with a label in her hand.

ROSE: What?

BILLY: They never put stamps on their letters, either. I always gotta remind 'em.

Rose wires label onto the can, viciously.

ROSE: And that god-damn *Merv*! Useless as tits on a bull!

BILLY *(carefully non committal):*   Umm.

ROSE: Sneakin' off tuh Meaduhlark every day! Leavin' *me* with all thuh work!

BILLY: Now Rose, maybe he isn't . . .

ROSE: Don't you stick up for him! *I* know what's goin' on! *(She sits down.)*

BILLY: Wonder if he'll be here—in time for thuh train?

ROSE: Who cares? *(silence)*

BILLY: Gonna rain.

ROSE: Eh?

BILLY: Might rain before thuh day's out. More'n likely, anyhow.

ROSE: Tuh hell!

BILLY: Yuh know how I kin tell?

ROSE *(finally):*   How?

BILLY: Yuh see all them clouds buildin' up to thuh west there? *(He points out left.)*

ROSE: Yeah.

BILLY: Cumulo-nimbus.

ROSE: Huh?

BILLY: Rain clouds.

ROSE: *Radio* said it was gonna be dry *aaall* day.

BILLY *(crushed)*: Oh.

ROSE: Whatsa time now?

BILLY: Twenny to. *(Rose rises and yawns, shuffles along platform to lower right.)* Hey. *(pause)* Hey—Rose! *(At the signal tower, she turns.)* You said *I* could, you know...

ROSE: What?

BILLY *(already defeated)*: Change the signal.

ROSE *(incredulous)*: *You?*

BILLY: You said... *(She laughs, harshly.)*... if I told yuh about—Dave...

ROSE: Billy, I was pullin' yer leg!

BILLY: Oh.

ROSE: I can't let *you* put the signal up.

BILLY: No.

ROSE: What if the inspector found out?

BILLY: Yeah.

ROSE: It's against the *rules*.

BILLY: Okay.

ROSE *(condescending to sympathy)*: Merv could get intuh trouble.

BILLY: I said okay!

ROSE: Anyways, yer so fulla doughnuts—you'd prob'ly *fall off the box*! *(Her laughter continues as she reaches the lever from the box. He diverts his attention to a piece of dirt on the mail bag in his wagon, then moves to the other end of the platform to sulk.)* Well—just about all set! *(silence)* So who needs *Merv*, eh? We kin do it all *ourselves*, can't we? *(silence)* Aw, I s'pose Merv ain't so bad. Eh, Billy? *(silence)* A bit rangy-tang, yuh know, but what-the-hell. Need soma that once in awhile, don't we? Merv got paid yestiday and yuh know what? Took me intuh Meaduhlark last night tuh celebrate! Me an' him! *(laughs)* Boy—did we git *hammered*! *(Her laughter runs down in the silence. Billy mumbles something.)* Whujuh say?

BILLY: I said, *big deal*.

ROSE: Hey, what's eatin' *you*?

BILLY: Nuthin'.

ROSE: Boy! Yer thuh *touchiest* guy I ever met!

BILLY: Ferget it.

ROSE: Person can't say *nuthin'* to you, 'thout yuh goin' all—pukey!

BILLY *(very low)*:   Yuh promised.

ROSE *(a major concession)*:   Okay! I shouldena promised! *(pause)* There! Feel better now?

BILLY *(mumbles):* A little.

ROSE: How'zat, Billy?

BILLY: *A little! (a long silence)*

ROSE *(cheerily):* So! Not much mail this week, eh?

BILLY: Not much.

ROSE *(trying hard):* Still—it's a lotta responsibility, izzen it?

BILLY: Well—yeah. I giss.

ROSE: I woulden mind bein' a postmaster.

BILLY: There's a lotta—scope, yuh know.

ROSE: Sure! Wimmen ever get tuh be postmasters?

BILLY *(thinks a minute):* I dunno.

ROSE: Hmph. Think Minnesota's playin' today, too.

BILLY: Can't see any reason why not, though.

ROSE: 'Gainst thuh Pirates, I think.

BILLY: I mean it izzen like it's *heavy* work, is it?

ROSE: Havin' a real good season, Minnesota.

BILLY *(pause):* Giss you useta *play* baseball, eh?

ROSE: Naw. My dad woulden let me.

BILLY *(eagerly):* Bet yuh bin tuh lotsa games, though. *(pause)* Eh?

ROSE: A few.

BILLY: Back in Eston?

ROSE: Better load thuh wagon. *(She goes to the platform wagon, and tries to pull it toward the cream cans.)*

BILLY: I'll give yuh a hand, if yuh like.

She does not reply, but he goes anyway, and pushes the wagon across the stage while she steers it with the tongue.

ROSE: Merv'll never make it now.

BILLY *(cheerfully)*:   Aw, he never does.

ROSE: Lissen, if yer gonna get *snotty*...

BILLY: Oh no!

ROSE: ... then I'll do it myself!

BILLY: It's—*okay*!

The wagon is quite heavy, and Billy is trying to align it in front of the cans. Rose is hindering, if anything. Billy is breathing hard with the effort.

There!

ROSE: Now thuh cans.

BILLY: Justa—minute.

ROSE: Huh?

BILLY: Get—my—breath.

ROSE: *I'll* do it.

BILLY: No! I—can. *(He wrestles the heavy cans onto the wagon. Each seems to get heavier, and he barely survives the last one. Again Rose gets in his way.) There! (Collapses onto the bench.)*

ROSE *(applauding):*   Yuh did it!

BILLY: Yeah!

ROSE: You sure got good muscles, Billy!

BILLY *(grinning weakly):*   Yeah.

ROSE: Comes from eatin' good, eh?

BILLY: Exercise—too.

ROSE: Yeah?

BILLY: Get the mail—every week—down here.

ROSE: Yeah—exercise. That's what Merv needs.

BILLY: Hey! I bet Merv—couldena lifted them cans that good!

ROSE *(hesitates):*   Oh—I—bet he coulden either! *(Laughs self-consciously.)* The old drunk!

BILLY: Yeah—he'd be too *drunk*! *(He laughs, too long.)*

ROSE *(offended):*   Pirates got a good team, too.

BILLY: Oh?

ROSE: Got a new—knuckleballer.

BILLY *(feigning interest):*   'Zatso?

ROSE: What thuh radio says. Could win 'em a lotta games.

BILLY *(pause):*   *Dave* useta play baseball, yuh know. *(A very long silence.)* Know thuh hottest tempature ever recorded in Wheat City? Rose?

ROSE: Nope.

BILLY: Try.

ROSE: Hunnert above.

BILLY: Nooo!

ROSE: Give up.

BILLY *(playfully)*:   Try, Rose!

ROSE: Two hunnert above?

BILLY *(triumphantly)*:   A hunnert and *six*! *In the shade!*

ROSE: Yuh don't say.

BILLY: August thuh second, nineteen fifty-three.

ROSE *(she's got him)*:   Thought you said *today* was thuh hottest!

BILLY *(thinks for a bit)*:   No—no—that was differnt.

ROSE: Well, yuh sure got a head fer figgers.

BILLY: Giss that's why they gave me the job.

ROSE: Postmaster?

BILLY: Weatherman!

ROSE: *Weatherman!* Whudder you *talkin'* about? Since when are *you* the weatherman?

BILLY: Since Alex Garvey left. Nineteen sixty-four.

ROSE *(with a sarcastic snort)*:   Alex Garvey!

BILLY *(imperturbable)*:   March thuh ninth. Just

packed up his family one day and moved tuh Moose Jaw. Didden even *try* to sell his lumber-yard. Took what he could load on his truck and left the rest tuh rot.

ROSE *(not biting)*: So? Where is it?

BILLY: Oh, nuthin' left now. *(pause)* Didden have nuthin' *then* hardly. *(Points off, down centre.)* Useta be just over there. Across from the Wheat Pool elevator. *(Pause as he gazes.)* Just empty space now.

ROSE: Whole town's empty space now!

BILLY *(still looking)*: Yeah.

ROSE: Merv says it's finished.

BILLY: Oh, I dunno.

ROSE: What Merv says.

BILLY: Alex Garvey, he ran the guvviment meteor station, and when he left, they asked me tuh do it.

ROSE: Wasn't nobody else, eh?

BILLY: They needed somebody with a head fer figgers!

ROSE: Oh yeah?

BILLY: Mom always said: "Dave got the looks and Billy got the brains."

ROSE: Dave ain't so good-lookin'.

BILLY: Oh, maybe not *now*...

ROSE: How come he never got married then?

BILLY *(thinking hard)*:   Well, he's waitin' fer the right... *(Rose laughs. Billy, defiantly)* Dave coulda married lotsa girls around here!

ROSE: You know what they say about you and him?

BILLY: Who says?

ROSE: All thuh farmers. Guys in thuh beer parlour at Meaduhlark! *(Moving closer.)* You know what they say?

BILLY: No.

ROSE: Yuh want me to tell yuh?

BILLY *(frantically)*:   I gotta keep thuh meteor records, yuh see. Guvviment want it fer their weather maps and stuff. So I take thuh tempatures and hemmedity and stuff, and send it back to them once a week. *(Points to mail sack.)* Got it all right there! I'll let yuh look at thuh insterments some time. Got 'em out in a little white box behind the old chicken house!

ROSE: Yuh want me to tell yuh?

BILLY: There's nuthin' tuh tell!

ROSE *(shrugs)*:   Okay.

Baby begins whimpering, off. It gets louder through the scene.

BILLY: That's *Meaduhlark* guys for yuh! People *here* never useta gossip.

ROSE *(pause)*:   Wish they still had that beer parlour.

BILLY: Well, they don't.

ROSE: Could just cross that street there and order up a coupla cool ones. Woulden need Merv and his old truck then!

BILLY: How about thuh kids?

ROSE: Aw, they kin look after theirselves.

BILLY: I s'pose.

ROSE: Mind you—thuh baby's a problem. Hadda leave her in thuh truck last night. On thuh seat.

BILLY: Gee.

ROSE: Oh, I kept goin' out tuh check on her!

BILLY: Um.

ROSE *(testily)*: She was asleep, yuh see—so it was okay.

BILLY *(dubious)*: Yeah but still—it's not...

ROSE: *Not what?*

BILLY *(pause; he looks around)*: Not too hot yet today.

ROSE: Be different if there was a baby-sitter around.

BILLY: Yeah.

ROSE: Trouble with this place.

BILLY: Hmmm?

ROSE: No baby-sitters!

BILLY: No.

ROSE *(thoughtful pause)*:   What do you do—after supper, Billy?

BILLY *(quickly)*:   I gotta look after thuh phone exchange!

ROSE: Whaddaya mean, *phone exchange?*

BILLY: Thuh telephone! I gotta be around tuh answer it. In case there's an important call, yuh see. It's wunna thuh rules! That's why I never leave home at night!

ROSE: Are you nuts? Nobody ever calls here!

BILLY: I *always* gotta be there! That's why they made me operator.

ROSE: *There izzen any god-damn telephones left!*

BILLY: Sometimes the superintendent phones from Moose Jaw just tuh make sure thuh line's clear! *(Baby is now crying hard.)*

ROSE: Billy, it'd only be for a few hours.

BILLY: Lissen!

ROSE *(listens a minute)*:   Aw, she'll quit in a minnit. Jus' wants attention. Brenda'll look after her. *(Billy listens to the crying, concerned. Rose, shouting)* Bren-n-n-n-*da!* Look after that kid! *(Crying continues. Billy goes down right, gazing off thoughtfully.)* Awright! I'm coming! *(She stomps into the station; Billy does not move. Rose off)* Brenda! *(pause)* Okay, sweety-sugar, don't cry. There, there now. Mommy's gonna get yuh a nice bottla milk. *(pause) Wheresa god-damn milk? Brenda!*

CHILD'S VOICE: *What?*

ROSE *(off)*: Wheresa milk?

CHILD'S VOICE: *In the fridge!*

ROSE: *Didden yuh hear thuh goddamn baby bawlin'? (pause)* Okay, sweetie-pie, there's a nice bottla warm milk. *(crying stops)* Drink it *aaall* up now. Whoopsy-daisy! Gotta hold onto it! *(Rose re-enters.)* Can't trust 'em fer ten minnits. *(pause)* Just like Merv. Where were we?

BILLY *(very faint)*: Baby-sitters.

ROSE: Oh, yeah.

BILLY: I hafta—keep Dave company, too.

ROSE: Tuh hell! He izzen here any more'n *Merv* is! *(long pause)*

BILLY: Train be in, ten minutes.

ROSE: So what?

BILLY: So what? Well, it's your. . .

ROSE: No, it ain't!

BILLY: . . . job. What?

ROSE: It's *Merv's* job! And you know where *he* is! Off enjoyin' hisself in thuh beer parlour. And I'm stuck here in this—*ghost town* with a ganga bawlin' kids and a. . . a. . .

BILLY *(helpfully)*: Weatherman.

ROSE: *A fatso! (He retreats right again. She goes after him.)* Yuh know what I'd do fer two cents? For *one* cent? I'd just let that train go runnin' on through! Without even stoppin'!

BILLY *(horrified)*:   Yuh couldn't!

ROSE: Then we'd see what happens tuh *Mister Merv*. If it wasn't fer *me*, that sunnuvabitch woulden even *have* a job! Who does all the work? Liftin' them heavy cream cans?

BILLY: Well, uh. . .

ROSE: *Me!* Right?

BILLY: Yeah—I guess. . .

ROSE: Yuh wanna know *why*?

BILLY: Ummmm.

ROSE: 'Cause if I *didn't*, we woulden even have *this* dump tuh live in. *A train station!*

BILLY: Gee.

ROSE: Wanna know somethin' else? They don't even *need* an agent here. They transferred Merv here 'cause it was easier than *firing* him. They felt *sorry*—for me and the kids.

BILLY: Awwww. . .

ROSE *(almost in tears)*:   Which is more'n I kin say for *some* people!

She slumps onto the bench with an outburst of tears. Billy goes awkwardly to her. After a moment of agony, he reaches out his hand and lays it on her shoulder. She reaches up and clasps it. He almost withdraws it, hesitates, and stays.

BILLY: You'll be—awright—Rose.

ROSE: Oh Billy, I—can't. . .

BILLY: Would yuh like something?

ROSE: I don't s'pose yuh gotta—drink?

BILLY: Gee, I—don't uh—think so . . .

ROSE: Nuthin'?

BILLY: Well, uh—water? *(Rose snatches her hand away.)*

ROSE: Aw—siddown! *(Billy sits, uncomfortably.)* Whaddaya *do* for kicks, anyway?

BILLY: I—dunno.

ROSE: What a dumb-head! *(pause)* Yuh wanta know something? *(silence)* I'll only tell ya if yuh *wanta* hear it!

BILLY: Yeah—okay . . .

ROSE: I nearly—didden marry Merv!

BILLY *(beyond his depth, very uncomfortable)*: Yuh don't say?

ROSE: Wasn't shotgun, neither. *We* didden have tuh get married, like a lotta people I could name but won't mention.

BILLY: That's—nice.

ROSE: Know who I coulda married?

BILLY *(thinks)*:   No-o-o.

ROSE: Archie Willmott!

BILLY *(pause)*:   Who?

ROSE: Archie Willmott. Useta pitch fer thuh Moose Jaw Millers!

BILLY *(never heard of him)*:   Oh yeah!

ROSE: Coulda had him easy as pie.

BILLY: Yeah, well—that's the way things. . .

ROSE *(dreamily)*:   Had real clean, white teeth. Dark hair. Had sort of a—brush-cut. *(pause)* He was a southpaw.

BILLY: Hmmm.

ROSE: And yuh know what else? *(silence)* I let him—you know—in thuh back seat of his car. *(in a reverie again)* We were parked behind thuh hamburger booth at Sandy Lake, in some chokecherry bushes. Moonlight just *streamin'* down. *(long pause)*

BILLY: Hymie Cantor was a south paw.

ROSE *(snaps out of it)*:   And ole Merv. He didden even get a *sniff* till we was married!

BILLY: That's—nice.

ROSE: Not even a *feel*!

BILLY *(pause)*:   How come yuh didden marry Archie Willmott?

ROSE: Ah—one thing an' another. Giss I didden feel like it at thuh time.

BILLY: Uh-huh.

ROSE *(pause)*:   He was only in town fer one night.

BILLY: Oh.

ROSE: They lost. Four tuh three.

BILLY: Were you there?

ROSE: No—no—he told me.

BILLY: Aw well. Least it was close! *(Pause. Billy checks his watch.)*

ROSE: Who the hell is Hymie Cantor?

BILLY: Hymie Cantor? I told yuh about him! Ran thuh General Store. *And* thuh Cockshutt agency.

ROSE: Oh yeah.

BILLY: Jew. Useta have thuh Post Office there, till he sold out and moved tuh Winnipeg. That's when they asked me tuh be thuh postmaster.

ROSE: Boy, yer just about *everythin'*, arncha?

BILLY: Somebody's gotta look after things.

ROSE: Aaaah!

BILLY: If I wasn't here, there woulden be *nuthin'* in Wheat City.

ROSE: Yeah? How about thuh *railway?*

BILLY: Oh yeah—forgot about that.

ROSE: Smart-ass! How 'bout thuh Wheat Pool elevator?

BILLY: Yeah, but thuh elevator agent lives in Meaduhlark, don't he?

ROSE *(pointing down left)*: Well, thuh *elevator's* here, ain't it?

BILLY *(looking up)*: Yeah.

ROSE: Wish it was a beer parlour.

BILLY: Hymie useta sell liquor in his g'radge.

ROSE *(interested)*:   Really?

BILLY: All thuh farmers would stop there an' have a drink when they came intuh town. Him and Alex Garvey. Almost like a bar or somethin'!

ROSE: You ever go there?

BILLY: Me? No!

ROSE: Well, it ain't here now.

BILLY: Dave useta go sometimes.

ROSE: Ain't *nuthin'* here now.

BILLY: When I was a kid—I useta hang around outside Hymie Cantor's g'radge. Sometimes guys comin' out would gimme a nickel fer a chocklit bar.

ROSE: The Candy Kid! Ha!

BILLY *(ruefully)*:   Useta be a lotta fun in them days. 'Specially on mail nights. Train came three times a week then! Town was *fulla* people.

ROSE: Tuh hell.

BILLY: They'd all stand around on thuh board-walks, shootin' thuh breeze, yuh know, talkin' about the crops and so on. They'd walk up and down thuh street, sayin' "How yuh doin'?" to everybody else. All us kids would go over to thuh community hall and play Auntie-Auntie-Aye-Over!

ROSE: Yeah.

BILLY: And in the summer, it'ud stay light a good long time, and there'd be a baseball game!

ROSE: Huh.

BILLY: Oh, you'da *liked* it, Rose!

ROSE: Maybe.

BILLY: Then, one night, thuh Mounties came from Moose Jaw and pinched Hymie fer bootleggin'. *(pause)* That's when he moved tuh Winnipeg.

ROSE: Rotten bastards! *(long pause)* Hey, Billy.

BILLY: Yeah?

ROSE: How long since you started comin' down here?

BILLY: For thuh mail?

ROSE: I mean early. Tuh—you know, talk.

BILLY *(apprehensive)*: Oh...

ROSE: Coupla months, right?

BILLY: Yeah—I guess so.

ROSE: Woulden yuh say we was—friends?

BILLY *(warily)*: Yeah...

ROSE: Then yuh gotta tell me a secret.

BILLY *(startled)*: *Eh?*

ROSE: I told yuh wunna my secrets. Now you gotta tell me wunna yours.

BILLY: How come?

ROSE: That's what friends do. If one guy tells a secret, then the other does.

BILLY: I just told yuh one!

ROSE: Huh?

BILLY: About Hymie Cantor's g'radge!

ROSE: No, *no!* A really *personal* secret—about *yourself*. Like the one I told you.

BILLY: Oh.

ROSE: 'Cause we're friends, see?

BILLY: Giss you're right.

ROSE: Well?

BILLY *(pause)*:   Don't think I got any.

ROSE: How 'bout—you and Dave?

BILLY: Me and Dave?

ROSE: Yeah.

BILLY: Thought yuh just wanted one about me.

ROSE: Hell, *I* don't care.

BILLY: Umm—let's see...

ROSE: A real *juicy* one.

BILLY: One time. Dave and me...

ROSE: Yeah?

BILLY: We was only kids, yuh see! We snuck in-tuh Alex Garvey's old Dodge truck and—drove it all the way up the c'rection line and back! And he never even noticed it was missing!

ROSE *(pause)*:   *Look*—Billy. Didden yuh ever— you know, *do* it with somebody?

BILLY *(faintly)*:   Do it?

ROSE: *Yeah! Do it!*

BILLY *(turns away, alarmed)*: Oh, I coulden— talk about. . .

ROSE: It's okay, Billy *(seductively):* You kin tell *me.*

BILLY: You might tell.

ROSE: It's a *secret* izzen it?

BILLY: Yeah—but. . .

ROSE: Anyways, who could I tell? Izzen nobody *left* tuh tell.

Billy sits down, facing away from Rose. It takes him a while to begin.

BILLY: One time. . .

ROSE: Can't hear yuh!

BILLY: One time! I went. Tuh Moose Jaw. With Dave. Was after I finished school. After Mom died. Dougal McLeod give us a ride intuh Moose Jaw. Dave was gonna find me a job, yuh see. There wuzzen any jobs here! Even in Meaduhlark! Hymie still had the post office, and Alex Garvey was still here, and Melody Winters was thuh telephone operator —so there was nuthin' fer me tuh do. I hadda work, yuh see?

ROSE *(helpfully)*: Needed money.

BILLY *(turning to her)*: Yeah! I coulden live off Dave, *could I?* He had a job on thuh section gang, but I coulden expect him tuh keep *both* of us alive, could I? So we looked around Moose Jaw all day fer somethin' I could do, and then we went intuh a beer parlour and had a few beers.

ROSE: *You?*

BILLY: Only a few. Dave *said* we was s'poseta! Thing was I coulden find a job nowhere. 'Cause I coulden *do* nuthin', yuh know? Anyways, I was feelin' kinda...

ROSE *(sympathetically)*:   Blue?

BILLY: Yeah, blue. Dave was, too.

ROSE: I know the feelin', boy.

BILLY: Anyways, Dave got chewin' the rag with this guy in there, and when the beer parlour was gonna close, the guy said for us to come along to this party.

ROSE: And you went.

BILLY: Well—it wouldena bin polite *not* to. Dave he was feelin' perty good. *(Pause. A tiny grin.)* And I giss I was feelin' perty good, too. So we went along the street tuh this guy's hotel, and... *(a sudden thought)* Maybe it *wasn't* his hotel.

ROSE: Go *on!*

BILLY: Well—this guy, Perry was his name, had some more beer in his room. There was—some other people came—and this girl.

ROSE: *Girl?*

BILLY: Well—lady. She was a real byootiful lady. *(pause)* After a while, Dave tried to get her tuh go in the other room, and Perry did too.

ROSE: Ooooo!

BILLY: Perry took this beer bottle and *broke* it

on the radiator! So Dave woulden fight, 'cause he didden wanta get, y'know, all cut up. They just stood there, cursin' each other out!

ROSE: What were *you* doing?

BILLY *(surprised)*: Oh, I was sittin' beside the window, watchin' this neon sign outside. Said "Star Hotel." Kinda shone intuh thuh room, all red-like. Kept goin' on and off. *(pause)* On and off.

ROSE: Well, what *happened*?

BILLY: I wanted Dave and me tuh go home, yuh see.

ROSE: About thuh *girl!*

BILLY: Oh, she—woulden *go* in the other room with Perry after that, even when he kinda won thuh fight. She asked who I was, sittin' by thuh window, lookin' like a dummy, and Perry laughed and said, that's Dave's little brother Billy, and she came over and—and said— *'Hello, little brother.'*

ROSE: I be, go-to-*hell!*

BILLY: Everybody laughed, 'cause I was—yuh know, *fat*, even then. She made them all stop laughin' and—asked me if I wanted tuh—go in the other room with her. *(pause)*

ROSE: *Go on*, fer Crissakes!

BILLY: I—I—didden wanna go, but Dave—made me! *(pause)*

ROSE: And didja—do it? *(Long pause. Billy's head sinks to his chest. He shakes it slowly from side to side. Rose, incredulous) Ya didden? (His head is still shaking.) Then what's the god-damn secret?*

BILLY *(directly to her, apologetically):* I—dunno, Rose.

The horn of a diesel train sounds in the distance, introducing the shuffle of a train, faint at first but growing in volume right to the end of this scene.

ROSE: Jeeze, I dunno about you, Billy. Tuh get that close and yuh don't even. . . *(She laughs sharply.)* It's just *like* you though, ain't it?

BILLY: Yeah, I guess so. *(Pause. He listens, checks his watch.)* Train's comin'.

ROSE: Betcha that was the only chance you ever had, eh?

BILLY *(standing up):* Yeah.

ROSE: Well—*(shrugs)*—Merv'll get a bang out of it, anyways.

BILLY *(horrified):* What?

ROSE: Merv. I said, *he'll* get a good old laugh.

She goes to the wagon. Billy is struck dumb, rooted to the spot.

ROSE *(not noticing):* Gimme a hand with thuh wagon, will yuh? *(She turns and looks at him. Tears are welling from his eyes.)* What thuh hell's eatin' you? *(Billy tries to speak, but can't. He gestures in despair.)* Come on! Thuh train's nearly here!

BILLY: You—you—*you said!*

ROSE: Huh?

BILLY: *It was a secret! You can't tell secrets!*

ROSE: Aw, don't be so dumb. What's thuh point of a secret if yuh don't *tell* somebody? You told *me* didden yuh?

BILLY: Rose—please. . .

ROSE: Anyways, Merv ain't gonna spread it around.

BILLY: Maybe I kin—get yuh somethin'. . .

ROSE: Don't need nuthin'.

BILLY: *Nuthin'?*

ROSE: 'Cept a baby-sitter once in a while.

BILLY *(stunned)*: Baby-sitter?

ROSE: Once in a while.

BILLY: You did that— on *purpose!*

ROSE: Did what?

BILLY *(blurting)*: I'll tell *your* secret!

ROSE *(amused)*: Which one is that?

BILLY: About Archie Willmott!

Rose laughs aggressively. The diesel has become very loud.

ROSE: You dumb-head! *I made all that up! (Billy retreats to his wagon.) So you go right ahead and tell—little brother!*

She laughs again. Billy begins pulling his wagon to the edge of the platform to meet the train. The stage goes black as the "diesel" roars in, drowning out

Rose's laughter. A strobe light will indicate cars flashing by. There is the sound of brakes. For a minute, the sound of the engine idling. Then it starts up again, and "leaves" the station. The lights go up. Rose is slinging the empty cream cans—five of them—back against the station wall from the wagon. Billy stands beside his wagon, gazing at the fresh mail sack in it.

ROSE: See what I mean? I get left tuh do all the work myself! As if I didden have enough just lookin' after them kids! *(Billy slowly begins edging toward the ramp up right, pulling his wagon behind.)* Can't rely on Merv, that's fer sur. Sittin' over in Meaduhlark, swillin' it down. What kina father is that, eh? Eh, Billy? *(pause)* Well, he izzen gonna get away with it! 'Cause I ain't puttin' up with any more! I mean it, it's too much tuh expect! Izzen it? *(Pause. She watches him go toward the exit.)* Tell yuh what, Billy! Hey! *(Billy stops, does not turn.)* Tell yuh what. You come over after supper, and we'll lissen to thuh ball game on thuh radio. *(pause)* Minnesota and thuh Pirates! *(Billy begins moving again.)* Don't think I kin git it, eh? Well, I can! K. W.B.X.! Butte, Montana! *(pause)* Maybe Merv'll bring some beer home from Meaduhlark, and we won't go out tonight! You don't *hafta* have none, though! *(pause)* Wait! *(She runs after him.)* Wait, Billy. Okay! I won't tell him! *(pause)* After all—it's a secret, izzen it? *(He stops at the point of exit.)* It's just—well, yuh shouldena *told* me! Stuff like that yuh shoulden tell *nobody.* Yuh know what I mean? It's too—tempting. *(Billy nods.)* I'll—see yuh next week—eh Billy? When yuh come down for thuh mail? *(He finally turns to face her.)* And—maybe some time—I kin come and see yer—meteor station. Whaddaya think? *(He smiles, rather sadly.)* Maybe we kin—set a record or somethin', eh? Ha, ha! *(pause)* Will yuh—will yuh—come early next week? So's we kin—talk? Eh? I'll letcha put thuh signal up! *(Billy turns and exits, still smiling, pulling his wagon. Diesel horn in the distance.)* Tell yuh what, Billy! *(Calling after him.)* I'll git thuh place all cleaned up and we kin have coffee or somethin'! Whaddaya thinka that? *(pause)* Gotta stick together, *don't* we? Right, Billy? We're thuh last people in Wheat City! Okay—Billy?

She stands looking off to the right in both hope and despair, as the stage goes to black.

A TIME TO SOW

All that week in April, I watched Bucky for some kinda sign that he remembered. I knew he was gonna disappoint me, just like he always did for the important things, and sure enough, he never even let on, even though I went so far as to draw a circle around April 19 with a brown crayon the day before, and sat in the kitchen with a mug a coffee in my hand while he looked right at the calendar and never even noticed it.

Every day since the first of April he'd gone through his whole routine, the one he went through every spring, looking out the kitchen window and watching the sun come up over the sand hills to the east, checking the time against his C.P.R. pocket watch and the calendar. Seeding-time was the only season he even looked at the Wheat Pool calendar up beside the fridge, and I'll never figger out how he always knew when one of the kids was having a birthday, but he never disappointed any of them yet, even if it meant tearing off to town in the old Fargo to pick up some comic books at the last minute for Jody's birthday. For Wendy's Grade

Eight graduation, he got a nice camera at the Pay'N 'Save and kept it as a surprise till after the ceremony. It was a neat thing Bucky had about dates, and that was why I was still hoping, even though my brain knew better, that he would remember the nineteenth of April.

He never even mentioned it once. That didn't mean anything, of course; the problem was there are so *many* dates to remember. We got three birthdays in the month of December alone, just when everybody's thinking about their Christmas shopping. That's Jole and Randy and Darlene, and sometimes they get short-changed on the presents because you start thinking, well, those three are gonna get two this month and the others'll feel put out, so you end up getting them one big one and one little one, or sometimes combining them into the same one. Then Carol-Ann was in February, Dale in March, nobody at all in April thank God, Little Buckman in May, Wendy in July, and Gloria in August. No, Gloria is July, and Wendy is August, then poor Andy on November the third when everybody else had lots of left-over Hallowe'en goodies, and gave him all their black-and-orange candy kisses that otherwise would only lay around for weeks getting stale. And then came frantic December, when I always ended up dithering over all the Christmas things that had to be organized, and three birthdays on top of it. But Bucky always remembered everybody, and would find them neat presents, like the time he got the dog for Randy.

When the nineteenth came, a Tuesday this year, he went through the usual routine in the morning and then sat down for his oatmeal porridge. It was hard to tell; nothing ever made a dint in those pale blue eyes of his. He must've waited there for a good three or four minutes, with no noise in the whole house except for the electric clock humming away, before he finally looked up and said, "Where's alla kids?"

"Didden think you'd notice," I said. "They all went over tuh Burtons' while you were feedin' the cattle."

"What the hell for?"

"They're gonna watch TV there while they're waitin' fer the school bus."

"What's wrong with our TV?"

"I sent them over there and I don't wanta talk about that for a minute. I wanta talk about today."

"Today? What about today?"

"You know what I mean. What day is today?"

He made a big show of concentrating and squeezing his forehead. "Tuesday."

"Yeah, Tuesday, Mr. Einstein. Tuesday, the nineteenth of April."

His eyes didn't flicker an inch. "Yuh don't say."

"Now we gotta talk about this, Bucky. It won't do no good to start butterin' yer bread, neither, I'm not puttin' out no breakfast till we get this sorted out once and fer all."

"What sorted out?"

He made me so mad, I grabbed the bowl he was turning round and round in his hands, and just skimmed it straight at the wall, where it broke into a million pieces. "The wedding sorted out!" I yelled. "This is our engagement anniversary!"

"Yeah, guess it usually comes right after the first big thaw."

"And you said we could go ahead and *have* it this year!"

"There was conditions, though," he said.

"Conditions to hell! You promised me! You agreed last year we put it off long enough. You said I could go ahead and plan it—if—"

"*If*," he said, as though that meant something, and hitched up his belt as though he was getting ready to go out to work, which both him and me knew he would never do until he got a bellyful of breakfast inside of him.

"*If*," I said, "you weren't stuck in the middle of seedin' when the date come! That was the only condition."

"Well, I'm just about ready to go now."

"That's what you said last year. And the year before!"

He just shrugged and sat down again, looking at the stove for his porridge.

"And you're not gonna snaggle your way out of it that easy. The kids heard what you said last year, and they're all planning for it. They awready told their friends and everything."

"Well, they shoulden've."

"They're gettin' older, Bucky! They got a right to expect *some* kind of decency. You wanta ruin their chances for a happy life of their own?"

He looked at me finally, right into my eyes, and for a minute I could see the way he looked at me that night at the Genesis Sports Day, the first time we done it. I *saw* his eyes that night. There was a big light just behind the baseball field and I could see them shining with something like hope, and something like real true love, and even a touch of downright scaredyness that went right through you, but ever since then we always did it in the dark, and I never saw the look again till just that minute in the kitchen.

"I can't," was all he said, then he stood up and went to the kitchen window, pushing the curtains to one side. The sun was already up, but it was cloudy and still dark, so maybe out of habit he took out his watch and started waiting for the sun, as if there might be a way around it that way.

"We gotta do it, Bucky. It's now or never."

"I don't wanta hurt yer feelin's, Vesta, but I'm just about ready to start diskin', and I can't take no time out for all this foolishness. I s'pose Wagner's bin stickin' his long beak in again."

"Mr. Wagner's got nothin' to do with it. And we got plenty a time to get everythin' done before the first of May."

"May!"

"You're never gonna get out onto that summerfallow before the first of May."

"Might do," he said, going through the whole routine again of the window, the watch, the calendar, and back to the window.

That did it then. I just up and lost my temper, went over and grabbed him by the front of the overalls and pulled him back to the table. "You siddown," I yelled. "We're gonna have a heart-to-heart talk like normal people do. Just you and me."

I waited for him to say something, but he never moved, so I took a deep breath and gave it to him good: "You might as well know it now as later on. We're gonna have another one."

That got him. "Oh no," he said.

"Oh yes. Another one. In August, looks like. And I don't mind tellin' you it's gettin' tough to explain it to all the women in the hospital. When Little Buckman was born, I swore I was never gonna do it again. You should see 'em, sittin' there just as smug as fence-posts, enough to drive you up the wall. Who can relax with all them starin' at you? Some rest!''

"Who said it was supposed to be a vacation?"

"Don't try to change the subject! I'm tellin' you I done it for the last time! And tryna tell them nurses that I like it this way! I gotta have some re-speck, you know!" Then I broke down bawling, right in front of him.

"I know, I know," he kept saying, and I let him get feeling good and sorry, which he does when I start crying, which isn't very often, 'cause it only works if you do it once in a real long while. Last time was when I wanted to get all the other kids baptized, and Bucky wouldn't let me because of this thing he has about churches. The only thing that upsets him worse than churches is somebody bawling. Finally he said, "Well, as long as it don't inter-fere with gettin' my crop into the ground..."

"We kin do it?"

"Yeah, if the fields don't dry up in the mean-time, 'cause if they do, there won't be any damn weddin', nurses or no nurses!"

"This is the wettest spring we had in ten years," I told him. "It'll be the tenth of May before you git started sowin'."

"We'll see. Anythin' kin happen in this country."

I made him shake hands before he could back out of it. "It's a deal, then? We'll have it on May the first. A Saturday."

He looked at me fer a minute. "You planned all this."

"The kids and me planned it," I said, going to

get his breakfast, which wasn't oatmeal porridge after all, but scrambled eggs with tomatoes and bacon, his favourite. "Course you'll hafta get a new suit."

"I'm not buyin' no damn new suit for a *weddin'*!"

"Don't worry, I got money put aside for the whole thing. We got everything planned."

Well, the kids nearly raised the roof when they got home from school, they were so happy. They never believed I'd talk Bucky into letting the wedding go ahead. Every time they bugged him about it before, he always found a way out. Wendy just about broke down and cried. "Is that right, Daddy? You really gonna go and get churched?"

That made him mad. "Don't you go and start talkin' like that, or it's all off! I want the proper respeck!"

"You really goin' ahead?" Dale said, his little eyes as big as saucers.

"Unless the weather clears up and dries them fields. In which case you'll be passing out the weddin' cake from the back of my tractor!"

Everybody took a hand in planning the big event. Even Little Buckman got caught up in it, holding paper while the other kids cut out the flowers and things for decorating the car. They had them spread out all over the living room floor, with streamers going out to the kitchen. Randy and Carol-Ann got started on the coloured wedding bells they were cutting out of Styrofoam, big ones to put on top of the old Plymouth. Wendy took Darlene and Gloria into the kitchen nearly every night to make cookies and sandwiches for the reception, which was scheduled for the Legion Hall in

town. I decided to look after the wedding cake my-
self, 'cause I always swore when I got married I
wouldn't have one of those store-bought cakes; they
always seem so dried-out and scarce with the nuts,
it's better to do it home-made. I never figured then
it would turn out the way it did.

Reverend Wagner was really swell, too. He'd
been trying for years to talk Bucky into this, and it
all came to nothing, so he was real happy to help
out. I didn't tell him I was expecting again, though.
It was hard enough on him the time we got the other
nine baptized. Even so, he really liked Bucky, and
thought it would be worth whatever snooty looks he
got from Mrs. Horsnall and the rest of them old tur-
keys.

We just kept getting busier and the days kept
getting longer. On the twenty-eighth, the sun broke
through early in the morning, and Bucky spent the
day on his machinery, getting it all greased for the
second time, tightening nuts and bolts, throwing oil
around like crazy. He was just dreaming, though,
'cause there were still big snow-drifts around the
farm in every gully and pot-hole. It was warm okay,
so it was melting fast, and there was water laying
everywhere.

On the Friday it was still sunny and he did some-
thing even sillier. Maybe we shouldn't't've been teas-
ing him so much; the kids got a big kick out of
humming the wedding march, dum dum da da, and
you can hardly blame them for that. But he
stomped out after breakfast and drove his tractor all
around the farmyard to see if the ground was get-
ting dry enough to start seeding. It held up in the
yard, so he drove out onto the summerfallow south
of the buildings, and not fifty feet past the cara-

ganas the right wheel of the Massey hit a soft spot and bogged down like she'd hit quicksand.

You'd've thought all hell had broke loose the way he carried on about that tractor. It wasn't enough he had to go and get stuck, but he had to make a big production out of getting it out of the mud-hole, when any fool could see the only common-sense thing to do was leave it there till the field dried up. But no, he had to go and get the big grain truck and a bunch of chains, and proceed to make a *real* mess. When the kids got home from school, he made the older boys go and help, till everybody was just covered with gumbo, and the truck ended up stuck, too.

Bucky always found it hard to admit when he was licked, and this wasn't no exception. He couldn't even admit the tractor was stuck, 'cause that would've meant that seeding wasn't ready to start, so he wouldn't call a tow-truck from town. On the other hand, if he was determined to get it out of there, he'd end up working all night in the mud, and still be no better off, because that field he was mudded down in was always the earliest field he could plant. I have to admit, I chuckled once or twice, thinking of him out there, swearing.

At supper time, he sent Dale and Randy in to the house to say he was going to be another hour or two, and to send out some sandwiches to keep him going till he was finished.

I cut some sandwiches from the roast of beef I was keeping in the oven and took them out myself. "Buckman, what do you think you're doing?"

He looked out from under the front end of the tractor, which was down to the axles in the mud-hole. "Nearly got her out now." He was so covered with muck, about all you could see of him was his little blue eyes peeking out.

"You're just bein' stubborn now. You better come in and get a good rest tonight 'cause we gotta be ready to go first thing in the morning."

"Ready to go where?"

"There's gonna be a rehearsal at the church in the morning. You gotta get cleaned up for that."

"You go and get ready, I'll be in in a little while. Nearly got her outta this little patch of mud."

"Here's yer sandwiches," I said, dropping the bag and the thermos of tea on the tool-box.

I let him stay out there getting good and cold while the kids and me iced the wedding cake. The older ones were decorating the car out in the garage, where they had their record player set up. They were all talking about what a good time they were gonna have at the wedding dance. Wendy was the brides-maid and she was just having the thrill of her life. She would probably be the first of our kids to get married, 'cause she was such a good-looking girl, with a real lovely laugh. I used to think sometimes how awful it'd be if she got married before I did, and I had to go to her wedding supper with no ring on my hand. That reminded me.

"Jole," I said, "run and get the box." He left off the icing he was doing on the bottom layer, and ran to the bedroom to get the blue velvet ring-box. I put a down payment on that ring at People's Credit Jewellers after Wendy was born. Lots of times, the kids would bug me to take it out of the drawer, and I'd let them look at it. The band was all white gold, with hearts engraved around the inside of it, and Bucky's and my initials sort of twined around them in a perpetual wreath. The man at People's designed it, and kept it for me till I got it paid off. The kids never got tired admiring it. They always tried to get me to slip it on my finger, but I wouldn't do that. Bucky was the only person who'd ever put that ring on my finger.

"How's he doin' out there, anyway?" I asked.

Carol-Ann went to the south window in the upstairs hallway and looked out to the field, where the truck headlights were shining on the tractor. "Still at it!"

"Well, let's git this cake done, anyway," I said, and sent Jole back with the box to put it in the dresser. When the kids came in from decorating the car around ten o'clock, we were just getting the top layer finished. Gloria had bought this little plastic bride-and-groom set they make for the tops of cakes, and we were having a bit of trouble getting them on level. That sort of operation was right up Bucky's alley, and I wished he was there to help, 'cause he had the straightest eye for balance I ever saw. But the kids went to bed finally after ten, except for Wendy and Darlene, who had to help me get the white shirts and dresses ironed and laid out on the dining-room table. That way everybody could come down in the morning and jump into their good clothes and go straight to the rehearsal, before Bucky found something else to get us all sidetracked.

After rehearsal, we were gonna have lunch at the Chinaman's restaurant in town. There was too many of us really for my sister Pearl to feed all at one go just before the wedding, even though I was tempted by her offer, if for no other reason than the Chinaman wouldn't hold four booths for us on a Saturday unless I gave him a deposit. There was some extra time after lunch for an hour or two, and I thought we could all maybe take a drive out to the regional park and see if the crocuses were up yet. Then Wendy and me and the little kids would take the car back to the church, while Bucky drove in later with the rest of the kids in the half-ton. They'd got it all decorated up, too.

Anyways, Bucky still wasn't in by midnight, when we finally finished the ironing. I dithered for a while, trying to decide whether to take out more sandwiches and coffee, or whether I should just go and tell him to stop being such a danged fool, or whether I should leave him out there, freezing himself in the mud. I decided to take coffee, but no food.

I couldn't find him at first because he wasn't under the tractor. The truck had the lights on and the motor running, though, so I walked around beside it and there he was, laying on a tarp near the toolbox, snoozing. Or I thought he was snoozing, till I got closer and saw the hose from the truck exhaust, and his little blue eyes staring into space with that same lost look they had at the Genesis Sports Day.

All the guests stayed for the funeral anyways; they made short work of the perogies and everything. We put the wedding cake in the freezer till Wendy gets married. Bucky woulda wanted that, I think. But I'll tell you something—we're not gonna have it at seeding time. It's the least I can do for him if we have it in a church.

COMING DOWN MORIAH

*And he said, Take now thy son, thine only
son Isaac, whom thou lovest, and get thee
into the land of Moriah;
and offer him there for a burnt offering
upon one of the mountains which I will tell
thee of.*

> Who loves me
> must love my sons
> like the hidden side
> of the horizon,
> the clear distant surface of
>   lake
> seen from the clutching
>   weeds.
>
> We are as whole
> as the firmament,
> moulded as a spruce forest,
> perfect as river pebbles
> rounded into spheres.
>
> Who divides us
> can split a flight
> of Mallards surging north,
> shall separate the sea.

IN THE CANCER CLINIC

In the cancer clinic figures walk
the tiles as silently as wraiths.
Even the toilets have been silenced
though the radio stays locked
on some loud official decibel.
Jingle Bell, Jingle Bell,
Jingle Bell Rock.

My lady of despair wears white
terrycloth armour.   It repels
eyes faster than lead shields
can bend an x-ray.
Smiling volunteers appear
at certain routine intervals
with styrofoam cups of tea.
Their calm murmers grate
the ear.   *Jingle Bell Croon,*
Jingle Bell Spoon, Jingle Bell,
Jingle Bell, Jingle Bell Tune.

Some inhuman instinct
craves the smell of blood
the white of naked bones.

GIVE ME YOUR ANSWER, DO

When Jasper arrived at Daisy's mother's house, nestled in its fringe of pink-and-green hollyhocks, there was a new bright red Mustang parked in the driveway. And no sign at all of Daisy's battered old Volkswagen with its mag wheels and yellow racing stripes. So he hesitated for a moment on the front step, unnerved by the implications of the Mustang. He stood there until he noticed the old man in the next yard staring at him, or more likely, at the large wicker basket he held in his left hand. He pressed the bell.

Mrs. Gelber came to the screen door, squinting into the harsh sunlight.

"Howdy," Jasper said, unsure—as always—how to address her. "Is Daisy in?"

"*Daisy*?" she said. "Daisy who?"

"I mean Doreen," he said, snatching the striped denim cap from his head so she could recognize him. There was the beard, too, but it was too late to do anything about that.

"Doreen's out in the garden." She opened the screen door and peered at him. "Is that *you*, Jasper?''

"Yeah." He grinned and put the cap back on top of his hair.

"So. You're back."

"Can I see her?"

"You wait here. I'll go get her." She stepped back from the door into the darkness, with a harsh glance that travelled down to the wicker basket, his cut-offs, the sandals, his large hairy toes. Then she disappeared down the hallway.

The old man in the next yard edged closer along the fence, pulling weeds from his beds of tiger lilies and pretending he wasn't listening. He wore a fine wide-brimmed straw Stetson hat, which bobbed among the green and brilliant orange flowers. Mr. Allpress, Jasper remembered, that was the name.

When Daisy suddenly appeared around the corner of the house and saw Jasper sitting on the step, she stopped abruptly, still grasping the side gate, her incredible green eyes stunned and accusing. She wore the red shorts, crisply pressed as always. Her legs were the same rich brown they had been the summer before, though now they were smeared with mud at the knees. She had been kneeling in the garden. Probably drawing pictures of tomatoes.

"Oh!" she said. "It's you."

Jasper stood up, his eyes suddenly gone unfocussed. He could not see the wicker basket in his hand, or Mr. Allpress leaning on the fence. He made out the mysterious Mustang in the driveway.

"What'd you do with the Berlin Bomber?" he said.

"The guts fell out of it in March." She laughed a short relieved laugh. "I got a thousand, though, on the trade-in."

"You mean you *bought* that thing?"

"I know. Perverted, isn't it?"

They had debated cars to the edge of boredom. He still could not look at her. Mr. Allpress finally coughed to break the silence.

"So," Daisy said. "You decided to come back after all."

"I brought your basket. And some smokes!" He swung the wicker basket into the air with the flourish he had practised all the way from the bus depot, and a blue carton of cigarettes fell into his left hand.

"Gauloises!" she sighed.

"Yeah."

"Well! How much were they?"

"No charge."

"You got them at the duty-free, didn't you? I won't take them if you don't let me pay for them."

"Fifteen dollars."

"*What*?"

"It's a *gift*, for Christ's sake!"

"Listen Jasper, I *remember* this conversation. Now how much do I owe you?"

"He said it was a present, didden he?" Mr. Allpress called from the fence. "Whynchuh just take 'em and be grateful?"

Daisy turned and shot a glare that actually seemed to strike the old man, making him stagger back from the fence and start bobbing up and down in the tiger lilies again. Without softening the deadly ray of her green eyes, she turned back to Jasper and said, "Come in and have a beer, or a lemonade."

"No thanks—I just brought your uh—"

"Shuttup. I'll give you a cup of oolong tea."

She led him through the front door into her mother's living room, unchanged from the year before. A den of china cats lurked on every table and shelf, captured in horrible postures of kitty-cat elegance. They appeared to guard the display of Daisy-photographs which went round the walls in chronological order, from the snapshot of bare-bottom Daisy on a cowhide rug to the cap-and-gown picture which posed in a frame atop the *Encyclopaedia Britannica*. He rushed through the hallway to the kitchen, where Mrs. Gelber was cutting rhubarb on a newspaper on the table.

"It's Jasper, Mom!"

"We met." She was slicing the stalks with sadistic vigour.

"But did you *recognize* him? Under that mop of hair?"

Mrs. Gelber looked up, her mouth held in a neat, tight grin. "I recognized him."

"Well. Is there any tea?"

"We're out. Used the last of it the other night, didn't you?"

"Oh. How about some lemonade, Jasper? Or Tang?"

"Okay—lemonade."

"No lemons either," Mrs. Gelber said.

He laughed, to make her think he didn't care. "Well, I'll have some Tang then."

"I *know* we have some of that. Listen Mom, if you're going to the store for tomatoes, anyway, why don't you pick up some tea?"

"Thought you said when that last lot went, you weren't going to drink it any more."

"We should keep some around."

"Anyways, I don't know when I'm gonna get to the store. I have to get this rhubarb done for supper."

"It's only two o'clock! Mom, I'd go for you, but I have to talk to Jasper for a few minutes."

"Talk!" Mrs. Gelber nearly slashed her hand with the knife. "He'll give you lots of talk, all right. I know his talk."

Daisy went to her mother and untied the apron at the back. "Why don't you pick up some cucumbers, too? I'll fix the salad tonight."

Mrs. Gelber grabbed her purse from the window-sill and stomped out into the hall. The screen door slammed; they could hear her footsteps snapping down the front walk.

"What's with her?"

"You make her nervous."

"*I* make *her* nervous?"

Daisy took the Tang down from the cupboard above the sink and measured it into two glasses. "When did you get back?"

"Got to Toronto on Friday. Came from there by bus."

"Had lots of time, did you?"

"Just sick of planes."

"Oh. Bad flight?"

"Not bad. Direct charter from Munich." As she stirred the drinks, her hips stirred too, like a dancer. "Funny thing happened."

"What was that?"

"Well, you mightn't think it was funny. Lady got stuck in the women's can."

"Where?"

"Right over the middle of the Atlantic!"

"This is one of your stories, Jasper."

"Whuddayuh mean, *stories*?"

"I won't believe any of it." She placed the glasses on the table. "So don't bother getting started."

"No—really! I was just sitting there reading my *Time* magazine when I noticed a great long line-up outside the toilets. Then a stewardess started banging on one of the toilet doors. Turned out it was this fat lady in the can."

"I hate stories about physical disabilities."

"She wasn't disabled—she was *fat*. Fat as a bear fulla chokecherries! She was sitting on the can—right?—and reached back to flush it. Well, they work on some kind of suction principle, and before she knew what was happening, she was sealed onto the toilet! Tight as a clam."

"I *knew* you were making this up!"

"That's not all! She—well, there was a big crowd gathered around the door of the toilet. You could hear her hollering her lungs out, and banging away on the inside. The crew finally had to rip the door off its hinges."

"My God, how embarrassing."

"Then they had to pry her off the seat!"

"What did she do?"

"Well, when she came out, she tried to ignore the whole thing. No way. Whole plane stood up and applauded her. She spent the rest of the flight in the galley with the crew."

"It's not right to laugh at fat people," Daisy said primly, before bursting out in a shriek of giggles. She tried to stifle them with her slim brown fingers.

"*Proost*," he said, saluting.

"Accidents always find you, don't they, Jasper?" She leaned across the table, cupping her hand under her chin, gazing at him. "I mean, you're always *there* when something horrible happens—like a catalyst."

"Jasper the Human Lightning Rod."

"About your letters," she said, almost in the same breath, as though they might even be talking about the same thing, not looking at him now. "It wasn't that I didn't want to answer—because I *did* —want to. I just didn't know what to say—I mean it was really heavy here, worse than you realized, just one heavy after another. You have to understand that."

"Sure."

"I did start to write once."

"Oh?"

"Yes—the time you sent the money—"

"I never sent any money."

"Okay, the *airline* ticket. But—I mean I couldn't just turn around, after going through all that crap when I got back—and everything really coming down on me—"

"I know," he said, taking a deep breath. Then another. "But how—are things now?"

"Things?"

"Generally." He waved his hand toward the front of the house: Mrs. Gelber's exit, Mr. Allpress pulling weeds, the red Mustang. "Everything."

"Well, I don't know. Getting better. I'm moving out next week."

"Where?"

She shook her head, and he noticed her knuckles whitening as she gripped the glass of Tang. "Stan and I are getting an apartment," she said. "Near the university. He's going back to classes.''

He almost said something violent, which he had vowed he would not do; instead he set his glass on the table and walked to the back door. Through the aluminum screen he saw tall green corn. Silk already. In July.

"Listen," Daisy said. "How much did it cost?"

He did not seem to hear.

"To mail my clothes and stuff, I mean. I'd like to pay you for that. It must have cost a fortune! Oh, and the pictures—I'd like to keep them.''

"Pictures?"

"The enlargements you sent. The ones we took in Vondel Park. Remember? The day you sold the Noorder Straat paintings! We went down there to celebrate with Harry and Charlotte and the kids—''

"How's your mother?" he said, not turning from the door.

"Oh—better now. They think they got it all in the second operation.''

"Not malignant?"

She looked out the kitchen window. The delphiniums and hollyhocks had grown so high they showed above the sill. "It might be. They're still testing.''

"Well—it's a good thing you came back, eh?"

"I *had* to, Jasper. There is no point even arguing about that. I had to." Daisy turned back from the flowers. "You didn't have to bring that basket, you know. It wasn't really mine. We bought it with the household money. That was your money.''

"Listen, I had a bitch of a time getting this onto the plane as hand-baggage. Don't make me walk out of here and throw it in some garbage can." He lifted the basket over to her side of the table.

"Yes," she said, picking it up and running her fingers across the diamond patterns in the rough brown wicker. "I guess I would like to keep it."

The moment had come for the phrases he had polished for nearly six months (and six thousand miles, too, all the questions and answers as well, flashing past in an instant), watching her fingers trace the patterns on the market basket (full of peppers and cheeses and round, linen-wrapped loaves of dark bread), the one thing he had known she would want.

"How is Harry, anyway?" she said. "And Charlotte and Sammy and the baby?"

"Fine."

"Good."

He sat down at the table again, pressing his hands flat. "If you're moving into this apartment with Stan—does that mean you're going to stay with him?"

Her eyes turned away, searching for an answer among the silly pink hollyhocks. "I guess so."

"I suppose there's a reason."

"Yes. There is a reason."

"What is it, if that's not too personal?"

"The reason is he needs me."

"That's not a reason."

"It's as good as you're going to get, Jasper."

"But you don't even *like* him! He'll drive you round the bend again. In six weeks! That's not an answer!"

Her direct unswerving eyes came at him again, dazzling like green lightning. "You're right. It isn't an answer. There are no answers."

He slammed his fist onto the table, jangling the spoons and glasses.

"All right," she said. "It's an answer because he's my husband. And because sometimes I do things that don't have a reason. As you know."

"Like marrying him in the first place."

"I suppose."

"Or running off to Holland to 'find yourself'."

"If you like."

"And concocting a tragedy about your mother's cancer—so you could run back again?"

"Yes!"

She suddenly seized the carton of Gauloises, ripped out a package and mauled it open, finally managing to light a cigarette, despite trembling hands. "It might interest you to know," she said, exhaling a shudder of blue smoke, "that I quit smoking when I came back to Winnipeg."

"Oh. Well, I'm sorry."

"You're always sorry, aren't you?" She blew a thin stream across the table. "I'd forgotten how good they were. Thank you."

"You're welcome."

"And don't go thinking I flipped out, either. I thought that for a while. I was going to make an appointment with Wilhelm and get my head looked at, but I sat down and said, 'Daisy, you're *not* a loony! It's just that your mother is dying.' She really was sick, Jasper. I *had* to come back. That isn't craziness."

"But for Christ's sweet sake—*Stan*?"

"Oh, I don't know. Being alone, I guess. Yes. Loneliness."

"Couldn't you at least have gone out and dragged some stud off the *street*? It would've been better than—"

He stopped.

"They didn't really have to pry her off the seat, did they, Jasper?"

"Yes, they sure as hell *did*."

"Tell me—about the apartment! How's Mrs. Hookstraten?"

"Okay."

"Tell me about her!"

"She still collects the bird cards from the tea packets for you. Every Saturday she comes to see if you're back."

"You're a bull-shitter, Jasper. She never asked once! What about Simon and the crazies at the Pampam?"

"They're still there." He stood up suddenly. "Anything else?"

Her eyes flashed him the same startled look as when she had appeared at the corner of the house. "You're not going?"

"I've got to catch the bus out to Souris. See my folks."

"I meant—to Amsterdam."

"Yes." He looked away. "Back to the work."

"The work," she said, dropping the half-smoked cigarette into her glass of Tang. It sizzled and bobbed on the surface. "How's 'the work' going, anyway?"

"Fine. Show in London, October."

"If you'd been here, Jasper, it would have been different. Just been here…"

"Yeah—well…"

He had to leave before it all began happening again. Trying not to walk too quickly, he reached the living room, then the front door. She followed but remained inside as the screen banged behind him.

"I'm sorry," she said. "It's the way I am."

"Yes," Jasper said. "Yeah, I can see that. So long, Daisy." Mr. Allpress was still watching from his yard.

She waited until he had walked past the Mustang to the front gate, then yelled, "My name isn't Daisy! It's Doreen."

He would have argued, but the green light from her eyes had already faded into the shadows of Mrs. Gelber's hallway.

"So long, Daisy," he said anyway, but only the old man in the straw Stetson—a fine, *fine* hat—could hear him, and even he never let on.

RAFFERTY AND THELMA
(from WANDERING RAFFERTY)

When Japan lashed the Pacific into war, and the port was closed down except for war shipments, Rafferty was out of a job again. Still the government would not accept his enlistment, concentrating instead on uprooting all its citizens of Japanese descent from the coast and packing them to internment camps in the Interior. Once again, Rafferty packed up his cannon and caught the last ferry south to Vancouver before the commercial shipping lanes closed.

It was the very day he walked off the ferry into the drizzle of rain in downtown Vancouver that he saw Thelma, her calm face etched like the Virgin Mother's in the dark interior of the taxi. He was about to step off the curb into the traffic when he shuddered with ecstatic recognition. He leaped to the door of the cab and found himself staring down at her, his mouth hanging open.

"Is—is this taxi taken?" he finally stammered.

"It certainly is," she said, not looking away from the parcel in her arms.

"Can I share it with you?"

"Don't be ridiculous. Driver, what are you waiting for?"

"Red light, lady."

"Well, do *something*."

"Push off, mac. You're buggin' my fare."

"Maybe I'm headed the same way you are," Rafferty pleaded, ignoring the driver. "Where are you going?"

"None of your business. You must be drunk—hopped up or something. Get away and leave me alone."

"I'll tell you why I came over. When I saw you here, looking down at that parcel, your eyes filled with gentle grief—"

The taxi rocketed away with a roar across the intersection. Rafferty pounded down the sidewalk after it, catching up just as it stopped in the line of traffic behind another red light. He tried to open the door, but she—cunning Madonna indeed—had pushed the lock down, and he seemed to be on the outside for good. He rapped his knuckles against the window. She looked up with a frown. He pointed at the lock. She rolled the window down about an inch.

"Go away!"

"Your eyes," he said. "I thought you were the image of the Pieta."

The window went down another notch.

"I beg your pardon?"

"I couldn't stop myself from coming over to see if you were real. My name's Rafferty." He flashed his most charming and persuasive smile. "I just stepped off the boat from Rupert, and I don't have a place to stay."

"I recommend the Royal Vancouver," she said,

as the taxi shot along Georgia again. It caught a green light at the next intersection, and Rafferty sprinted for a block to catch up. He was gratified to see her window still open; in fact, she had turned once to see if he was still coming.

"Is it—expensive?" he gasped.

She laughed. "Does that bother you?"

"Only—indirectly. I've got about ten bucks. Do you—" he paused for a couple of quick breaths "—have any other suggestions?"

She thought for a moment, tapped her gloved finger seriously against her cheek. "I do recall seeing one place. Why don't you try—?"

Her words faded into the roar of traffic as the cab accelerated once more. Rafferty cursed the taxi-driver, who was laughing, and for one hesitating second he almost abandoned the pursuit. But his legs knew better, already pounding their way along the crowded sidewalk, driving him like a madman to catch the taxi carrying the exquisite face away.

It was a losing effort because traffic grew thinner the farther east they went, and the taxi collected more green lights. They went through three before Rafferty caught up at another red and fell against the side of the car, nearly collapsing on the sidewalk.

"Well run," she said, smiling encouragement. "What is that thing you're carrying?"

"Cannon," he gasped, his breath rasping in his chest. All his heaving lungs seemed to draw was the taxi's exhaust fumes. "What was that—" he sucked more carbon monoxide into his chest "—hotel again?"

"The Oxford Arms."

"Thank you. Now—" he gasped, "—now tell

me—"

But she was gone. He tried to take off once more in pursuit, but the exhaust fumes had finished him. After a few faltering steps, he collapsed onto a bus-stop bench and stretched out, his feet at the curb and his head on the back of the bench, looking like a stiff corpse someone had propped up at a bus-stop for a joke.

He was still like that five minutes later when the taxi screeched to a stop in front of him. The Madonna stepped lightly out, flashing an expensive spring coat along the sidewalk, and walked over to his inert form.

"Do you have a job?" she said.

Rafferty managed to wag his head, and she took a business card out of her purse.

"Here." She dropped it on his trembling chest. "If you come by tomorrow morning there might be some work for you."

Rafferty turned up at 8:30 the next morning at the door of the Fortunato Tobacco Shoppe, an exclusive-looking store in the mall of the Royal Vancouver Hotel. He would no more have bought his own cigarettes there than he'd have purchased condoms at the Prince Rupert recruiting station. In fact, he had almost decided not to go at all, having spent a nearly sleepless night in the Oxford Arms, where the insects were gigantic and the clientele maniacal; it was without a doubt the grubbiest flophouse he had ever stumbled into. He had paid the bouncer a dollar extra to store his cannon.

Inside the tobacco shop he found a mousy-looking spinster behind the counter, and an old man putting stock on the display shelves. "I was sent to get a job," Rafferty said.

The woman leaped into the air and began dashing back and forth behind the counter, staring at him with enormous, hurt eyes.

"You must be Mr. Rafferty," the old man said. "Miss Harrison said you would be over."

"Miss Harrison?"

"She seemed to have great faith in you."

Rafferty's scalp tingled. He almost jumped at the old man to embrace him. "What do you want me to do?" he said.

"Well, ah—we contemplated your working at first with the stock: controlling, invoicing, and so on." Rafferty could have tallied all the stock in the shop without moving his eyes. "Then, of course, as you become proficient—master your trade, so to speak, after a short probationary period—why, you will join the sales staff."

"The sales staff."

"Yes," the old man said enthusiastically. "I don't want to hold out false hopes for you, but I shall be retiring in not *too* many years, and Miss Tingley has never indicated a desire to manage the Fortunato Tobacco Shoppe." He waved his hand at the wasted old maid behind the counter, who was still squeaking back and forth in agitation. She smiled wetly.

"Never, Mr. Crawley," she whispered.

Rafferty couldn't shake his impression of stepping into a Dickens novel. Not a single customer had yet appeared. "Does Miss Harrison work here too?" he said.

"Bless you, no. Miss Harrison is Mr. Harrison's *daughter*."

"Who is Mr. Harrison?"

Mr. Crawley's face showed a mottled blend of

surprise and terrified respect.

"Why—Mr. Harrison *owns* the Fortunato Tobacco Shoppe. He also owns KBL Industries and the Burnaby Tugboat Company, and—and Consolidated Forestry Products!"

"Oh," Rafferty said, taking off his raincoat, ready for work. Crawley showed him to the stockroom in the hotel basement, stacked with enormous crates full of bulk tobacco and boxes of cigarettes. There was a bench where tobaccos were blended.

The biggest customer, it turned out, was Harlow B. Harrison himself, who showed up every Thursday to collect two pounds of rolled Egyptian cigarettes. Rafferty discovered he had bought the Fortunato Tobacco Shoppe because it was the only way he could get his cigarettes without a lot of personal trouble—hang the expense. Apparently it didn't matter whether the place made money or not.

"I don't give a shit," he told Rafferty the first Thursday morning he met him in the stockroom, with Crawley at one side wringing his hands in shudders of anxiety.

"The place can go to shit, money-wise, as long as you bastards keep laying in my 'gyptian baccy. Give me a light, son. Old Crawfish here never carries 'em around—makes him feel like a murderer. Haw, haw. Right, Crawfish?"

Mr. Crawley nodded weakly.

Miss Harrison, on the other hand, did care about the state of the ledgers, having assumed an *ad hoc* managerial role in her father's empire. One of her greatest irritants, like the pea under the princess's mattresses, was the financial drain incurred by the tobacco store. It annoyed her partly because she did not smoke herself, but mostly because she appreciated wealth; it was precisely this appreciation which had sent Rafferty to work. Although an extra stock-controller and salesman was expensive, she hoped that Rafferty—a genuine *entrepreneur*—would eventually force old Crawley out. She had given up trying to persuade her father to get rid of the place, and her ambition, bordering on obsession, was to make it pay its way.

"How are you doing?" she demanded of Rafferty after his first week.

"Well," he said, "I don't think much of your taste in hotels. I'm waging a losing battle against the bedbugs. How did *you* stand it?"

She paid no attention to him. "Are you selling anything?"

"Well, no. I'm only the stock-controller, hoping to work my way up to salesman."

"You mean he keeps you down *here*?"

"Well, there isn't too much room up there. Miss Tingley is wearing a hole in the floor because she's got such a short track to run on."

"I'll fix that."

"Tell me something," Rafferty said. "How much am I getting paid? Mr. Crawley doesn't seem to know."

"How much do you want?"

He looked at her slyly. "Thirty dollars a week, and dinner every Friday."

"I'm tied up on weekends."

"All right. Every Monday then, starting tonight. But first, you'll have to ask Mr. Crawley to pay me."

"I'll do more than that," she said, her long legs going *flash-flash* out of the half-darkness of the stockroom. That afternoon, Rafferty and Miss Tingley traded places and he was paid thirty dollars cash out of the till. Miss Tingley's departure into the depths was a heart-breaking sight; she and Mr. Crawley clasped hands and cried. Rafferty managed to shut the sight out by thinking of his dinner date.

That night, he rolled up in a taxi to the Harrison house in Shaughnessy. "If they have money," he thought, "this must be the place." He was wearing the Royal Vancouver's chief bell-hop's best suit, which fit not too badly but was five years out of style. He rang the bell and a pimply-faced young man about his own age answered the door. The young man avoided looking at Rafferty and spoke instead to the juniper bush beside the door.

"Hello."

Rafferty glanced quickly at the bush. "I'm Tom Rafferty," he said. "Does Thelma Harrison live here?"

"Thelma Harrison? Thelma Harrison? There's no Thelma Harrison here. Perhaps if you tried—"

"Rafferty?" Thelma's voice rang out from inside somewhere. "Is that you, Rafferty?"

Rafferty watched the man in the doorway squeeze pimples on the back of his neck and flick his eyes crazily around the shrubbery-landscaped garden.

"Yes it is," Rafferty called past him.

"Come on in and sit down. I'll be right there."

He started past the man into the house, but the man stepped into the way to block him, his eyes still skittering madly around Rafferty's silhouette.

"She's not here," the young man said in a

clipped monotone. "There's no one here. You've got the wrong number. Are you lost? Where were you heading for?" He stopped for breath, gasping and mauling his disfigured face with long finger-nails.

"Thelma!" Rafferty roared. "This nut won't let me in."

"That's only Herbie," she called back. "Don't pay any attention. Just walk in!"

Again Rafferty motioned to go past, but Herbie moved with him, blocking the way. Rafferty heard a distinct growl. Herbie spoke again, his voice squeaking like a record on a high speed.

"This is a private home. You'll have to go before I call the police. There's no one here to see you! Now go away. You've got the wrong place! If you're lost, maybe I can find the right number—"

Rafferty turned and sat down on the front step to wait for Thelma. He hoped she wouldn't be long; the taxi was waiting in the driveway, ticking away. Herbie slammed the door; Rafferty could hear him shrieking incoherently inside the house. Thelma came out ten minutes later, calmly putting her gloves on.

"My brother Herbie," she told Rafferty as they got into the taxi. "He's been a big disappointment to father."

"I can't imagine why," Rafferty said. "He's a *great* watchdog."

He hoped to impress her at a Chinatown restaurant the chief bell-hop had recommended. She crushed him by greeting the manager by name and ordering the meal for both of them in Chinese. The bill came to $18.35, including the tip. With the taxi-fare, it didn't leave Rafferty much to live on for the rest of the week.

"Would you like to change the terms of your contract?" asked Thelma with a smile, as Rafferty dismissed the cab at her front door. He had decided to walk back downtown to the Oxford Arms.

"Just keep your Mondays free," he said. "I'll be here. Maybe you could arrange to have Herbie locked in his room or something?"

She laughed. "I'd invite you in, but he hasn't gone to bed yet. And he's always worse when he's tired and cranky. Good night, Tom. It's been delightful."

He contemplated Herbie as he trudged along Burrard Bridge, trying to thumb a ride back to town.

"Looks a little different around here," Mr. Harrison muttered the following Thursday. "Where's that weird dame?"

"Here's your tobacco, Mr. Harrison." Mr. Crawley was squirming in between them, holding out the package.

"I opened up a display area at the front," Rafferty explained. "Pipes and accessories. There were boxes that've never been opened."

"So you have," Mr. Harrison said.

Mr. Crawley forced the package into his hands. "I hope you don't mind, sir," he said. "I've taken the liberty of adding a dash of something new to your blend. Just on the market. I think you'll enjoy it."

Mr. Harrison looked at him as if for the first time. "I better," he said and walked out, leaving Mr. Crawley looking very faint.

Within a month, Rafferty had become manager of the Fortunato Tobacco Shoppe, having made it a

nearly worthwhile business venture. He relieved his
guilt with the knowledge that Mr. Crawley's and
Miss Tingley's retirements were more secure. And
when he felt his pride inflating over his accomplish-
ments, he reminded himself curtly that almost any-
one above the level of a moron in Vancouver in
1942 was making money. The Pacific war was creat-
ing fortunes left and right.

But there was a limit to the amount which could
be made in the Fortunato, and after a year, when
Rafferty felt he had reached the limit, he men-
tioned it to Thelma during their weekly dinner. He
could now afford both the Monday evening and a
comfortable room in a Kingsway rooming house.
At seventy dollars a week, he had even bought his
first suit.

"But where will you go?" she said.

"A couple of tobacco wholesalers have won-
dered what I'll do next."

"What if there was an opening in the tugboat
company?"

"What do I know about tugboats?"

"What did you know about tobacco?"

They kissed good-night on the doorstep of the
Harrison mansion that night, although Rafferty—
as always—kept stepping back nervously at the
thought of Herbie sitting at a window somewhere
above the door, preparing to drop a bed or some-
thing on top of him. Since he hit seventy a week,
Rafferty had kept the taxi waiting on Monday
nights.

"Why don't you send the cab away?" Thelma
said.

"Don't worry about it. I can afford—"

She breathed out a long sigh which caressed the

inside of his ear. "I mean, *why don't you send the cab away*?"

The hair on his neck shifted. "What about Herbie?" he said.

"I locked him in his room before I left. He'll be asleep."

Rafferty had never made love to a young, independent woman in his life, with the possible exception of a ridiculously flat-chested Navy lieutenant's wife who had been a virgin. But this was different. Thelma was, well, knowledgeable, and their love-making ranged across two bedrooms, a sun porch, and a dressing room. Rafferty suddenly realized what the metaphysical poets were writing about; an elation kept surging up which beat back exhaustion. He was still hours away from needing sleep when an alarm clock went off somewhere in the house. Herbie's whine rose to a penetrating shriek as he clamoured to be let out of the locked bedroom.

"Good God!" Rafferty said, dragging his pants and shoes together. "How am I going to get out of here? I have to get to work."

"Don't panic," Thelma said, rising luxuriously from her bed. "You can go down the back way." She showed him the staircase descending into the back yard from the sun porch. "Don't bother going to the tobacco shop; they don't need you any more. Get some sleep and try to make it over to the tugboat offices by three o'clock."

Rafferty's new job involved the dispatching of tugs to and from all points in the Pacific Northwest. The war was almost over and commerce thrived. The complexity of the job led to creativity, and it wasn't long before Rafferty's diligence and efficiency were attracting contracts for Harlow B. Harrison from all over the west coast. Harrison was ecstatic over discovering an intelligent employee, and gave him a raise almost every month to keep things going up, up, up, beating hell out of the competition even though—Harlow B. Harrison knew goddam well—Rafferty was screwing his daughter almost every night down the hall of his own house before descending the back stairs. But he didn't mind as long as she had no crazy notions about getting married.

"Father, I want to marry him," Thelma said one day as they drove to the tugboat office to see Rafferty.

"Sweet Jesus Christ!" he said, firing his Egyptian cigarette out the window. "You're as crazy as that Herbie son-of-a-bitch. What do you want to do that for?"

"He's the only one I ever met."

"Only one *what*?"

"The only man I could live with."

"*Live* with him. Just don't get married. Think of your mother."

"*What?*"

"Okay, think of Herbie then. He'll go buzzerk. We'll never get him back out of the trees."

She shrugged. "That's your problem."

"Fine attitude about your own brother!"

"I've lived for eight years, father, with him crying on my shoulder and messing up my social life. I feel sorry for Herbie, but I can't be his mother. Have him put in an institution, if you don't feel like looking after him yourself."

Harrison drove in silence, squinting ahead along the road. "How can you afford to move out? Rafferty isn't earning enough to buy a house.''

"You've forgotten how well people can live on four hundred a month. We'll get along. I bet Tom's never earned so much in his life. Besides—'' Thelma turned to her father and beamed a smile ''—you'll give him a raise—won't you? When you make him manager?''

"Sweet Jesus Christ!'' Harrison exploded, pounding the steering wheel with his fist.

Rafferty turned down both the promotion and the raise. In fact, as he said to Harrison, he wasn't sure he wanted to marry outside his class. He maintained his dignity and independence, finally, by resigning from his father-in-law's company and going to sell cars for a used-car dealer who was an old boy friend of Thelma's. She went ahead and rented a house for which she selected the furniture herself but allowed, on Rafferty's insistence, a prominent place in the den for his old brass cannon barrel.

The wedding was held four months later, a small, private affair with three dozen guests including Herbie, who had been liberated from his new rest home in the Interior for the occasion. He behaved well, too, until the point in the ceremony where the assembly of old boy friends, cousins, Thecla Rafferty, and the bridesmaid, gathered to hurl rice and confetti at the newlyweds. Herbie misconstrued the activity entirely, and began hurling at his sister and her captor everything he could lay his hands on: lamps, rubber boots, pieces of wedding cake, dishes, bottles. Finally, as his rage reached spectacular heights, he tried to lift his own father and throw him under the wheels of the new Monarch convertible which Rafferty was desperately urging down the driveway under the hail of missiles from the front door. The car itself was a wedding gift from Herbie, bought on his behalf by Harlow B. Harrison, who suffered a cracked rib from landing on the crushed gravel driveway, vowing that his son would never see the light of freedom again. Thecla Rafferty was so offended at the immorality of it all she returned on the next bus to Penticton and refused to speak of her in-laws again.

When they came back to Vancouver after the honeymoon, he spent all his time making love to Thelma and selling cars. He had a facility for disposing of old wrecks, a facility which astonished him; Rafferty was a sales genius. It was soon a very rare day at Marco's O.K. Used Cars that Rafferty had not sold at least one old can, and often two, to unsuspecting veterans or college students. His method evoked wide professional admiration across the city. He would carefully explain all the faults of the car—old tires or broken radio—before explaining what qualities the wreck *did* have for the money asked. After a carefully controlled pause, he would come down five per cent in the price. He soon had a widely recognized, if totally false, reputation for honesty and generosity. Suckers flocked to Marco's to buy from "Smilin' Tom" Rafferty—a name bestowed by his cynical colleagues which stuck for twelve years. Finally he was regularly selling three cars a day; his income had never been higher; and Thelma was already planning their takeover of Marco's.

Then Rafferty cracked up in the English Bay Hotel.

INCIDENT IN MICHIGAN, WINTER

Ahead in the black spruce
forest a red glow beats
mocking the half-december dusk,
omen of life on this long
empty road from Sault to Duluth
graveyard turn on a long trek home.

A mile away a car is stopped,
red tail lights peering
like rats' eyes
trapped on the road
by three-foot walls of snow
ploughed up on either side
no escape   the tunnel
floor pebbled ice and
glistening treachery.

Beside me Harvey peers
through the tiny frost-
cleared circle in his corner
of the windshield, mutters
"car stalled up there" meaning
you are only seventeen
behind that wheel
first Toronto to Moose Jaw
forty-hour transcontinental
in the dead of winter —
even overdoing it, speeding
when everyone is asleep
dreaming of Christmas
with the boys.

"I see it" snarling
gripping the wheel
then seeing the set
of yellow clearance lights
rounding the slight curve in the road
(beyond which the red glow still beats)
a truck approaching on the far side
of the stalled Dodge,
the coincidence too extreme
for contemplation,
a rush of adrenalin while
shifting down to third
(too late to brake on the ice)
trying to see meaning
in that strange red light
out of sight around the curve,
must be a neon sign
a roadhouse or tavern
or the sun going down,
the truck barrelling toward me
as I pull out to pass
the idiot in the old
Dodge   South
Carolina plates   tires

iced-under dashes of white
paint flashing by
goddam the Beetle traction
fingers squeezing the wheel
Harvey whining about his precious car
till he wakes Muzz and Jack
in the back, luggage
unpiling around their ears
and one of them likely Muzz
suddenly yells

making me crimp the wheel
at the precise second we
slip past the Dodge,
some yo-yo in front
pissing in the snow amazed
as we *swoosh* straight at him
who is not even aware
of the big semi
hurtling toward the darkness,
cursing our faces, four
gawking through the frosted glass
as we breeze past him,
snowbank wheeling around us
beckoning of cushion
flicking at the car
(not enough to slow it down)
the mad Volkswagen
spiralling down the road
like a curling jam pail
though I'm geared into second
and stomping like a fiddler,
Muzz and Harvey yelling advice
while Jack maintains a deep
respectful silence
our eyes locked
on the red neon
beaconing out
of the swirling
darkness, a star
winking like heartbeat
from the looming black windshields,
driver's white mask staring
at our doomed pirhouette
down the tunnel, both of us
knowing that no help will come

from inside this thin
tin can   gears   wheels
brakes   all useless
as Harvey's advice
on buckling the seat belts
as we slide to the wrong lane
I grind it into low anyway
the sphincter's pressure
bulging my eardrums
eyeball fluid boiling
at the sight of this
juggernaut falling
on us like Armageddon
blotting out the last arm
of the astral welcome
two hundred yards beyond
an impossible future
red glowing star
Christmas perhaps
Marxist Utopia
my retinas black but obsessed
with the fading scarlet image
like a babe spinning headlong
down the channel of life
to the pink bloody light
all hope drowned in the tide
of grinding metal
like Harvey's shrieks
dreaming a death so black
I think I've passed beyond
when the glass screen
clears to grey
shows us
spinning
to a halt

in the centre
of this twilit
magic road
foot still pumping
eyes staring back
at the truck plunging
through the white foaming ditches
knocked through the tunnel wall
by a piece of silly German tin
bouncing off its side
harmless as a child's ball,
though one second sooner
and we'd all be an inch thick and piling
through the snowy ditches,
the new silence
reverberating in the air
like gongs,
the light of life
pulsating everywhere red:
texaco texaco texaco
texaco texaco
texaco

texaco.

IN OLD MEXICO

I knew something horrible would happen if I listened to The Old Bat. It always happened.

"You never know, you might even *like* Mexico," she said, mewing at me like she always did when she was trying to get on my good side. "Good Lord, Bix, how do you ever hope to be anything when you don't have the gumption to poke your nose outside of Toronto? That's why you're just a salesman!"

A salesman, for crying out loud. That really got me. There I was, promoted to district sales-rep five years before, and she still said things like that. It proves she never listened to a goddam word I said.

"What's so special about Mexico, anyway?" I said. "Who wants to see a buncha Mexicans standing around?" I was planning a jaunt to Kakabeka Falls, where we'd always had a good time before.

"It's different, that's what—somewhere new and exciting. If you won't think of yourself, at least consider Sally and the children. The least you could do is take them somewhere different and—and exotic!"

Well. I nearly exoticked her, on the spot. Those little creeps of mine wouldn't recognize an exotic *hot dog* stand if I ran into it at seventy miles an hour. They wouldn't even look up from their exotic *Spiderman* comics. Anyway, it all turned out pretty exotic for her.

Sally wasn't any help, naturally. She just sighed, "Maybe it would be educational for the kids." I saw right away The Old Bat had already got to her.

"What about *me*?" I said, hitting my hand on the table in the breakfast nook. "Did anybody ever ask me what I wanted?"

"Well I don't know, Bix. . . " she said, trailing off like she always did.

"I think it would be very educational for the children," The Old Bat said, barging through from the dining room. She'd been listening outside the door again. "Heaven only knows they need *some*-thing to help them out in school."

That did it. That's when I put my foot down. Here she was, supposedly worried about my kids' education when all she wanted was to finagle a free trip to Mexico, all expenses paid, courtesy of me. Well I was goddamned if she'd get as far as Hamilton in *my* car.

It was no use, of course. We went anyway. I should have known Sally wouldn't stand up to her. And one of the first things she did was leak word to the monsters that they *might* be going to Old Mexico. From then on, my life was hell.

"Whennerwe gonna go, Dad? Hey, Dad? Whennerwe gonna leave for Mexico?" Jimmy'd be hollering in my ear while I was trying to read the *Sun* in a little peace and quiet before supper.

"We're not going! For the billionth gol-darn time, we aren't going anywhere!"

"Aw Daddy," Shelley would say, on the other side of the La-Z-Boy. "Why can't we Daddy?"

I wouldn't answer for a while, to make them go away.

"Daddy? We never go *anywhere*. Why can't we go to Mexico this summer?"

"Because they all talk *Mexican*! Who the heck talks Mexican around here? They'd cheat us blind."

They'd sulk for a day or two, then it would start all over again when I got home from work. Hey Dad, Aw Dad. It finally started to get to me, the whole business, when the Mexican tourist brochures started coming in the mail. That and The Old Bat playing her "Learn Spanish Easy" records every night in the living room, until one night when I stood up and hollered that I was going to the bar at the Bellevue Golf Club and I wasn't coming home till they shut it off and kept it off.

They finally wore me down, though, keeping after me like that all the time, day in and day out, all winter long, till about Easter I said, "Okay, we'll go! But you're not gonna get me to talk like a Mexican! I'll do the driving, and you guys can do all the parley-vooing."

Well naturally, they all hugged me then and said what a great Daddy-Dads I was. Even The Old Bat was nice to me, but I didn't let on I noticed. I knew who was responsible. Of course, none of them ever thought what it would be like in Mexico in the middle of July. Kakabeka in the summer is perfect. I could have told them Mexico would be hotter than four hells, but nobody would've listened to me anyway.

No. We listened to her. All the way down here, through Buffalo and Pennsylvania and Mississippi and all those weird Dogpatch places that gave me the willies just to drive through. All the way. Every morning when we finally got on the road—after I got the bags packed, the Fury III filled with gas, the campground paid for, soft drinks bought; when I got a map, found some new comic books, and finally, *finally* drove out onto the highway—she would roll down her window in the back, take a deep breath of air and say:

"My, Bix, isn't it a *lovely* day?"

She goddam nearly sent me round the bend was what she did. It was a hundred and ten in the shade, if you could find any, the inside of the car baking like a steel furnace, sweat pouring down the crack of my ass, and she'd warble away like some skylark about the joys of the open road.

I tell you, the only thing that kept me from going berserk and driving straight into the next cement wall was a kind of game I made up. I got a funny sort of kick out of making up foul curses—not yelling them at her, but keeping them in long strings inside my head in case Sally wasn't around to really hold me back.

Regular as clockwork, she'd roll down the window the second we pulled onto the highway—I could hear the handle going *rasp, rasp*, and feel the hair on the back of my neck prickle in the sweat—then she'd sing out:

"My, Bix, isn't it a *lovely* day?"

All I could ever see was an endless stretch of highway disappearing into the heat-haze, and millions of camper-trucks and Winnebagos zooming past in both directions—and she would say that. Of course the kids had to mimic her every time, snorting and giggling until I had to turn around and scream at them to shut up. Then they'd settle down and read their comics. The only halfway entertaining thing on the whole trip was when Sally and The Old Bat would practise their Spanish on each other.

"Tiene usted fosforos?" one would ask.

"Mi cunado es arquitecto," the other would reply. It was ridiculous. They were going to make fools of themselves.

If the States was hot, you wouldn't *believe* Mexico. When we crossed the border at Laredo, Texas, I nearly turned around and drove straight back to Toronto. I would have, too, but I wanted to see her suffer—really *suffer*—for getting me on this crazy trip. They'd all be good and sorry they didn't listen to me for once.

The Old Bat didn't even flinch, just handed the map over my shoulder and said, "Take this road straight to Zacatecas."

Now I could tell by the map that the road was going to run through two hundred miles of solid Mexican desert, but I didn't say a word, not a word. Just clenched my teeth and tramped on the gas, and we roared off south in a cloud of dust.

That night we camped at a place outside Monterrey where they had back-houses for rest rooms, and a pipe sticking out of the ground for water. The next morning, on the road heading into the desert, she was a lot quieter. I listened for the window handle to start its *rasp, rasp*.

Nothing. Blessed peace and quiet. "Do you feel okay, Mother?" Sally said, turning to the back seat.

"Cramps," she said.

By the time we got right into the desert, even I

started to get a little worried about her. It was *really* goddam hot. I decided to stop and let everybody get a drink from the canvas canteen I had hanging in front of the rad. The kids ran off behind some cactus to have a pee while I went to get the water. That's when I discovered what that Mexican kid with the gold teeth had been doing at the front of the car at the last gas station. Stealing the canteen. I was standing there trying to decide what the hell to do when I heard a funny gasping sound behind me. I turned around just in time to see The Old Bat stagger out the back door of the Fury III and proceed to have some sort of heart attack on the spot.

I'm goddamned if it wasn't the weirdest thing I ever saw. One minute she was standing there, sort of hunched over, leaning against the car, and before I knew what was up, still thinking about that kid with the gold teeth, she took off in a couple of pirouettes like some nutty ballet dancer, then flopped over onto the desert, her heels beating a kind of two-four rhythm on the sand.

A sudden picture flashed into my mind. I don't know why, because I hadn't thought of it for years, but it was the picture of a kid who used to play third base, in my former pitching days with the old Hagersville Hurricanes. I had lobbed a ball to him, just a gentle kind of toss, the way you do after picking off a pop fly, but he wasn't looking, and the ball hammered him right in the old guts. I thought he was going to die, the way his face turned blue and his tongue hung out while he scrabbled on his knees down the third-base line, clutching his stomach. But he turned out okay, just winded.

"*Bix!*" Sally was screaming at me. She must have been hollering for nearly a minute, because her voice was hoarse. "Bix! *Do* something!"

I shook my head to clear it and walked over to where The Old Bat was lying on the sand. A little thread of spit drooled from the corner of her mouth. It was so hot out there, the sun dried it up as fast as it ran. Her eyes were open but she didn't seem to be breathing. I tried to bend over and feel her pulse, but all of a sudden my back wouldn't bend. It was really stupid; I couldn't move. "Looks —dead," I said, as respectful as I could.

Then one of her feet suddenly kicked out at me. I jumped back, stopping myself in the nick of time from letting go with a really good curse.

"What is it?" the kids yelled, tearing out of the cactus bushes. "What is it?"

"Ooohhhh," Sally moaned. "It's Gramma!"

"What's up, Dad?" Jimmy said, staring at her stretched out on the sand. "What's with Gramma?"

"I don't know! Now you kids go back where you were till I get all of this straightened out. Go on!"

I didn't know where to start. My muscles were going numb and there was an awful pruney taste in my mouth whenever I tried to bend over and touch her. Her skin was all dry and wrinkled.

"Do something, Bix!" Sally was howling. *"Do something!"*

Then there was a snap inside my head like a broken elastic, and I yelled, "For cripe's sake, will you shut *up*? Isn't it bad enough I'm getting a headache without the rest of you getting my goat? What the heck are we doing here, anyway? If you'd all've listened to me instead of—that—*that*—!"

I barely managed to hold back the flood of

swear words I'd been storing up in my head for three thousand miles, but I couldn't stop myself from shaking. My finger was jabbing away like a bayonet toward The Old Bat laying there on the sand, staring at me pop-eyed like it was my fault.

"Ooooooooooooohh," Sally moaned. She staggered too, like she was going the same route as The Old Bat and might collapse right beside her.

Right away I felt terrible. I could have cut off my tongue. After all, The Old Bat *was* her mother. I put my arm around her and apologized, moving her toward the car so she could sit down. That's when I noticed the big scratch in the right rear fender. Probably done by the kid who stole the water-bag. At least thirty-nine-fifty at Fender-King.

"Can we come back now?" Shelley whined from the clump of cactus where they were sitting in the shade.

"What's up with Gramma?" Jimmy said.

"Nothing!" I roared at them. "And stay where you're told!" I got out a cigar and lit it to calm myself, wishing I was back in the bar at the Bellevue Golf Club with a big highball full of rye and Coke in my hand. If they'd all just quit *bugging* me.

Anyway, it was too late for *her*, that was for sure. No point in panicking and trying to get her to an emergency ward in—whatever that place was—Zacatecas. I went back and looked at her again. When people die on TV, they at least have the decency to close their eyes. Not her. Maybe if I kicked a bit of sand...

"*Bix!*" Sally shrieked from the front seat.

It wouldn't work if she was watching. I walked around to the other side of the car where at least I didn't have to look at The Old Bat. It certainly was a disgusting fix.

"Da-a-a-d! Shelley says Gramma's dead."

I just rolled the cigar in my teeth and ignored them. It occurred to me there might be real trouble about this thing. There was no telling what the Mexican cops would do if I reported the death to them. Probably arrest me. But for what? I hadn't done anything. All I wanted to do was go home without any trouble. *Why did I let them talk me into this crazy holiday?* My teeth suddenly bit through the cigar and it fell on the sand still smoking.

I made up my mind to act, and marched straight to the trunk of the car, rummaging through it for the little snow-shovel I keep behind the spare.

"Bix? What are you doing?"

"Just keep the kids away from here. I'm gonna dig a hole."

"What for?"

"What *for*?"

"No!" She stamped one of her blue sneakers, and it sank a couple of inches into the sand. "You are not going to bury my mother out here in this godforsaken desert." There was something new in Sally's voice that made it sound like her mother's, as if the minute she passed away, The Old Bat had handed on her voice, like that bit in the poem about the failing runner who tossed the torch.

I just about gave up. "What do you want me to do? Leave her lying there? So the *vultures* can come and pick her bones?"

She got this stricken, mournful look in her eyes, and sat down in the car again. "We're going to give my mother a decent Christian burial, Bix," she said.

"Okay, I'm—sorry."

"Daa-a-ad!" Jimmy yelled. "I have to do a

number two."

"Go *ahead*, for gosh-sakes! Why do you always have to tell me?"

"You told me not to do it outside until I asked you first."

I had this trapped, suffocating feeling, as if the desert was slowly sinking in the middle, and the sides were coming in on top of me. "Go away," I said, and turned to Sally. "All right, what're we gonna do? We can't have a funeral here, can we?"

"I've been thinking," she said. "The first thing we have to do is report it to the authorities."

"To the *what*?"

"Otherwise, we could get into serious trouble."

"Are you crazy, for cripe's sake? The police down here are a bunch of hired killers! They're liable to throw us all in jail if they think we had something to do with her kick—passing away. Do you want to spend the rest of your life in a dungeon? Eh?"

"We will go to the next town," she said, her teeth clamping down hard on each word. "Zacatecas. And report it to the police. We can make arrangements to have her shipped back to Toronto for burial."

"How are we going to take her to Zacatecas? Just throw her in the back seat with the kids? She isn't gonna last long in this heat, you know."

That didn't even faze her. "Why, I thought we'd put her in the front, and I would sit in back with the children."

This was getting more insane by the minute. "Listen, Sally, think of the kids! It could give them a trauma or something, driving along with their dead gramma in the front seat like that."

She thought for a minute. "Maybe you're right."

"Daddy!" Shelley yelled. "Jimmy's saying dirty words about my tooney!"

I decided to ignore this and not say anything, like they suggested in *Tips for Pops*.

"I was not, Dad! She was watching me go to the bathroom!"

Well, I just blew my stack. *"Shut up!"* I screamed. "Shut up or I'll come over there and beat the pants off both of you!"

Sally was giving me a funny look, which was only natural because my nerves were certainly going strange. Finally she said, "I suppose you thought of putting her on the luggage rack?"

To tell the truth, I hadn't. I looked around at the aluminum rack on top of the Fury III.

"You wouldn't *have* to look at my dead mother then."

"It isn't that, it's just—her eyes—"

"I see."

"Maybe we could wrap her up in something." I thought maybe we could use a sleeping bag or a newspaper, and then I got a bright idea. I rummaged through the plastic bags full of souvenirs in the back seat until I found it. The Old Bat had haggled for two hours in Laredo for a "genuine Indian blanket" to show her friends in Leaside. It was me who found the Made in Hong Kong label on it. I'd been saving it up to show her.

Sally gasped when I brought it out. "Not my mother's *Indian* blanket!"

"We can't just strap her down on top of the tent, can we? It's either this or a sleeping bag."

"Oh, all right," she sighed.

We wrapped her up and tied the blanket with a tent-cord. It looked pretty colourful, I had to admit, what with her red sandals sticking out. We were just lifting her to the top of the car when Jimmy came out of the cactus and saw us.

"What's in there?" he said.

Sally looked at me to say something, but I didn't know how to break it to him. I tried to think of some proper way of explaining, standing there with The Old Bat's feet on my shoulder, sweat pouring down my face. She was a lot heavier than she looked.

"Nothing," I said.

Sally gave me a dirty look and cleared her throat. "Gramma had a heart attack," she said, her voice quivering with bravery. "Now you two go and sit in the car. We're going to take her to Zacatecas."

They looked solemn for a minute. Then they climbed into the car and giggled. They knew what was in the blanket. They were just trying to get my goat again. I heaved the feet-end onto the luggage rack, then went to help Sally at her end. There was only a bit of space between the side of the rack and my Travelgaard suitcase to fit her into.

"Watch my Travelgaard," I said, not wanting it to get all polluted by The Old Bat. Cost me a hundred smackers at Markham's Discount.

"Your Travelgaard! What about my *mother*?"

"Couldn't we bend her knees or something?"

"You move your Travelgaard," Sally said, glaring at me.

"Okay!" I climbed up onto the roof to move the bag. The top of the car was like a stove, and I could tell it was going to get worse. "But it's a heck of a note when a guy's brand new hundred-dollar suit-case doesn't merit *some* consideration. After all, the living have to go on living, don't they?''

When we finally got her packed on, Sally would only let me drive forty miles an hour all the way to Zacatecas, and I had to stop every ten miles to check the ropes and make sure The Old Bat was still with us. At least the monsters in the back seat kept their mouths shut. If they were like me, they were too whacked to say anything. My back and neck felt like I'd been carrying her across the desert by my-self. Not to mention I was dying of thirst.

We never did make it to Zacatecas that night. Without any warning at all, the sun suddenly dis-appeared and it got so dark I was afraid I'd miss a turn in the road; so at the next small town we came to, I pulled into the square. There was a building a little bigger than the others, with a sign above the door, lit by a bare bulb. It said, ''Policia.''

''Well?'' Sally said.

''Do you want me to go in?'' The street was empty, but I thought I could see a bunch of hood-lums watching us from the shadows behind the buildings. There was nobody walking anywhere.

''What if they think *we* killed her?'' Shelley said.

''Don't say that!''

''It's all right, Bix. You stay here in your pre-cious car. I'll go in and explain the whole thing. Af-ter all, I speak the language.''

''Maybe you better let me,'' I said, but before I could get the door open, Sally was already out of the car with her purse and her Spanish-English dic-tionary in her hand.

''I'll be right back.'' She disappeared inside the door.

Twenty-two minutes later, I started to get nervous. "You kids stay out here," I said. "I'm going in." Then they wouldn't stay in the car by themselves, so we all got out and moved toward the police station.

"Hey Dad!" Jimmy whispered. "What if Mom's being raped and pillaged?"

"You moron!" Shelley hissed. "It's not raped and pillaged! It's raped and quartered!"

"Shut up both of you!"

I pushed the door open, but the room was so dark, it was a few seconds before I could see Sally standing at a long counter which divided it in two. On the other side of the counter were two Mexican cops, a few sticks of furniture, and a door with bars. I couldn't see anything but darkness beyond that door.

"Muerte!" Sally was saying loudly. *"Muerte!"*

The two cops looked at each other, bored. One was a fat sergeant who looked exactly like the sweaty bandit leader they always have in movies. The other one was a constable who stood there picking his nose.

"Muerte!" Sally shouted again. She started flipping through her Spanish phrase book, muttering, "Heart, heart." She turned back to the sergeant. *"Muerte Corazon!"*

He looked at his sidekick and yammered away in Spanish for a minute. The other one shrugged, not understanding either; then he made a circle with his thumb and poked his finger through it in an obscene gesture. The sergeant laughed and pointed at poor Sally, and made a gesture, too. They still hadn't seen us.

"Stop it!" Sally was outraged, rising up on her

toes. "My mother! *Madre! Corazon!*"

This made them laugh all the harder, saying, "*Madre muerte*," and making the obscene signs. They hadn't spotted me yet, and it occurred to me that it might be a good idea to run back to the car and take off for Zacatecas to bring help before something serious happened.

"Bix!" Sally shouted. The cops looked up and saw the kids and me standing at the door. Too late. We were all doomed.

"*Estudo el marido?*" the sergeant said, sneering horribly. The kids, my own bloody kids, were pushing me toward the counter.

"No comprenez," I said. "No comprenez. Je suis Canadian."

The constable shouted something and they made more gestures, looking back and forth between Sally and me. I was edging back to the door in case I had to make a break for it.

"It was an accident!" I yelled. "She had a heart attack!"

"Ask if they got any soft drinks here, Dad," Jimmy said.

"Stop it—all of you!" Sally shrieked. The two cops looked at her, jolted into attention. "*Me madre is muerte*!"

"*Su madre es muerte?*" the sergeant said cautiously.

"*Si!*" She nodded sharply and pointed outside toward the Fury III. "*On le cotch.*"

The sergeant stared at her, his eyes bulging, "*Su madre muerte es en el—?!*"

"*Si.*" She started flipping through the phrase book again. "Luggage rack, luggage rack. *En la vaca del cotch.*"

For a minute, the two cops could only blink at each other, then back at us. *"Chingada!"* they roared together, and scrambled through the flap in the counter, kicking each other in their rush to get outside and see. They nearly bowled Sally over. The kids and I stepped out of the way as they came charging through the screen door. It banged behind them, and for a minute it was so quiet you could hear the bugs crawling on the walls. We stood there, afraid to move until the Mexicans finished inspecting the luggage rack. Even the kids kept their mouths shut for once.

Suddenly the sergeant gave an angry bellow, and I knew something else was wrong. I didn't know what more could happen to us before we got out of that fix, but I did know there was a limit to what a guy could tolerate without flipping his wig completely. And I was getting close.

"Well?" Sally said. "Aren't you going to see what they want?"

I eased the door open. I could make out the dim outline of the Fury III, but there was something screwy about it. I edged toward the voices muttering in the darkness.

"Uh—pardonny-moy! What seems to be the, uh, trouble?"

They switched on a flashlight and aimed it at my face, blinding me.

"Bueno," the sergeant said sarcastically. *"Encontraste la madre muerte!"* The flashlight beam stabbed at the luggage rack. It was completely empty.

I couldn't say a thing. I couldn't even move. But my mind was whirling like crazy. All our bags, our clothes, the good lawn chairs. My new Travelgaard.

"My mother!" Sally screamed in the darkness behind me. "What did you do to my mother?"

Even The Old Bat! God Almighty, was there *anything* Mexicans wouldn't steal?

"Usted tiene que par explicaciones, señor," the sergeant said.

"Me madre! Me madre! Thieves! *Ladrons!"*

The constable stepped back, looking nervous. *"Que?"*

"Hey Dad," Jimmy said, pulling at my sleeve. "Didn't we come here with wheels on the car, Dad?"

I turned and looked at the Fury III again, but a blur hit my eyes like I was going blind. It was as though I finally reached the point of no return, and my whole system just up and quit working, my brain wiped as clean as the mirror behind the bar in the golf club. I was past feeling scared, beyond humiliation. I seemed to be floating somewhere above, staring down at my bald spot, watching myself step calmly and coolly into the driver's seat and lock all the doors and windows. Slamming it into low gear, I roared off into the black, baking desert, leaving the whole rotten business behind. I could see myself crouched down behind the steering wheel, peering ahead like a Grand Prix driver and speeding across the desert, riding on the brake drums and throwing up huge clouds of dust to blind my pursuers.

"Do something, Bix! *Do something!"*

I was still standing there. I hadn't moved an inch.

There was nothing I could do, of course. It was

Sally who browbeat the cops into staying up all night and searching the town for her mother's remains, while I tagged along behind. The kids slept in what was left of the car.

I could have told them they'd never find anything. The thieves would have been so peed off at finding The Old Bat wrapped up in her Indian blanket they would have just taken the whole kit and kaboodle and dumped it into one of those bottomless mud-holes they always have around Mexican towns.

In the morning, one of the cops drove us into Zacatecas, where we scrounged around the old garages till we found four second-hand wheels that fit. They weren't much, but at least they got us back to white man's territory in Laredo, where we got a motel and a decent night's sleep. Before we could leave the next day, I spent four hours pleading with the manager of Lone Star Quick Cash to get $20 on my Timex, for food. Then I drove forty solid nonstop hours to get back to T.O., stopping only at gas stations and McDonald's Hamburgers, with Sally waving a leather strap to keep the kids in line.

The only thing that kept me going—no, *two* things—was the memory of the Bellevue Golf Club and a notion which had been nudging around in the back of my mind ever since the moment I saw The Old Bat twirling in circles like some crazy sundancer in the desert. It was the realization that finally, after putting up with that whining voice of hers all those years, *finally* I was going to cash in! She had at least twenty thou in the bank, money she squeezed out of poor old Frank before nagging him to an early grave.

Ha. Little did I know.

After a while I might have forgiven her about

Mexico, because the insurance covered all the luggage and stuff, and after a few rounds at the Bellevue, I blotted out the memory of the heat. But to my dying day, I will forever curse her rotten remains wherever they are in Mexico. Exotic Old Mexico. Because the day after we got back, the bank manager and his lawyer told me that without a body there is no death certificate, and without that we don't collect a cent for seven years.

But that's okay. I'll wait. You hear me? I'll *wait*, you tight-fisted old Babylonian—penny-pinching old rotten—breath-stinking, mother—money-grubbing battle-axe son of a—

TEACHERS

"Well, I don't know what to say," Miss Steinecker, the Grade One teacher, said. "We told them the *last* time he couldn't be registered. I can't imagine why they'd bring him back again."

"It's all right. I'll examine him, anyway," Dr. Walcott said.

She glanced past him into the hall, looking for the principal. "I don't understand it. Mr. Ballard made it quite clear he could *never* be admitted to the school. You'd think they'd learn, wouldn't you?"

"May I see the boy? If it's not an imposition."

Miss Steinecker's winged blue eye-glasses almost took off flapping around her classroom. "Yes! Oh yes, of course, doctor. They're waiting with him in the movie room."

She retreated briskly to her desk and pulled a clump of keys from the centre drawer, her moment of fluster already fading. "I'll be back in two minutes," she told the pupils who sat wide-eyed, their pencils still poised in mid-air from the moment of Walcott's knock on the door. "Three demerits for anyone who leaves his seat. Garin is going to be the monitor. Aren't you, Garin?"

Garin was a gnomic-looking child with the face of a born informer. He grimaced self-consciously. "Yes, Miss Steinecker."

She led Walcott down the hall to a series of doors along a rear passageway that had once been the old school. The corridor was unlit and dark, despite the bright September sunshine outside.

"You have a movie room?" he asked politely. It was a luxury, even in a school as large as this, serving one of the biggest school districts in the province. Nearly all the students were bused in, some from as far as forty miles away.

"Mr. Ballard has assembled the biggest audio-visual library of any school in the unit."

"Why did you put the boy in the—movie room?"

"It's got a lock."

"You locked him in?"

"Well—the mother's there. Mrs. Achtzner. The grandmother, too."

"What about the father?"

"He didn't come in last time, either. All he did was drive the truck, and the women brought the—child into the school." She stopped in front of a door, and separated a key from the bunch. "This is the room."

"What happened the last time?"

"Well," she whispered, drawing Walcott by the arm away from the door. "It was unbelievable, doctor! They brought him in last year on registration day. Then ten minutes after they left, he started to moan and holler and I don't know *what* all. And the minute I spoke to him, he *shrieked*. At the top of his lungs." She stared at him from behind the blue wings. "Well—you can imagine the effect *that* had. The other little kiddies just went wild. A bunch of them tried to run home. Mr. Ballard came tearing into the room, and grabbed this Achtzner kid by the arm and tried to haul him out."

"Was he violent?"

"He bit Mr. Ballard on the wrist! Clear through *to the bone*! I had to pry his teeth apart with a ruler."

Walcott smiled. Miss Steinecker, staring at him, suddenly giggled and clapped her hand to her mouth. "Poor Mr. Ballard's shins were *covered* with bruises."

"And the boy?"

"Oh, we finally got him into one of the janitor's broom closets. The father came back after four and loaded him into the truck."

"Okay," he said. She opened the door.

The room had black-painted windows; bare unfrosted bulbs hung on long cords from the ceiling. The silver-pebbled screen on the far wall was severely pitted after years of a steady barrage of paperclips and chalk. Walcott made out a few rows of metal chairs, perhaps forty in all, and in the front— waiting patiently as though for a movie to begin— sat two rather shapeless women and a boy of about ten. Miss Steinecker cleared her throat forcefully and whispered: "*Mrs. Achtzner!*"

One of the women stood up stiffly and walked toward them. She carried her heavy purse at one side like a shopping bag, tilting that way as she walked. Walcott could see now that she was somewhat younger than the other one, who continued to gaze at the screen.

"This is Dr. Walcott, the new school-unit doctor,'' Miss Steinecker said. ''Whom you wanted to see.'' She tip-toed primly out the door and closed it behind her. The key rattled in the lock.

Mrs. Achtzner gazed at him defiantly.

''You thuh one sez if Ray kin go tuh school?''

Walcott nodded.

''Well, he kin read now, an' he izzen as spooky as he used to be, so we figgered he should get the same chance as anybody else's kid. So if you could just give him some a that medicine—''

''Just a minute.'' Walcott took his leather-bound notebook out of his breast pocket, and un-clipped the tiny gold pen from inside it. ''What is the boy's name?''

''Raymond Ernest Achtzner.''

''And his—problem?''

''No problem.''

She maintained her defiant stare, waiting for him to write this down. The pen remained poised above the notebook, almost hidden in his fingers.

She shrugged toward the door. ''*They* say he's retarded. Well, I don't need no school principal to tell me Ray's a little bit slow. I'm not denyin' he's a little slow.''

''What's the background?''

''Eh?''

''Do you know—what might have caused it?''

''Nope, we coulden even *tell* till he was a year old. Didden move very much if yuh know what I mean. Woulden kick his legs or nuthin' like other babies. Just sorta laid in his crib starin' at yuh. Cried kinda funny, too—like he had his—dinky caught in the zipper.''

''His what?''

''You know. His *dinky*. What he pees with.

When he gets it caught in his zipper, he sorta squeals."

"Ah."

"Willy figgered it out first. 'Somethin' funny about that kid,' he sez. We took him to Maple Crick finely, and the doctor said he'd never be a normal, yuh know, kid."

"Mmm."

"Willy, he just about blew his stack. Kep callin' Ray a feeb and everythin'. 'I'm not gonna have any goddam feebs in this house,' he kep sayin'. Useta make Gramma cry. She really likes Ray, just like he was hers, yuh know. She stuck up for me."

Walcott glanced at the grandmother still watching the scarred movie screen, her hand resting on the boy's shoulder. His rough blond hair spiked out over his collar.

"How did your other children react to this?"

"Somepin happened when I had Ray, Doctor Waldo. Coulden have no more kids, thuh doctor said."

"A difficult delivery?"

"Oh, it was offul. He woulden come and he woulden come. Doctor said he was all backwards."

Walcott wrote "Anoxia" on his notepad, and put a question mark after it. "May I see him?"

They walked to the front row of chairs. He started to take a small flashlight from his jacket to look into the boy's eyes, but the boy suddenly shouted and threw his hands up, his eyes rolling in terror. Walcott waited for the fear to pass, and put out his arm to shake hands. "Hello, Raymond," he said. The boy flung his hands behind the chair, squealing with alarm. He was small for ten years, but seemed otherwise normal. His hair had been combed down wet, without being washed; it looked like dirty wheat straw. When Walcott looked closer, he saw a layer of chaff spread across the shoulders of Raymond's new denim jacket.

Walcott held out the flashlight for him to see what it was. The boy yelled and fell from his chair, scrambling crab-like to a corner of the room. He tried to squeeze into the angle of the walls.

Walcott turned to the mother. "Do you *beat* him?"

"Gramma and me don't. Willy, if he ketches Ray goin' outta thuh barn, sometimes takes a length a britchin' to him. But he hasn't caught him fer a couple a months."

Without turning to look at Walcott, the grandmother moved quickly to the corner and began stroking the boy's hair. He kept up a shrill whine, and tore at his bare arms with dirty fingernails.

"D'you think he remembers all them whippin's Willy gave him?" Mrs. Achtzner said.

"It wouldn't surprise me." He could not keep the angry edge from his voice. "How long has he stayed in the barn?"

"Oh. Since thuh doctor tole us. I giss he was aroun' three then. Willy said he wasn't gonna 'low any loony feebs in the house."

Walcott made a sudden gesture with his hand, and she blurted, "Willy isn't mean, Doctor Waldo! It's just that he wanted a boy baby so bad, yuh see! And then he was mad when I coulden have no more babies. He was offul mad, Doctor, and when he found out Ray wuzzent, you know, so smart..."

"But he was only three! It's a wonder the cold didn't kill him!"

"Oh, it ain't so cold as yuh might think. The cows help to keep it warm in winter and we fixed a place in the calf-pen. I useta think he'd be lonesome, but Gramma and me went out and talked to him a lot. We taught him ta read."

Walcott almost dropped his flashlight. *"He can read?"*

"Gramma taught him mostly."

He glanced at the old woman. She had calmed Raymond to a whimper, and was spitting on a Kleenex. She stroked it along the red welts covering his arms. Walcott realized he had left his antiseptic and cotton in his car, but it didn't matter. The boy would throw another fit if he approached him.

"Yeah, we taught him tuh read. When we brought him to thuh school, they said he coulden learn nuthin' and not to bring him back, so Gramma and me taught him tuh read."

"What can he read?" Walcott asked, hardly daring to believe her.

She opened her purse and removed a cheap cardboard book. It was an alphabet book with animal pictures and large black letters. There was excrement smeared across the cover, but whether human or bovine he could not tell. Yet anything was possible. If the boy *could* grasp the alphabet, he might just be eligible for a class of slow-learners. It could be the spark needed to fire his intellect, if there was any there.

"Read it." Walcott showed him the book but Raymond cringed, then roared incoherently. His eyes turned up until there was nothing but white showing in them.

Mrs. Achtzner grunted and removed the book from Walcott's hand. She opened it to the first page, where there was a drawing of an ape with the letter "A." She touched the top of her son's head to quieten him. "Read," she said.

The boy stared at the book, his eyelids blinking slowly, his body shivering. "Hay!" he shouted.

Mrs. Achtzner turned to Walcott with a hesitant, pleased smile. Raymond had said "ape."

"Try another one," Walcott said.

She showed Raymond the page with "Bat." Again he stared at the book, and back to her, his eyelids sliding open and shut like valves. He struck his head several times with his fist.

"Banh!" he shouted. This time, the grandmother turned to Walcott and smiled triumphantly. The two women stood beaming at him, and the doctor felt sick. Before he could stop them, they flipped the page to "Cow."

"Hownh!" Raymond roared.

Walcott lifted the book from Mrs. Achtzner's hand, and it fell open at "Porcupine."

The boy stared at the book, and beat his head with his fists again. "Haw!" he shouted.

Mrs. Achtzner blushed in embarrassment. Their secret had been exposed: Raymond couldn't read at all. He had merely memorized the animals by rote. And he had just called the porcupine a dog.

The grandmother's eyes floated in tears of shame and defeat. She spoke for the first time. "He isn't feeling good today. It scares him to come in here."

"Have you ever thought—" Walcott hesitated, then went on quickly. "Have you ever thought of sending him to the Training School? In Moose Jaw?"

Mrs. Achtzner shook her head violently. "*Willy*

wanted tuh send him there, to thuh nut-house, but I woulden let him. Ray izzen a loony, yuh know, just a bit slow."

"Yes," he said. "That's true."

"*Ennybuddy* kin tell that."

"There's no point in putting him in the school system, Mrs. Achtzner," Walcott said, as gently as he could. "They can't teach him anything here."

"But the medicine! They said there was pills."

"There are no pills," he said.

The grandmother grasped his sleeve. "Doctor Walcott, *please* let him into school. Darla and me can help him learn. He'll listen to us."

"I'm sorry." He reached down and detached her clinging fingers from his coat. "If there was any chance—"

The door opened suddenly and Miss Steinecker peered around its edge. "How are we all doing?" she said brightly.

The doctor shook himself to settle his jacket, a professional habit, and walked to the door. When he turned around, he saw the two women take Raymond and lead him to the front row of chairs, each holding one hand. Miss Steinecker closed the door. She clicked the key into the lock.

"You don't have to lock the door," he said.

She hesitated. "He bit Mr. Ballard clear through to the bone. I can't take responsibility for—"

"Leave it open," Walcott said, raising his hand in a sharp threatening gesture. "I'm *telling* you to leave it open."

GONE THE BURNING SUN

Gone the Burning Sun is a dramatic biography of Norman Bethune, one of Canada's greatest heroes. There have been many attempts to portray this complex and contradictory man on stage and film, but none even came close to the exciting character that lay below the surface.

I had been doing research on Bethune for ten years before I discovered in Scotland in 1980 that I was related to him, through my great-great-grandmother. Norman's predecessors, she was a Beaton of the famous clan which derived from the Isle of Mull in the Hebrides. The following year, while teaching in China (and being mistaken for the legendary Chinese hero nearly everywhere), I realized that Bethune was the ideal subject for a one-man drama, one that I might conceivably perform myself some day. That dream was made real in 1983, when I toured the People's Republic of China, performing *Gone the Burning Sun* in several cities, at universities and language institutes. The audiences were astonished and delighted that a Western play could come so richly alive for them, and their reaction was essential to placing the final bricks in the structure of this international play—designed for both Chinese and Western audiences, thanks to the music of composer David Liang. It was the superb performance of actor David Fox, however, that brought it to life at the Guelph Spring Festival in May, 1984.

Bethune in Montreal

BETHUNE: Good morning, gentlemen! Welcome to the Montreal Royal Victoria Hospital, jewel in the crown of international Medico-Pulmonary Surgery. Now—what does that mean to innocent young interns like yourselves? *(pause)* You're absolutely right, son—sweet bugger-all! Because in fact it's no better than some waterfront abortion-den, if you look at the statistics. Riddled with bureaucracy and rotten with incompetence. So don't expect a medical utopia, here or anywhere else. The inefficiency will make you sweat. The hypocrisy will make you puke. More patients die in the Royal Vic from the cautious fumbling of old men, than they do from T.B. in the slums of Verdun. *(pause)* Cynical? Not at all. *Realistic.* To expect better would only create disillusionment. And God knows, there are enough disillusioned doctors already. When *I* was given a second life—through radical pneumothorax, I left general practice and became a lung surgeon. One of the best, according to some. Oh, not these fossils, of course. There are people here who say Bethune *kills* his patients. Well, it's true: I have a high mortality record. In fact, I operate on cases they're all terrified to allow into their offices—the hopeless dying. *(rises angrily)* So to hell with them! If you want to be lung surgeons, you'll follow *my* technique—fast diagnosis —out *there*, in the reeking streets of Montreal—fast operation, fast treatment. Yes, they die on my operating table—but remember—Bethune gives them a sporting chance.

(He pulls a stethoscope from his pocket.)

BETHUNE: First demonstration this morning. Identify this object. *(points)* Right! I believe you have a future in medicine, son. Well, take a good look at "the stethoscope." The symbol of life, right? Wrong! This little device has killed more lung patients than all the cigarettes ever manufactured by Imperial Tobacco! My advice: wear it around your neck like a magic amulet—bit of voodoo never hurt anybody—remember the doctor is the holy priest— but for *results*, stick to your x-ray machine. Five hundred percent more reliable. And when you're ready to work—these!

(He presents a set of heavy rib shears, rather like hedge shears.)

BETHUNE: Rib shears. My proudest invention. Look dangerous, don't they? Well, they're not made for delicacy. They're made to cut through *bone* in one stroke, to get *at* the disease, to collapse the lung, and give it—rest. We're dealing with an extreme disease, gentlemen—and it demands extreme remedies. Make no mistake. You will get blood on your hands. And other unpleasant organisms. You'll have to overcome some pet aversions, see them for what they are. Maggots, for example.

Last month, I introduced forty-six live fly maggots into the chest cavity of one of my patients. Having trouble getting the septic fluids to drain. Now maggots *love* to eat rotting flesh—and would you believe it?—within ten days my little maggots had made him healthy by consuming the entire infection. The despised vermin of this world can be valuable, gentlemen, if you allow yourselves to think in extremes.

Well, I don't want to shock you—but you'll hear lots of shocking things about Norman Bethune. Playboy—alcoholic—eccentric. Now I'm a Red! Ha! But if I'm remembered for anything, it'll be the development of the artificial pneumothorax machine.

(He shows an advertising poster of it.)

BETHUNE: A pump to collapse the lung. With this machine, I actually maintain my patients' lives —including my own. Yes? *(Chuckles)* No, laddie— medical inventions will not make you rich. Unless you're a psychiatrist. Or a plastic surgeon.

(Bell rings.)

BETHUNE: Consider these thoughts as you memorize your Latin. Tomorrow's lecture: Bedside Manners and Bigger Fees.

(Lights to black.)

Bethune in China

BETHUNE: Alright, what've we got here? Dzuxin. Take the splints off that leg. Phew. Okay. Gangrene. Get the chloroform ready, Xiao-hua. We'll have to take it off. Dzu-xin, you can start washing the leg. Tell the attendants they've got to hold him down. Tight. And bring two buckets full of *kai-shui*.

(He sets to work, laying instruments onto the table.)

BETHUNE: Good God! Where has this man been kept? Those officers have got to send the wounded here straight away—not let them lie around rotting for three days! What's the point in *being* at the front, if we can't get them in here? Right now—ready? Hold him down. *(To the patient)* Tong-zhi—ni hao? (Laughs) Good. *Hao-hao!* But—lost too much blood. Have to fix it, right now. Tell him we're short of anaesthetic. He's going to have to endure it. Good man. *Kuai-kuai—dong-bu-dong*? Okay. Give him a slug of *mao-tai*. It's all that'll help now. Hang on. I'll have one too. Right. *Gam-bei. (Drinks, takes his knife.)* Let's go. Streeetch it out—nice and easy. That's it.

(A sudden explosion shakes the table.)

(Cuts with a scalpel) You see the angle? Remember now, keep these blades sharp. You want to be doctors, you've got to learn the skills of four workers: blacksmith, tailor, carpenter, and butcher. Dammit, hold him *down*! Give us more chloroform! Now. Cut, you bastard, cut! *(He hurls the scalpel at the floor.)* Knife! Gimme a knife! And it better be sharp, or I'll have your guts for garters, young lady! *(Works)* Alright. Fine. Forceps. Good. Another needle. Right, that's it. Okay. Xiao-hua. Finish up the stitching will you? I need a smoke.

(He steps aside, pulls a battered cigarette from his pocket, lights it. The sound of battle in background eases.)

BETHUNE: Good morning, General. Morning, evening—what's the difference? The guns. Destroy all sense of time. Rest? How can I rest when I'm needed every minute? No, I *don't* have to sleep! We did 68 straight hours last week, during the battle at Chi Hui. A hundred and fifteen cases. So I don't think I'm ready for bed yet, General. Oh? Why? Any complaints of negligence? Okay, you were right about the hospital. I made the wrong decision. Broke my heart, to see three months work blown up in ten minutes. We were lucky to get our equipment out. Now we're going to mobile units. See? I'm learning to take your advice, control my arrogance. But that doesn't mean you're right this time! I don't need to be relieved. My medics are already working twice as hard as I am. What kind of a teacher would I be, if I didn't set an example for them? An *order? (Laughs shortly)* Well, I can't disobey an order, can I, General? *(He flops down on the table.)* All right. Here I am. Lying down. Resting. No objection if I smoke, I hope? *(He smokes furiously for a minute, until he realizes he is being ridiculous. He flings it down, leaps up, stamps it out.)*

BETHUNE: Dammitall, this is ridiculous! How can a guy sleep with a battle going on a mile away? General, I came here to serve the people. That's what Chairman Mao asked of me. Now, you gonna let me serve the people or not? Never mind "orders"! Exhaustion is a medical question, right? Not a military question. And in the medical command, I issue the orders—not you. So I'm giving an order. Bethune—get back to the operating table. Look! Another soldier going in. See that arm? My medics can cut it off. But they can't set it. You want that arm to carry a rifle again, General? *(Pause)* Dzuxin, where's my knife?

THE VILLAGE IDIOTS OF GREECE

In Astros a broken cripple haunts
the bus stop in the square
cart-wheeling through the diesel fumes.
He enjoys a measure of self-respect
laughing rudely at alighting tourists.

The morning coffee drinkers of Spetsa
torment a mongoloid who hops
around the ancient stone mosaics
a bald mandrill dancing
for their laughter.

The clown in Agios Petros grins
with gnarled teeth and scrapes
his head in frenzies but
he wears a clean white shirt.
His mother must be still alive.

Here in Kastri, like elsewhere,
there are no pinball machines.
Our pastime is a crazed beggar
who shrieks in Oriental chords
and turns his eyeballs back

so far he shuts us from his sight
to watch the demons
grappling in his skull.
But why exactly one in
every town? Exactly one.

Does a village blessed with two
donate its extra to less favoured towns?
And if our present moron dies
will men appear outside my door
with ropes and hooks?

DEMETRIO

The evening ritual begins
with Lassie reruns dubbed in Greek.
Following the Three Stooges we
climb the mile of cliff-face
to his parents' house, whitewash
dripping in the endless rain.

He always treats the corpse with cheer.
On good days the old man groans back;
on the bad — silence as
Demetrio lifts the old fisherman
dying of broken leg and bedsores
from his pool of fecal slime.

For fourteen months, nine days
Jimmy has spooned mush to the mask
of pain, a mask that still
can laugh at the stupid things
the nets of village fishermen
heave daily to the village pier.

The conversation gets to doctors
though only Jimmy does the talking.
Together they consider
the nursing homes of Athens.
(Jimmy turns to say in English
"In hospital, my papa is *kaput*.")

The final rite is classic
television of the fifties:
Gramps and Lassie save the world in Greek
(Jimmy rehearsed it all the way).
Larry pokes Moe and Curly in the eye.
Tears of laughter burn our cheeks.

(CLEAN MONDAY), 1974

We are Orthodox by accident
made pious by a five-day rain.
The rivers of Tripotoma
plunge like avalanches.

But one is grateful for a stone room
in this olive-pickers' house
dense with candlesmoke and icons.

For our first meal of Lent
we enjoy a sack of sour olives
one tin of salted squid (allowed,
but grey as hand grenades).

If a week from now,
crazed for meat and
eyeing the only mule,
we haven't broken our fast
God's will be done.

Across the rock-grinding torrent
three fat hens cackle
in the sunlight over eggs.

GETTING TO KITHIRA

1

From the window of the Sparta Tourist Police Office, the sergeant could see a young foreign couple approaching. He yawned and gestured at the constable to get up and attend to them. The sergeant thought it beneath his dignity to talk to foreigners unless they drove a car or came in one of the luxury tour buses from Athens. The constable was perfectly capable of dealing with backpackers.

The constable stepped to the counter as the pair entered the door. The sergeant remained beside the interrupted *tavli* game, clicking his amber worry-beads and watching them from behind a newspaper.

For a moment the couple looked around the office, as tourists nearly always did, studying the posters and the racks full of brochures. The young man stepped to the counter. He wore a faded denim jacket and blue jeans. A dark moustache plunging downward at the corners of his mouth made him look more sinister than he might have been, though his eyes were sharp and critical. He had the thickened and scored fingers of a workman. A drifter, but perhaps educated.

The sergeant could not be sure about the girl. She looked English or Swedish, with her fair sun-burned skin and one of those silly straw hats they always wore to keep the sun off their faces. Although it was still very early in the season, she wore shorts, and as he noticed her thighs, the sergeant thought he could see why. He put the newspaper aside and stood up, so the counter did not obscure his view. Yes, they were spectacular legs; beautiful. She must be an athlete, or perhaps a dancer. The muscles of her calves and thighs strained against the skin like rising bread. However she was rather flat-chested, and when she smiled at him nervously, she showed a set of small white teeth. Definitely English.

"*Melate Eglaisika?*" the young man said.

"I speak a little English," said the constable.

"Good. We are heading for the island of Kithira. What I'd like to know is where to catch the boat, and when it goes."

The constable turned and looked at the sergeant. They all looked at the sergeant, who was still staring at the young woman's calves. He sat down again in some embarrassment and clicked the beads through his fingers. He had an index finger-nail at least an inch long and filed to a sharp point, of which he was very proud. He displayed it toward them as he considered. "No boats to Kithira," he said finally, in Greek.

"I'm afraid there are no boats to Kithira, sir."

"I don't get it."

The constable held up his hands. "Sir, here in Sparta we are many kilometres from the sea. What would we know about boats, anyway?"

The girl dropped her bag to the floor with an irritated gesture and stepped up to the counter. She pointed at the map of southern Greece on the wall behind the policeman. "On the map, it shows a domestic boat service that operates from Githion. What about that?"

"Anyway, there is nothing on Kithira," the policeman countered. "Not even hotels. Why would you want to go there?"

"We just want to go and have a look at it."

"You must have some information," the young man said. "Even a tourist brochure."

The policeman shrugged again. Then he returned to his seat at the *tavli* table, across from the sergeant. "Your play," he said in Greek, and picked up his own set of beads, which began to click.

The pair of foreigners stared at the map for a moment, as though trying to memorize it, then stepped back out into the street. As the door opened, the wailing chant of the lottery ticket sellers drifted inside, and the still air was filled with a litany of *"Lucky numbers!"*

2

On the street, the couple stood for a moment, hesitating over direction. It was Amy who really wanted to go to Kithira, but Foster had agreed to scout the way, mostly because he had mastered a few rudimentary fragments of the language. "Why not spend a few days in Sparta? There's a lot to see here," he said.

"There's nothing."

"How could there be nothing? Sparta's famous, isn't it? The home of the hard-bitten soldier? The cradle of Fascism?"

"That is a gross distortion."

"Tell that to the boys in the tourist office. What's going on there, anyway?"

"You put them off with your arrogance. You could be more diplomatic."

"Bullshit! Are we going to explore Sparta or not?"

"There's nothing left of the ancient city, Foster. It disappeared long ago. It's just another country town. A rather nice one on the surface but not—significant."

"Well, goddamit, isn't that disastrous! Look, what are we going to see on Kithira, anyway? More ruins, right? Piles of crumbling rock! I had my fill of goddam ruins at Mistras. Four days of crumbled rock!"

One thing about the old Byzantine capital of Mistras that Foster *had* enjoyed was the little guesthouse they discovered in the nearby village. It was right beside a good fish *taverna* and the balcony outside their room overlooked a steep valley full of pine trees. On the third day of their stay, he elected to sit in the cool shadows of the balcony, drinking wine and playing his harmonica.

It was on their final morning there, while studying her map over breakfast, that Amy had noticed the island of Kithira. It lay off the southern tip of the Peloponnesian mainland, dropped into the Mediterranean like an egg from the Greek underbelly. As they had travelled in a general southerly direction, through Corinth and Argos and Mistras, it seemed inevitable they would reach the strange

Greek island they had never heard of before.

Amy's curiosity was stimulated by a brief reference she had discovered in the ancient *Baedeker* she'd brought from London: Kithira was the legendary birthplace of Aphrodite, goddess of love. But they could find no other information. EOT, the Greek tourist bureau, gave out dozens of coloured brochures, describing each of the hundreds of islands that surrounded the country like a universe of stars. But nothing for Kithira. This was enough to stir Foster's interest.

Why then was the place so inaccessible? There were ten boats a day from Athens to shopworn cruise stops like Mykonos and Hydra. But there was no apparent interest in the birthplace of Aphrodite; it simply was not mentioned in the tourist literature. And now, it seemed, there was no way of getting there.

They stopped at a small *souvlaki* stand near their hotel, and bought *gyros* pastries stuffed with meat and tomatoes. On the map Foster unfolded onto the table, there was clearly a dotted line showing regular boat service from the port of Githion, fifty kilometres further south of Sparta. He stared at the map and folded it back into his shirt pocket.

"Anyway, I could get into modern Greece. Sparta looks like a great little place. Lots of restaurants. Good climate."

"Alright, we'll stay overnight. We can take the bus to Githion in the morning."

3

Githion was a pretty little town, more a fishing

village than a port of call. They found the Tourist
Police office in the back room of a fish market on
the town square. The policeman here was more
helpful, informing them that a boat stopped at
Githion once a week on its way to Kithira from Pir-
eas. It left at 3 a.m. the following Sunday.

"Four days!" Foster said. "What are we going
to do in the meantime?"

"Well, explore, I suppose. This town, for exam-
ple, was the seaport of ancient Sparta. It must be
full of antiquity! And down the Mani peninsula,
south of here, there's some famous caves."

"Yeah, okay."

"I know! Let's take a three-day hike down and
back. It's the right distance."

It was an exceptionally beautiful walk, just the
right combination of clear sky, roadside taverns,
brilliantly coloured flowers. They came across
strange Mani towers frowning over the olive trees.
The Mani peninsula was the only part of Greece
never conquered by Turks during the middle ages,
but the fierce-looking defence towers were built for
protection from feuding clans, not the Turks. The
Mani people had mellowed in recent years, and the
towers stood empty and unchallenged.

The caves at Glifada were disappointing, much
less interesting than the surrounding countryside.
But like dutiful tourists, they took the little boat,
gliding past fairyland castles lit with red and green
spotlights. They pretended astonishment as their
youthful guide tried to make obscure shapes into
elephants or flowers.

Foster began to feel claustrophobic anxiety and
cut the tour short, to the chagrin of their guide.
Back in the sunshine, Foster sighed extravagantly

and stretched his arms. They climbed down the rocks to a quiet beach lying in a sheltered cove.

"This is better, eh? Sun and sand. Here—put the wine in the water to cool."

"Shall we start back to Githion today, or force-march tomorrow?"

"I don't want to think about marching right now. Where's the olives?"

"Foster?"

"Hmm?"

"You don't mind, do you? Going to Kithira?"

"One place is as good as another. We still have two months."

"It's been fine so far, don't you think?"

"I don't think about it. Enjoy and survive, that's my motto."

"God! More backwoods philosophy. Don't you have any sensitivity at *all?*"

"You don't talk sensitivity, you feel it. Like this."

"Don't."

"Or this. Is that sensitive?"

"*Please* don't! There's someone sitting over there."

"What?"

He looked where she pointed. A young man was sitting on a jagged rock at the other end of the tiny beach, reading. He was very tall and thin, and wore a black sailor's cap. Even at a distance of fifty yards, Foster could see his smooth, unlined face and trusting eyes. If that didn't give him away, his open-toed sandals and football jersey did.

"Don't look. He'll come over."

"I'd have thought you'd enjoy company."

"Maybe we can just roll behind those rocks

and..."

"It's too late, Mr. Smith. Here he comes."

The young man approached, his eyes cast shyly downward. He kept one finger separating the pages of his book, as though about to read them. Lawrence Durrell.

"Hi."

"Hi."

"Fantastic, aren't they? The caves."

"Wonderful."

"I thought they were tacky," Foster said. Amy glanced at him. "But then I'm not big on caves. Olive?"

"You're American!"

"No, I'm not."

"No? Canadian! Well, it's the same thing, isn't it? I went to Montreal for Expos."

"Fantastic. Well, my dear, it's time we began the long trek back home. What do you say?"

"Alright. The wine first?"

"No, let's keep it for some quiet roadside picnic."

"Where are you headed?" the boy asked.

"Well, nowhere definite. But we're generally headed for the island of Kithira. After that?" Foster shrugged. "Nice meeting you."

"Yes. Thanks for the olive."

"See you around."

"You bet. Have a nice day."

They shook hands and set out on the road toward their rendezvous with the boat. "You were not very affable," Amy said.

"Survive and enjoy."

"Barbarian."

"What you see is what you get. There were days

you *liked* a decisive male.''

Foster had met Amy at London Polytechnic. She was the instructor in an Anthropology seminar he had registered in because it kept him off the streets during the afternoon. He had come to London on the invitation of an artist friend who had a good thing going at the Hornsey Art College. Foster had never been in England, and was soon committed to the night-life in the West End, Sundays in the parks, forays into alien ghettoes full of Pakistanis, Arabs, Irishmen, and Maltese.

He had invited Ms. Amy Coleman out for a drink, and it wasn't long before they were going to plays together, then making excursions to Whipsnade and the North Downs in her little car. She had invited him to her bed one night, and they had repeated the experience at irregular intervals. Nothing special. Just good company. When Amy got a six-month sabbatical at Christmas, and Foster faced a long English winter, they decided to pool their resources and head south. She had always wanted to visit Greece; he was keen on covering distance, in any direction. The trip would squander the rest of the cash windfall he'd gotten wrangling for the Altman film in the Rockies.

And they both enjoyed walking. Minor irritations arose, as they always did over the washing or their eating habits or the jagged philosophical dialectic they occasionally undertook, and they walked them off. Walking absorbed so much concentration.

By mid-afternoon of the third day, they strolled into Githion, footsore and sunburned, carrying nearly empty packs, and satisfied with the 150 kilometres they had just covered. They were ready for

Kithira.

4

The landlady at the guest-house woke them at 2 a.m. Blinking away their exhaustion, they shuffled to the dock with their packsacks. There a rusted old trawler called the *Kanaris* coughed a plume of fiery smoke into the night sky. Amazingly, it had arrived on time, and if the activity around the gangplank was any indication, intended to leave on time. There were a couple of ragged Gypsy men carrying a huge bundle of carpets, half-a-dozen country people, presumably Kithirans heading home, and the tall American boy. He was wearing a T-shirt that said "Don't mess with this kid." Foster refused to respond to his greeting.

Once aboard, each group of passengers found a corner of the saloon for their bags. The *Kanaris* chugged into the darkness. The gypsies immediately rolled themselves up in their carpets and began a raucous, antiphonal snore. A steward appeared, serving coffee. The American boy approached their table.

"Are you on your honeymoon?"

"We're not married," Foster said. "This is a tart I met in England."

"Oh, *English*!"

"Born within the sound of Big Ben, pal."

"But you're going to Kithira, right?"

Amy interceded. "Yes. So mysterious, isn't it?"

"What do you mean?"

"Well, the boat schedule, for one thing. The lack of tourist promotion. It's like some enormous bloody secret. Why are you going?"

"No reason. When you mentioned it, I looked it up on the map. Lucky about the boat, huh?"

"Yes. You're from America?"

"Originally. I live in Hamburg now. Studying opera."

Amy's eyes lit up. "An opera singer? *Really*?"

"A conductor, actually. But I sing a bit, too. You want to hear something?"

"No, no!" Foster cried, though he realized no one else in the saloon would have noticed, much less objected. "Really—let's try to get some rest."

He wanted desperately to stretch out on the bench and sleep, but Richard was keen on telling about his travel adventures. Foster could not understand how he had made it that far without being robbed and beaten. It transpired that he'd hitchhiked through Yugoslavia. Only an American, Foster thought. That passport is a magic amulet.

The sun was well above the horizon by the time the ship chugged up to the dock at Kapsali, on the southern tip of Kithira. It would return in a week, though the steward thought there was a small boat that ran back to the mainland on charter.

Kapsali harbour looked deserted in the morning light, the gleaming crescent of white buildings like vacant shells along the beach. The main town was at least five kilometres away, on the high cliffs overlooking the harbour. Even up there, no sign of life could be discerned. Beyond the town, they could see only rock and sky, not a tree anywhere. It was a barren-looking place. Even their fellow-voyagers and the gypsies had already vanished from sight.

"*Pour ini to kafenion?*" he asked the solitary dockhand as the boat slid back into the Mediterranean.

"*Pamme*," the man said, waving them toward a new two-storey building near the end of the pier. It turned out to be his place, a hotel and coffee shop, sparsely furnished inside and so cold it seemed air-conditioned. There was nothing to eat but coffee and *friganes*, the dried bread crusts Greeks liked to crunch in their teeth for breakfast.

"It's no tourist season now," the owner complained. "What you doing here?"

"Just curious," Amy said. "We understand this is the birthplace of Aphrodite. Is it?"

The man shrugged. "Up in town is museum. Man there knows all about this island. Me, I'm from Kriti. Bus business is ver' bad."

"How do we get to the town?"

The dockhand-hotelkeeper shrugged. "There is a taxi, but today is gone to Agia Pelagia. Most people walk. Why bother? You stay here, wait till the boat comes back. I give you winter rates, okay? Nice beach."

"Is that right?" Richard said, as they climbed the long switchback trail along the cliff face toward the town, which was also named Kithira.

"What?"

"It's the birthplace of Aphrodite?"

"So they say. A legend, of course."

"What else do you know about it?"

"It's been over-run by the usual gangs of invaders: Franks, Venetians, Turks. Actually, it was a British colony for a while in the nineteenth century, according to *Baedeker*."

"So how come you speak Greek?" Richard asked Foster.

"It's nothing—a few words from phrasebooks. You pick it up fast. We've been here for a couple of months."

"Together?"

"Together."

The town appeared as a jumble of white plaster cubes piled above the shoulders of rock. An awesome, Venetian-style fortress jutted from the brow of the cliff, barely distinguishable from the rock itself. A few rusted cannon-snouts still threatened the Mediterranean. Behind the castle stretched a labyrinth of alleys. The clusters of houses gleamed like dice, the streets so narrow the travellers had to remove their backpacks to move between the buildings. At each corner a small child peeped out, watching their progress. A church-bell tolled somewhere.

A shutter suddenly banged open above their heads and a woman's black mandilla appeared. "*Zitate domatio*?" She beckoned them upwards. "You want sleep?"

"*Zitame.*"

The woman had a cousin whose sister-in-law sometimes rented out an extra room in her house. She led them along one of the twisting passageways, and a hundred yards along they were hopelessly lost. The cousin's sister-in-law examined the trio with dismay. She had visitors from Athens staying with her. The room was occupied.

"Isn't there a room anywhere?" Foster asked their guide.

The woman in black turned hostile, the flash of gold in her teeth disappearing behind a pursed mouth. "Perhaps the *taverna*," she muttered and vanished down a side passage.

Foster finally persuaded a small boy to lead them to the *taverna*. It was located on the main street, not far from the museum and castle. A sign painted on the wall said "Johnny's Hotel and Tavern." Hospitality enveloped them like a warm cloud as they approached. A woman ran out, chattering in English. She did not eye with suspicion their packs, or lift her nose at the spectacle of Amy's ringless finger.

"Sure, I got two rooms! You all together, or what?"

She was an attractive woman, not more than thirty. She tended the tavern while her husband worked in the terraced fields above the village.

"The lady and I are travelling together. Richard would like his own room."

"This way, please."

She took them up an outside staircase to the second floor. Richard was given a small room at the back, while Foster and Amy were shown to the front bedroom, overlooking the street. A boy was sitting on the bed, dressing hurriedly.

"*Vlahos*!" the woman shouted. "Get out." She cracked the boy on the side of the head and scooped a pair of evil-smelling socks from the floor. "My son," she said with a proud smile. "He's so stupid."

"I'm sorry we had to move him," Amy said, without sincerity.

"He only sleeps here in the winter. The sun coming in the window is so nice. But—soon it will be summer, *ne*?"

They unpacked their bags and washed, while the woman—who said her name was Galatea—went downstairs to prepare breakfast. Foster planned to spend the rest of the day sleeping, but Amy and Richard voted to eat, then do some exploring before retiring early.

Breakfast consisted of huge bowls of sheep's milk yoghurt, with hot pastries and Greek coffee. Richard ate two bowls. "I'm really into health foods," he explained. "This stuff is fantastic. Look, how fresh it is! You make it yourself?" he asked Galatea.

"Of course."

"No preservatives, see?"

But Richard's enthusiasm waned when he examined his bill. "What? Thirty drachmas for two bowls of yoghurt? That's more than a dollar! Ridiculous. You don't even import it. It's *made* here!"

Foster stood up, embarrassed, and walked to the back wall of the tavern, where a large map of the island was tacked up. Kithira was pear-shaped, about forty kilometres long by twenty across. There was a road along the spine of the island, with a village every five or six kilometres. The road stretched to the tiny harbour of Agia Pelagia at the north end. Along the way, several churches, monasteries, and caves were marked. Nothing indicated a shrine to Aphrodite, but it did look like an interesting hike. The sun had now warmed the buildings and streets, and the heat seeped through the open door of the tavern.

"I'll give you 25, and that's all. On the mainland, I only paid 15."

"For Christ's sake, Richard, don't be so cheap! You were lucky to get something you liked."

The boy looked at Foster with wounded eyes. He'd only been trying to bargain, as he had in all his travels across Europe. Everyone in Greece did. Why was Foster being so bitchy?

The woman smiled as she pocketed the money.

"*Efheristo*," she said to Foster.

"*Para kalo*."

"*Melate Ellenica*?"

"*Ligo, ligo. Essis melate Eglaisika poli kala, Kirea*."

She laughed and winked toward Richard. "German?"

"American. He's travelling with us for a while."

Foster stumbled upstairs to sleep while Amy and Richard went exploring. They all met for lunch in the *taverna*. Galatea had prepared an octopus in tomato sauce with fried potatoes, olives and fresh bread. She boasted that the food had all been gathered by her husband's hand.

"So? What did you find?"

Amy's eyes brightened. "Oh, *everything*!" The curator in the museum is a dear. He ran home to get a book in English that describes the island. Do you know there are three hundred and eighteen churches here?"

"That shouldn't be surprising. Greece is covered with them. What do you want to do this afternoon?"

"Well, there's supposed to be an interesting graveyard with some English crypts."

"With Richard?"

"Why not?"

"He's getting to me."

"Oh, you just didn't like him bargaining like that. He's alright, Fos."

"He's a big baby."

"All the more reason to take him along. He's lonely, can't you see that?"

"Hm."

"In Hamburg, he doesn't know anyone either.

We're the first people he's spoken English to, for months.''

"I don't believe it."

"Don't be a prig, Foster. This is a wonderful island—I'm glad we came."

"That's good." He stroked her cheek.

Theirs was an odd relationship: not quite lovers, more than friends. Since leaving England, they had neither grown closer together nor further apart. She was an odd creature, really, physically attractive but shy, and riven with insecurities. And having been married once, Foster was stingy in offering security.

5

That evening a party began in the *taverna*, which they joined with gusto. It was the usual thing, a *bouzouki* player in the corner, a dozen people rollicking through the country dances, many bottles of *retsina* drunk.

"What's the occasion?" Foster asked Galatea.

"No occasion."

"No?"

"Just you people are here."

"Come on. You don't hold a party every time you have guests, do you?"

Her teeth flashed a wicked smile. "Sure. Why not? Anyway, you are the first of the season. Always special. Come. Dance!"

Even Richard got into the swing of it, though he refused to drink any wine. For some one with musical training, he looked suspiciously inept on the dance floor.

"What makes you so sure he's really a music student?"

"Oh, Foster! Don't be ridiculous! I heard him sing."

"You did?"

"This morning, when we went to the graveyard. He has a beautiful voice. He did 'Recondita Armonia' from *Tosca*."

"Well, he's no dancer."

"We can't *all* be multi-talented, darling. Excuse me."

This was such a strange bit of sarcasm coming from Amy, that he found himself brooding on it, and watching the tall young American from a corner of the *taverna*. The boy was clearly infatuated with her. Should he let the flirtation go on? There was no harm in it, he supposed. It wasn't as if she belonged to him. Still, there could be trouble. The kid was such a fake.

"Eh, *cumari!* You not played out from dancing already, are you?"

"No, just fuelling up. Say, where did you learn to speak English, anyway?"

"Australia. My husband and me go to Melbourne in 1960. To make a fortune, *ne*? Beautiful city."

"But you came back?"

She sighed. "Sometimes is difficult. Iannis did restaurant work, and he started a dry cleaning shop. But—"

"Yes?"

"He was homesick. We saved our money to buy this little taverna. And of course, he wanted to raise the boy in the old way."

"Of course."

She was sitting beside him at the corner table, her bosom rising and falling from the exertion of the *Tchamiko*. She began to poke absent-mindedly at the deep-fried squid on the plate. Her husband had come in from the kitchen to take over the *bouzouki* playing.

"You'll stay for a few days?"

"I'm afraid not. We're on a walking tour. I think we'll leave in the morning."

Foster was alarmed to see tears rising in Galatea's eyes. He suddenly picked up her hand and kissed it, then dropped it again. She smiled nervously, glancing not at her husband, but toward the far map-covered wall where Amy and Richard were engaged in earnest conversation.

"Where are you going?"

"Agia Pelagia. We'll hire a boat to cross back to the mainland."

"Walk! But there is a taxi that goes to Agia Pelagia. Twice a day! Why walk?"

"It's the only way to get to know a place."

She stared at him. "*Sto kalo!* You English! You know, there is *nothing* at Agia Pelagia! A dirty little fishing village. If you want to see something, go to the monastery at Mirtidia on the west side. You can get there and back in one day."

"It isn't up to me to decide."

"No?"

"No. Not any more."

6

In the morning, Richard woke them, tapping politely at the open door. He was wearing his packsack. "Well, all set to go?"

"Go where?"

"Walking across the island."

"Coming along, are you?"

"Sure. If you don't mind. I don't have anything else to do."

Foster turned to look at Amy in despair. He had deliberately avoided any mention of Richard the night before. She raised her shoulders from the blankets and shrugged, then smiled brightly. "Had breakfast, Richard?"

"Yes, I found a little store behind the museum that sells yoghurt at a reasonable price. And look—a kilo of cheese for the hike."

"Good thinking," Foster muttered. His mouth tasted like turpentine, and there was no jug of water in the room to relieve his thirst. "Well, darling. Shall we get dressed and under way?"

For the first time in weeks, there was no sun beating against the white walls and the dust. A light mist drifted through the town's convoluted passageways, though the air was still warm. The countryside looked even more deserted than the coast below. Although the ground was covered with heather and struggling flowers, there was not a tree to be seen. Nearly every farm house lay abandoned, its pebbled stone walls crumbling back into the ground.

By lunchtime, they had ascended to the ridge of high rock that formed the backbone of the island. At one crevice a tiny village squatted like a white-plastered bird of prey. As they approached, several old people drifted out of the doors and stood in a semi-circle, watching.

"Are you foreigners walking to Agia Pelagia?" a black-robed crone asked.

"Yes," Foster said. "Can you give us some water?"

"Some water for the foreigners!" she shouted.

"Is there a *taverna* here?"

"Alas, no. We had one many years ago, but the boy went to Australia. Like everyone else. Leaving us behind."

"Is that where your children are?"

"All gone to Australia. There are no young people left."

"Still, it's a very beautiful island."

"Yes, but—" She gestured vacantly. "No money."

The old people surrounded them, staring at Amy's muscular thighs, at Richard's expensive bright-red pack.

"Let's get out of here, okay?" Richard muttered. He refused the glass of water, though it was he who had been the thirstiest as they'd approached the village.

"What's wrong?" Amy said.

"They make me nervous. And I want to get to the boat."

"Good God, man, we've hardly begun. What's your hurry?"

"I just like to keep moving. I promised some friends I'd meet them in Athens next weekend."

"Piss off then."

"Foster!"

"Listen Amy, he wanted to come along, right? How come *he* starts dictating the terms all of a sudden?"

"Don't make a scene, Fos. Not here."

The old men and women had backed away, staring at them. One pushed forward with a jug. "Here, take this with you. Leave it with the priest in Milopotama, when you're finished."

"Thank you, Grandma. Now we're on our way. *A dio.*"

"*A dio.*" They stood waving while the foreigners disappeared down the winding rocky path. The sun was beginning to burn through the mist, and they stripped to their T-shirts.

"I'm sorry," Richard said, "but you never know how clean those dishes are. A friend of mine got a bug in Italy that nearly killed him."

"Amy, do you remember the castle at Astros? And those yellow flowers on the slope below it?"

"*Manoosa!*"

"Right. There's a whole hillside of them."

They had crossed the spine of rocks and begun a long descent into a startling green valley carpeted with ferns and flowers. Here tiny white chapels appeared every few hundred metres. Most were deserted but several still reeked of incense. A few farmers were still around to light the candles. They began to meet more people on the road—a little family with a donkey, an old man leading a dozen sheep. Olive trees appeared in neatly tended terraces. Women working in the fields would run to the road to comment on their progress, as though watching apparitions. Few enough foreigners on Kithira, but *walking*? Unheard of.

Their legend grew as they strode along, until even Richard began to swell from the attention. People brought them oranges and tomatoes, cheese and apples, wishing them a good journey.

As they neared the village of Milopotama, Foster could see a crowd of people advancing up the road to meet them. At the front of the group was a priest, wearing a tall black Orthodox hat. A wide grin showed through his grey beard. The priest's arms swept open in greeting. "Welcome, my friends. Welcome to Milopotama. We heard you were coming, and we are delighted to see you. It's many months since we've had such distinguished visitors. *Yorgos*! Run and tell Vassilis to serve the coffee and *gleka*."

A ten-year-old boy split from the crowd and sprinted ahead into the village. The crowd settled around them, buzzing with words of welcome as the triumphal procession advanced toward the tall trees of Milopotama.

At the *taverna*, Vassilis had laid out coffee and snacks. The village elders were seated at tables, playing *tavli* and trying hard not to stare at Amy's legs.

"So, you have come to Milopotama. A thousand welcomes. How long will you stay?" The priest spoke with a distinct Australian twang.

"Just overnight, I think."

"Not long enough. Such a beautiful place! And you must go to visit the caves at Agia Sofia. One of the wonders of Greece! You've heard of them? That alone requires one day. And of course, at this time of year, the air is so refreshing, you could spend days just sitting by the river!"

"Why aren't there more tourists here, Father?"

He shrugged. "I don't know. Perhaps there are so few people. They've all gone to—"

"I know. Australia."

"But we have a hotel here. Did you know? Of course, it's empty now, because of the season. But people have gone to bring blankets and sheets from their homes right away, so you will have good comfortable beds."

Richard was poking at the dish full of candied

fruit in front of him. "Does this stuff have sugar in it?"

"Yes," Foster said. "If you don't want it, just leave it to one side."

"Will we have to pay for it?"

"No, no! *Please!*" cried the priest. "You are our guests. Just tell your friends about our island when you go back to America. We need more tourists!"

"Well, what do you think? Shall we spend a couple of days here?"

"It sounds enchanting," Amy said. "How far are the caves?"

"About five kilometres. Overlooking the sea."

"I *really* have to get back to Athens. Is there a bus to—what's the name of the port?"

"Agia Pelagia."

"Oh yes! A taxi once a day. But so hot and dusty! And the boat might take two days to leave," the priest said. Three bright gold teeth punctuated his smile.

"That settles it. We stay," Foster announced. "This place is a paradise. You know what *Milopotama* means? A thousand rivers."

The supper was not as elaborate as they might have hoped—*souvlaki* sticks with country salad—but even Richard filled up and paid a third of the bill without complaint.

A young woman entered the *taverna* to say their rooms were ready at the hotel, and the priest walked with them down the street. It was an old stone building, formerly a school which had been converted to a hostel. Most of the rooms were empty of everything but beds and bedsprings, but the villagers had prepared three rooms joined together by a screened-in balcony. The balcony overlooked a tiny stream full of waterfalls that filled the air with gurgling.

"Separate rooms!" Foster muttered.

"Don't be difficult. It's romantic! And these people are so hospitable!"

"Ask how much it costs, okay?" Richard still had his pack on his shoulders.

"It is fifty drachmas a night. Good rates."

"Not bad," he conceded. "Is there a bathroom?"

"At the end of the hall. Very nice. Tile floors."

Richard went to check it out.

"How are we going to get rid of this guy?"

"We don't get rid of him. He'll leave soon enough. Can't you see he's terrified? You make him nervous."

Richard walked back into Foster's room. "There's even hot water! I can take a bath!"

"You see?"

"Richard, are you going to the caves with us tomorrow?"

"Oh, I don't know! You always want everything so cut-and-dried! Are you going, Amy?"

"Well, yes, I think so. Probably."

"Wouldn't you rather come with me to the boat?"

She glanced at Foster, who looked away. "And then what?"

"You could make up your mind when you got there. Whether to go to Athens or not."

Foster could not be sure he was hearing this. Could she seriously consider travelling with this creep?

"Let me sleep on it, Richard? It's been a long

day. Well, good night to you both."

She went to her room and closed the door. Richard and Foster avoided looking at each other, but stood outside the door nonetheless, until Foster turned abruptly and walked out into the evening darkness, toward the *taverna*. He could hear the *bouzouki* and clarinet of the peasant music-makers.

The priest had already retired for the evening, but the welcome was no less boisterous for his absence.

"But where are your friends, Kirea Smith?" Vassilis asked.

"The hell with them," he said. "I'm here for the music."

"The young men will soon be dancing. Very beautiful."

"One glass of *retsina*, Vassilaki."

Whatever was going on back at the hotel didn't bother him. If Amy wanted to engage in this silliness with a snot-nosed kid from Madison, Wisconsin, that was her problem. What was she thinking about?

"They dance to express their feelings," Vassilis said. "So sad here now. The island will not last much longer unless something is done. Not many years ago, fifteen thousand people lived here. Today—only three thousand."

"All gone to Australia."

Vassilis nodded, his long grey moustaches drooping further as he watched the musicians play.

"Can't the government do anything?"

"The colonels? Pah!" He spat behind the counter. "They have ruined us."

"How? You mean with the tourists?"

"Ten years ago, we had plenty visitors. The

English, you know. We were almost a colony of England. Papadapolous—he doesn't know where a chicken farts from!''

"What's he got to do with it?"

Vassilis stared at him suspiciously. "You don't know?"

"No."

"When they made the *coup* in '67, they turned Kithira into a penal colony. The island was filled with communists."

"*Communists*?"

"Well, not real communists. Patriots, actually. Army generals who disagreed with Colonel Papadapolous. Politicians. Journalists. Anyone they thought was leftist. Six years ago. Down at Agia Pelagia, they used to walk up and down the beaches, their swords and medals dragging in the sand."

"That's why EOT doesn't want anyone to come here!"

Vassilis shrugged. "If they confessed their crimes, they were allowed back to Athens. The ones who stayed have all gone mad. They don't come out of their villas, except for drink. Funny, ay?"

"Ironic, anyway."

"What's that?"

"The birthplace of Aphrodite. A Devil's Island for political dissidents."

Half a dozen of the men were dancing now, a glass of wine in one hand and a handkerchief in the other. Foster could feel the music stirring inside, but he was not yet drunk enough to make a spectacle of himself. He ordered another glass.

One of the young dancers kicked a chair out from under a table into the centre of the floor. He kneeled, then picked it up in his teeth, maintaining the rhythm of the dance as he lifted it over his head. This evening the women were not present; even Vassilis' wife had gone to bed.

Foster took his blues harmonica out of his pocket and joined the music, trying to capture the high-pitched dissonance that reverberated inside his head. He drank and played and drank some more, and finally was on his feet dancing. It was true, he thought, wine did liberate the feet. Although he staggered, he was doing not at all badly by the rhythm.

Then he saw someone watching from the kitchen door. It was Galatea, the woman from the hotel in town. He lurched into the kitchen, but she had disappeared. "More wine!" he shouted, and Vassilis appeared at his side with a bottle, muttering about a cave.

"Maybe that's the cave of Aphrodite? Is not far."

"Where is the cave?" Foster said, but Vassilis was gone again, and the young men were more acrobatic than ever, urging each other on to more foolhardy weight-lifting and somersaults through the air. Foster stumbled out the door into the cool night. The overcast had cleared away, and the stars blinked like electric lights.

He had difficulty finding his way back to the hostel; the confusion in his mind kept leading him along the wrong rocky path. The mournful music from the tavern, sounding more Oriental than ever, was distracting his thoughts away from the destination somewhere ahead in the water-gurgling darkness. He reached a stone wall and could go no further. He sat against it and pulled his mouth organ out. He began to howl into it, wailing the loss which seemed to possess him. He thought he might be tapping on Amy's door, and hearing Richard's peculiar nasal snore, but decided it was the clarinet in the tavern.

Later, dead drunk, he fell into bed.

7

Richard was gone the following morning. He had risen early, Amy said, to catch the taxi. He had woken her up to say good-bye.

"Touching."

"He said to thank you for letting him come along, and we should go and visit him in Hamburg."

"What do you want to do now?"

"I'm enjoying myself. Aren't you?"

"Sure. You want to try St. Sofia's cave?"

"Of course." Amy jumped up and grabbed her hiking boots.

"You've eaten breakfast already?"

"Yoghurt and cheese. Richard brought them round."

"Jesus."

She stood up from lacing her boots. "Well, it made for a change."

On the way out of Milopotama, a cluster of children followed them, trying out their English. They were practising to go to Australia. The gabble attracted housewives to their front gates, where they filled Amy's pack with apples and cheese. As the path to Vassilis' cave was unmarked, Foster had to keep asking peasants for directions. Half a dozen times they got lost among the thorn bushes and rock slides, before finding the path again. The landscape grew harsher as they approached the sea on the west coast of the island, where the constant wind smashed and twisted the coast into chaotic patterns.

They emerged onto the sea-cliff finally, just before noon. The path became very narrow, a foot-wide ledge about ten metres below the lip of the cliff. On their left, the cliff dropped straight to the sea, surging and muttering a hundred feet below.

"Can you see it?"

"Not yet."

"You're sure this is the path?"

"It's the only one. Keep coming. Give me your hand."

They crawled around a promontory of rock. There was the entrance to the cave, somewhat larger than Foster had expected. Inside it they found a small chapel, with a domed ceiling far overhead. There was a dense smell of incense and candle-wax, but it did not completely obscure the odour of wet limestone emanating from the deep dark hole behind the altar. A single candle guttered its life away before the icon of St. Sofia.

"What's a chapel doing *here*?" Foster said.

"It's a good place for a chapel, I should think. No need to build a church around it."

There was a dangerous row of stalactites guarding the opening to the tunnel. Vassilis had assured Foster it was perfectly safe to explore the depths; it only descended a few yards beyond the altar, anyway. Foster lit two of the longer candles and they stepped into the darkness. It was so claustrophobic that Foster hesitated after a few paces.

"Let's go back."

"We have to go to the end now," Amy said.

"The candles don't throw enough light. What if the wind blows them out?"

"Come on." She stepped in front of him and led him around a pillar. They could see a flicker of light reflected on the wall ahead. Amy edged forward, stumbling on a fallen chunk of stalactite as she held the candle up. On the wall of the cave was an engraved figure, indistinct. Amy moved closer, holding the candle toward it as she peered. "A snake."

"It might be a sea serpent. Or a pair of wavy lines."

"It's the sea!" she said. "A symbol of the sea."

"Hmm."

"Foster, let's go! I feel strange."

He remained for a minute, staring at the engraving, trying to decipher its meaning.

"I have to get outside! I'm getting goose bumps."

Foster turned away and took her hand. They stumbled back through the forest of stalactites. By the time they reached the altar, they were running. Outside the chapel, a blue sky burst upon them like a wave of the sea throwing itself upon the cliff face.

They stood on the rock ledge just outside the cave, facing the dazzling light, the vault of sky, the thrashing sea below. Neither spoke, hoping the other could feel the same surge of ecstasy and liberation, hoping the sense was shared and known to be shared.

Foster turned. "What is it?"

"I don't know. It must be how a baby feels. You know, at birth."

They slid their backs down the rock-face until

they sat with their legs dangling over the edge. Dislodged pebbles bounced and spun into the sea below. Foster took the bottle of *retsina* from his pack, along with the *feta* cheese. But before he could open it, Amy threw her arms around him in a violent embrace. At first he had the crazy thought she was trying to grab him and throw him over the edge. But the kisses falling over his face and neck were passionate, erotic. Their lovemaking challenged the law of gravity at every shudder, as they grappled furiously among the rocks above the blustering tide, fighting for tenure against the long fall into the sea, plunging toward extinction of the senses.

By the time the sun had crawled round the southwest corner of the outcrop, they lay in each other's arms, exhausted. Once in the shade, the rock shelf cooled quickly under the influence of a rising breeze. Foster and Amy slept for the rest of the afternoon.

In the evening, they feasted on the wine and food, still not speaking, almost in a daze. It was dark when they returned to the hostel.

8

Two days later, they walked down the long sloping road to the north-eastern tip of Kithira. The village of Agia Pelagia sparkled in the sunlight.

"This is where the generals hang out," Foster murmured as they paused at a hair-pin curve, gazing down on the sleepy houses.

"They did what?"

"It's a place of exile for Papadop's enemies. That's why it was so hard to get here."

"Fancy that." She tightened her arm around his waist. "Now it's changed."

At the dock, a single fishing boat was tied up. The owner was mending nets, and said that he wouldn't be able to carry them back to the mainland until the following day. There was, however, a very comfortable tavern in the village where they could stay overnight. In fact, another Englishman was staying there now, also waiting for a boat.

"Richard!" Amy exclaimed.

"Couldn't be."

"It has to be! Let's go and see, darling."

Near the shore end of the pier was a small cabin with a wooden table and chair sitting in front, enduring the elements as they awaited a patron. The owner stepped through the beaded curtain.

"*Kafe*?"

"*Para kalo. Melate Eglaisika*?"

"Ah. You must be Mr. Smith."

"Yes?"

"I have a message for you. Mr. Richard wishes you well, and regrets his indigestion."

"*What*?"

"He means indiscretion," Amy whispered.

"Your friend was unable to hire a boat, and after he stayed here one night, he took the taxi back to the main harbour at Kapsali."

"A *taxi*?"

"He was very alone, Mr. Smith. A young man not accustomed to being alone, I will state. I gave him a bed inside, but he was pacing all night long."

"Do you have room for us?"

"Of course. See?" He swept the beads to one side. It was the smallest *taverna* they had ever seen, a room about eight feet by eight with a kitchen behind it. There was a table against one wall; against the other a single bed covered with dubious-looking blankets.

"We'll take it."

An hour later, they walked to the end of the pier, sated with fried fish and *kokoneli* wine. The sun was descending into the rocky hills behind them, throwing across the water the peculiar golden light of the Greek islands.

As they looked back from the end of the pier, Kithira glowed a green-and-blue sapphire.

"It's too—perfect—" Amy said.

"Can I ask you something?"

"I don't want to talk about Richard."

"That night in Milopotama. Did you?"

"There is definitely something unusual about this place. Beyond the legend. It's—primitive."

Foster looked out to the sea. "It's different, okay. But then there must be hundreds of islands. Every one is different. Some could be as beautiful."

"It would take a lifetime to explore them all."

"Maybe we'll live a full lifetime."

They sat down on the stone breakwater. It was low enough that their feet trailed in the water. They looked down and saw the bright golden sand, the shells of strange creatures advancing from the deeps.

THE GRAND BELL
(with translation assistance from Kang Oh)

The Great Void is a bell
Buddha said: The Cosmos is
a bell cast of bronze.

Man is an atom of the bronze
the clapper that rings the bell.
The clapper strikes, the bell sounds. . . .
A sonorous wave resounds
throughout the canopy of heaven. . . .

Pealing bell, it's you who brings
      messages from the battlefront
      it's you who proclaims birth
      and tolls for the dead
      it's you who sends good cheer
      and (yes) love
      it's you. . . .

Man is atom of the bronze
man is clapper of the bell.
The clapper strikes and o
the bell is charged with sound:
      a low gong from the depths of prisons
      a murmur from the survivors freed
      a clangor from the brave heroes
      a piercing shriek from the joyous young
        and old.

The world is a bell.
Man is the clapper that rings the bell.
The clapper moves, the bell chimes. . . .

THE GRAND BELL

钟

太空是钟
佛说　钟是大千
而世界铸以铜
人——是铜的原子
　——是鸣钟之锤

锤动　钟鸣‥‥
搏浪　坂宏‥‥

传送战火的信息是你
传送生和葬礼的是你
传送美意的是你
传送柔情的是你
传送‥‥

人————是铜的原子
铜是钟　是鸣钟之锤
锤动　钟鸣
飓溢那囹圄的低音

飓溢那群脱的弱音
飓溢那勇者的强音
飓溢那兜童和老人的欢乐
————无限高音

钟的世界————
人————是鸣钟之锤
————是铸钟之铜
锤动　钟鸣……

胡北疆

1980.11.1.

The THUNDER CREEK CO-OP is a production co-operative registered with the Saskatchewan Department of Co-operatives and Co-operative Development. It was formed to publish prairie writing —poetry, prose, songs and plays.

PUBLICATIONS

KEN MITCHELL COUNTRY, the best of Ken Mitchell, $4.95 pb.

FOREIGNERS, a lively, passionate novel by Barbara Sapergia, $4.95 pb.

MORE SASKATCHEWAN GOLD, exciting, imaginative, masterful short stories from prairie writers, edited by Geoffrey Ursell, $4.95 pb.

TERRITORIES, fresh, distinctive poetry by Elizabeth Allen, $6.00 pb, $14.00 hc.

DOUBLE VISIONS, the first release in the Wood Mountain Series, established to recognize the work of new writers. Poetry by Thelma Poirier and Jean Hillabold, $6.00 pb, $14.00 hc.

HERSTORY 1985, a practical and informative calendar featuring women in Canada, $6.95.

STREET OF DREAMS, poems that recover our lost experiences, our forgotten dreams, by Gary Hyland, $7.00 pb, $15.00 hc.

FISH-HOOKS, thirteen stories from an exciting new talent, Reg Silvester, $6.00 pc, $14.00 hc.

100% CRACKED WHEAT, an excellent source of dietary laughter from Saskatchewan writers, edited by Robert Currie, Gary Hyland and Jim McLean, $4.95 pb.

THE WEATHER, vibrant, marvellous poems by Lorna Crozier, $6.00 pb.

THE BLUE POOLS OF PARADISE, a document of secrets, poems by Mick Burrs, $6.00 pb.

GOING PLACES, poems that take you on a vacation with Don Kerr, $6.00 pb, $14.00 hc.

GRINGO: POEMS AND JOURNALS FROM LATIN AMERICA by Dennis Gruending, $6.00 pb.

NIGHT GAMES, stories by Robert Currie, $7.00 pb.

THE SECRET LIFE OF RAILROADERS, the funniest poems ever to roll down the main line, by Jim McLean, $5.00 pb.

BLACK POWDER: ESTEVAN, 1931, a play with music, by Rex Deverell and Geoffrey Ursell, $5.00 pb.

SINCLAIR ROSS: A READER'S GUIDE by Ken Mitchell. With two short stories by Sinclair Ross, $7.00 pb.

SUNDOGS, an anthology of the best in Saskatchewan short stories, edited by Robert Kroetsch, $7.95 pb.

SUPERWHEEL, the musical play about automobiles, with script by Rex Deverell and music and lyrics by Geoffrey Ursell, $5.00 pb.

NUMBER ONE HARD, an L.P. of songs by Geoffrey Ursell from the original Globe Theatre production, "an investigative documentary about the prairie grain industry", $6.00 pb.

EYE OF A STRANGER, poems by Garry Rad-
dysh, $4.00 pb.

ODPOEMS &, poems by E.F. Dyck, $4.00 pb.

All of the above may be ordered from your favour-
ite bookstore, or from:

coteau books

THUNDER CREEK CO-OP
Box 239 Sub #1
Moose Jaw, Saskatchewan
S6H 5V0

OTHER BOOKS BY KEN MITCHELL:

Chatauqua Girl

Sinclair Ross: A Reader's Guide

The Great Cultural Revolution

The Con Man

Davin: The Politician .

Cruel Tears

Horizon

Everybody Gets Something Here

Wandering Rafferty

The Meadowlark Connection

This Train

Heroes